910.4 Hemming, Robert J.
HE

  Gales of November

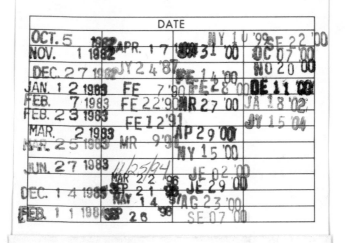

Gales of November

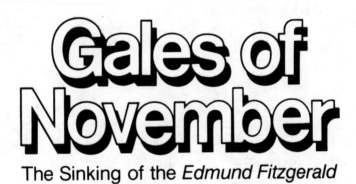

Gales of November

The Sinking of the *Edmund Fitzgerald*

Robert J. Hemming

Contemporary Books, Inc.
Chicago

Library of Congress Cataloging in Publication Data

Hemming, Robert J.
    Gales of November.

    Bibliography: p.
    Includes index.
    1. Edmund Fitzgerald (Ship).   2. Shipwrecks—
Superior, Lake.   I. Title.
G530.E26H45   363.1′23′097749   81-65182
ISBN 0-8092-5921-4   AACR2

Grateful acknowledgment is made to Gordon Lightfoot, Moose Music, Ltd., and to CACAP for permission to reprint portions of the lyrics of the song "The Wreck of the *Edmund Fitzgerald*."

Published by Contemporary Books, Inc.
180 North Michigan Avenue, Chicago, Illinois 60601
Manufactured in the United States of America
Library of Congress Catalog Card Number: 81-65182
International Standard Book Number: 0-8092-5921-4

Published simultaneously in Canada by
Beaverbooks, Ltd.
150 Lesmill Road
Don Mills, Ontario M3B 2T5
Canada

For my wife, Ann, and for all the wives of the men of the *Edmund Fitzgerald*.

The legend lives on from the Chippewa on down
Of the big lake they call Gitche Gumee—
Superior they said never gives up her dead
When the gales of November come early.

—From the song
   "The Wreck of the *Edmund Fitzgerald*,"
   by Gordon Lightfoot

CONTENTS

PREFACE

Shortly after seven o'clock on the night of November 10, 1975, the 729-foot straight deck ore freighter *Edmund Fitzgerald* sank during a violent storm on Lake Superior. It had happened suddenly—some say as quickly as ten seconds. One instant she was plowing through waves as high as a three-story building; the next she had been swallowed by the treacherous lake which bears the ominous sobriquet "the graveyard of ships."

The following day word had flashed around the world, telling of the ship's sudden and mysterious disappearance from the radar screens of several nearby vessels, and of the apparent loss of the *Fitzgerald*'s entire twenty-nine man crew. News of the sinking was carried in the press, on radio, and on television throughout the country on November 11; the news segments of NBC's "Today" show mentioned the loss; Walter Cronkite briefly noted it on the "CBS Evening News" that day; ABC and NBC reported the sinking on their evening news broadcasts. The *New York Times* carried a front-page story on the tragedy, as did hundreds of other daily newspapers; *Newsweek* and *Time* magazines also made mention of the *Fitzgerald*'s foundering.

And then the disaster was quickly forgotten by practically everyone. Within a few days the loss of the ship had apparently faded from the minds of seemingly all but the families and friends of the twenty-nine men who had sailed to their deaths aboard the *Fitzgerald*.

It was not too surprising that the sinking of the huge ship had little lasting impact on the public at that time. To most people, a ship—even one over seven hundred feet in length—being lost in the Great Lakes was tantamount to a rowboat foundering in a duck pond. Most Americans who have never seen them think of the Great Lakes as little more than knee-deep pools. Few fully comprehend the awesome size of what has been called the world's "eighth sea" or the dangers faced by those who sail upon these often cruel and bellicose waters.

Small wonder, then, that the sinking of the *Edmund Fitzgerald* sustained no lasting relevance in the lives of the public.

But then a strange thing happened. In midsummer of 1976 (about nine months following the *Fitzgerald*'s disappearance), Canadian folksinger and composer Gordon Lightfoot released a record album titled *Summertime Dream*. The haunting melody of one selection from the album, with its almost dirgelike quality and strange, mournful whining—like the wind whistling through a ship's rigging—quickly attracted attention. Radio stations throughout the Great Lakes area began receiving dozens of telephone calls each day asking that the selection be played; record shops quickly sold out their supply of the album. Within a few weeks a wave of interest in the song had swept beyond the Great Lakes region and had engulfed the entire nation with a rare fascination that was not limited to devotees of Lightfoot's esoteric musical style. Warner Brothers Records—producers of the album—responded to this interest by releasing a single (a 45-RPM record) of the song. Demand for the recording continued to increase, and before the first anniversary of the sinking of the *Fitzgerald*, Lightfoot's record had made its way to the top of the popular music charts. The song was titled "The Wreck of the *Edmund Fitzgerald.*"

Lightfoot had succeeded in acquainting a large portion of the public with the Great Lakes as something more than small, calm lagoons in which to splash in the heat of the summer and was able to tell the story of terror and death during a furious November storm on Lake Superior.

Still, much remains to be told of the ship and her crew, who lie today in 530 feet of extremely cold, murky water.

Each year, on the tenth of November—the anniversary of the terrible night when the *Fitzgerald* vanished—the newspapers and the electronic media throughout the Great Lakes region recount the loss of the ship and her crew. There is an almost reverential tone to these allegories, but not a great deal of new information has been added to the story since the days immediately following the U.S. Coast Guard hearings in 1976. Meanwhile, the Great Lakes sailors' axiom that Superior never gives up her dead has been reaffirmed; the bodies of the lost crew have never been recovered, and their spirits await a tangible memorial to their sacrifice.

It is my hope that telling the full story of the *Edmund Fitzgerald* and her crew, and of their final hours, will offer some more palpable tribute to these men than the ever-restless rolling of the lake; that perhaps their loss might be made a permanent symbol of the savage and never-ending struggle of all mariners against the "big lake" . . . *when the gales of November come early.*

This, then, is the story of those men and the last days of their lives. It is also the story of a great ship and the agony of her tragic and untimely death—an agony that is felt personally by everyone who has ever gone to sea . . . and by many who never have.

interviews, reliving not just the memories of happy times but the bitter, heartbreaking pain of the days that followed the loss of their loved ones, I owe a debt of thanks that can never be fully repaid. The list is a long one.

To Nellie McSorley, who from her sickbed graciously answered my many questions without complaint or hesitation; to Mary Catherine McCarthy, who not only contributed her recollections of her husband, John, but put me in touch with others whose knowledge of the *Fitzgerald*'s first mate, particularly in his boyhood years, was even more extensive than her own; to William and James McCarthy, who provided great insight into their brother's life and past experiences; to Father Nelson Callahan, who saw Jack McCarthy in a different dimension; to Brooksie Rafferty and her son, Randy, for their assistance in helping me to know much of Robert Rafferty's life, and to Pamela Rafferty Johnson, for her recollections of her father; to Mrs. Aaron W. Weiss, mother of Cadet David Weiss, who not only contributed her recollections of her son but encouraged me to complete this book; to Florence Simmons, Doreen Cundy, and Irmengard Kalmon, who were extremely helpful in their recollections of their husbands and in providing additional material on other crew members that proved invaluable, particularly where relatives could not be located; to the parents of Bruce Hudson (Mr. and Mrs. Odis A. Hudson) and Karl Peckol (Mr. and Mrs. William Peckol) for their contributions concerning the lives and personalities of their sons, and for recollections of the other members of the *Fitzgerald* crew. I would especially like to thank Ruth Hudson for the photos and clippings she so generously supplied me.

I wish to thank Louis, Wilmer, and Roger Holl as well as Lois (Mrs. William) Beardsley for the time they spent in recalling George Holl; Florence Bentsen, mother of oiler Thomas Bentsen, Maude Spengler, who spent part of her ninety-fifth birthday talking with me about her son, William Spengler, and Thelma Church and her daughter, Bonnie Kellerman, all of whom were very helpful in preparing those sections of this book which dealt with their loved ones; Mrs. Elaine Sespico for her gracious cooperation in providing information about her brother, Paul Riippa; and the mother of Thomas D. Borgeson, and Helen Bindon, wife of Edward F. Bindon, who contributed much. A very special thanks must go to Janice Armagost for her efforts in gathering material about her husband, Michael—she has the ability and the subject matter to do a book of her own. I hope she will someday write it.

There are a number of helpful individuals—most of whom are at present only faceless voices on the telephone—whose assistance has been most valuable. Included in this list must be Tom Fontaine, Carl Olestrom, and Andrew Rajner, men who knew many of the men of the *Fitz*; Gerard and Tim Spears, who contributed much valuable information concerning the day-to-day operations of iron boats such as the *Fitzgerald*; the personnel of the excellent libraries in Detroit, Cleveland, Chicago, Buffalo, and Toledo, all of whom patiently suffered my many intrusions in search of information and assisted me with uncommon professionalism; and the officers and men of the U.S. Coast Guard, particularly Lt. Comdr. C. F. Guldenschuh, Lt. J. G. Mark Bobal, Lt. P. G. Matyas, of the Ninth District, who were so very helpful in locating and supplying documents, transcripts, photos, and videotapes in connection with my research on this book. The assistance of Teraina D. Weaver, lead inquiries assistant of the National Transportation Safety Board, is also gratefully acknowledged.

I extend my appreciation to Elizabeth Locke as well as Capt. Calvin Durham, of Bethlehem Steel Corporation, and to Capt. William Chambers—master of the *Arthur B. Homer*—for their generosity and hospitality in arranging for my very pleasant and instructive hours aboard the sister ship of the *Fitzgerald*, which gave me a vivid understanding of the general layout of the *Fitz*; and to Jack C. Yewell and his public relations staff at Oglebay-Norton Company for their tireless efforts on my behalf.

I wish, also, to thank Clarence Edward Dennis, retired Burlington Northern boat loader, for his willingness to verbally take me through the day he loaded the *Fitzgerald* for the last time.

A special word of thanks must go to a pair of very popular "on-air" personalties at radio station WJR in Detroit: to Joe ("J.P.") McCarthy, who unknowingly inspired me to begin this book, who assisted me in attempts to get certain information and contact several individuals important to my research, and whose kind invitation to appear on his much-listened-to "Focus" interview show instantly put me in touch with persons I could not have located by any other means; and to Jim Davis, who generously broadcast my attempts to locate a tape recording of the radio transmissions between ships involved in the search for the *Fitzgerald* on the night of November 10 and early hours of November 11, 1975. It is a good indication of the size of his audience that within an hour of the broadcast I was in contact with the individual who had the much-needed tape recording. And of course I want to express my great appreciation to Richard Bell, of the *Ann Arbor* (Michigan) *News,* who was listening to Davis that day and possessed the very tape I had so unsuccessfully sought, and who readily made the prized tape available to me.

While I was extremely fortunate in obtaining full cooperation from almost all of the relatives and friends of the lost crew of the *Edmund Fitzgerald,* there were three instances where I was unable to secure the interviews I had requested. And while I was able to obtain sufficient information concerning the men involved through other sources, I regret the loss of the special knowledge these individuals might have been able to supply. But I fully understand and sympathize with the unwillingness of those persons to undergo the ordeal of reopening painful wounds.

I did find it puzzling, however, that spokesmen for U.S. Steel Corporation adamantly refused my requests for permission to interview crew members of the *Arthur M. Anderson,* the ore boat which first reported the *Fitzgerald's* disappearance. Although the dictum was not totally successful, a spokesman indicated that the company planned to advise the crewmen that they were not to speak with me.

Also, while permission was granted, as acknowledged elsewhere, to quote four lines of the lyrics to the Gordon Lightfoot song, "The Wreck of the *Edmund Fitzgerald*," the complete lyrics do not appear anywhere in these pages. This is on the decision of the holders of the copyright to the song. I mention this because I believe that readers whose first knowledge of the *Edmund Fitzgerald* disaster came through their hearing this beautiful and powerful folk dirge will want to know why those moving words are not presented here in full.

There are many close friends and relatives to whom I might direct a word of thanks for their encouragement, enthusiasm, and assistance during the writing of this book. However, to individually state my deep appreciation here is, unfortunately, not practical and must await a personal and private expression.

It would, however, be remiss on my part if I did not publicly thank Mary Margaret Carberry for her steadfast support for this project. Her gentle encouragement and wise counsel during the long months in preparing the manuscript has made the writing of *Gales of November* less of an ordeal. I can only hope the sleepless nights she must have suffered during the process will have, in her mind, been worth it. This same fervent wish applies equally to my wife, Ann, who spent many long hours transferring my handwritten and often illegible notes—complete with jawbreaking syntax—to the typewritten page. Any errors that remain in the finished product are there in spite of her quiet persuasion.

And finally, I owe a monumental thanks to John, Matthew, Janet, William, and Meredith ("Missy"), my children, who patiently endured the frequent loss of their father's attention and participation in activities they had a right to expect of him. I hope now to begin making it up to them.

AUTHOR'S NOTE

What follows is true.

The Oglebay-Norton ore carrier *Edmund Fitzgerald* sank to the bottom of Lake Superior on a stormy night in 1975, taking her entire twenty-nine man crew with her.

There is, however, one element of "fiction" involved in this account of the *Fitzgerald*'s final hours about which the reader should be aware.

No survivor came through the frightful ordeal to provide eyewitness testimony of the exact actions and statements of the officers and crew during the fateful last voyage of the ship on Lake Superior. Yet, some understanding of what was occurring aboard the vessel, particularly during the time she was in the area of "Six Fathom Shoals," is essential to providing possible answers to the question of why the *Fitzgerald* sank. Thus, it has been necessary to recreate the most *probable* narrative of what was said and done aboard the ship from the time she left Superior, Wisconsin, in the early afternoon of November 9, until the instant she slipped beneath the frenzied waters of the lake approximately twenty-nine hours later.

The material contained in chapters ten, eleven, and twelve must, therefore, be viewed as a hypothetical treatment of the *possible* actions, conversations, and mental processes of the officers and crew, based on the best evidence available. The reader is cautioned that this portion of the narrative is, at best, conjectural.

All other elements of this book are based on the several thousand pages of transcribed testimony from the hearings held and the reports written by the United States Coast Guard, the National Transportation Safety Board, and the United States Congress, and on the several hundred interviews I personally conducted with relatives and close friends of the lost crew and with individuals directly involved in the events surrounding the loss of the S.S. *Edmund Fitzgerald*.

Bob Hemming
Toledo, Ohio
March 1981

THE CREW OF THE
S.S. EDMUND FITZGERALD

McSorley, Ernest Michael	*Master*, Toledo, Ohio
McCarthy, John Henkle	*First Mate*, Bay Village, Ohio
Pratt, James A.	*Second Mate*, Lakewood, Ohio
Armagost, Michael Eugene	*Third Mate*, Iron River, Wisconsin
Holl, George John	*Chief Engineer*, Cabot, Pennsylvania
Bindon, Edward Francis	*First Assistant Engineer*, Fairport Harbor, Ohio
Edwards, Thomas Edgar	*Second Assistant Engineer*, Oregon, Ohio
Haskell, Russell George	*Second Assistant Engineer*, Millbury, Ohio
Champeau, Oliver Joseph	*Third Assistant Engineer*, Milwaukee, Wisconsin
Beetcher, Frederick J.	*Porter*, Superior, Wisconsin
Bentsen, Thomas	*Oiler*, St. Joseph, Michigan
Borgeson, Thomas Dale	*Able-Bodied Maintenance Man*, Duluth, Minnesota

CHURCH, NOLAN FRANK	*Porter,* Silver Bay, Minnesota
CUNDY, RANSOM EDWARD	*Watchman,* Superior, Wisconsin
HUDSON, BRUCE LEE	*Deckhand,* North Olmsted, Ohio
KALMON, ALLEN GEORGE	*Second Cook,* Washburn, Wisconsin
MACLELLAN, GORDON F.	*Wiper,* Clearwater, Florida
MAZES, JOSEPH WILLIAM	*Special Maintenance Man,* Ashland, Wisconsin
O'BRIEN, EUGENE WILLIAM	*Wheelsman,* Perrysburg Township, Ohio
PECKOL, KARL ANTHONY	*Watchman,* Ashtabula, Ohio
POVIACH, JOHN JOSEPH	*Wheelsman,* Bradenton, Florida
RAFFERTY, ROBERT CHARLES	*Temporary Steward (First Cook),* Toledo, Ohio
RIIPPA, PAUL M.	*Deckhand,* Ashtabula, Ohio
SIMMONS, JOHN DAVID	*Wheelsman,* Ashland, Wisconsin
SPENGLER, WILLIAM J.	*Watchman,* Toledo, Ohio
THOMAS, MARK ANDREW	*Deckhand,* Richmond Heights, Ohio
WALTON, RALPH GRANT	*Oiler,* Fremont, Ohio
WEISS, DAVID ELLIOT	*Cadet (deck),* Canogha Park, California
WILHELM, BLAINE HOWARD	*Oiler,* Moquah, Wisconsin

CHAPTER 1

"I Just Hope He Didn't Take a Nose Dive"

Wheelsman Harry C. Hilgemann stood at the aft bulkhead of the access tunnel and gasped. Looking down the 500-foot passageway connecting the forward and after deckhouses of the 767-foot ore carrier *Arthur M. Anderson,* Hilgemann watched in stunned amazement as the door at the far end seemed to be rising into the ceiling. It took several seconds for Hilgemann to realize that the ship was bending in the heavy seas, producing the illusion in the long, narrow tunnel just below the main deck. He stood and wondered if it would be safe to proceed to the opposite end.

In more than ten years of sailing as a crewman on the Great Lakes "iron boats"—the freighters that carry iron ore from the mines at the western end of Lake Superior to the steel plants in Detroit, Cleveland, and points east and south—Hilgemann had become accustomed to the rubbery bending and twisting of the boats in heavy weather. He knew that this incredible flexibility was engineered into these ships to prevent them from snapping in two as they were subjected to the tremendous stresses caused by the action of the waves. But never in all his years on the lakes had he witnessed the phenomenon as exaggerated as he was now seeing it.

It was 7:30 P.M. (1930 hours) on November 10, 1975, and Lake Superior was writhing in the worst storm veteran Great Lakes sailors had experienced in more than thirty years. Gale winds were being clocked at seventy knots (80.5 miles per hour), and gusts were reaching an incredible ninety-six miles per hour; waves were running thirty feet high. Men on the lake that night recall how the wind in the rigging sounded like "dozens of air raid sirens, all going at once." The waves, pounding on the sides of ships, were like "a hundred wrecking balls" banging on the steel plates of the hulls.

As Wheelsman Hilgemann debated whether to make the dash down the tunnel below deck, the men on watch up in the *Anderson*'s pilothouse were struggling with a more perplexing problem: What had happened to the *Fitzgerald*?

The *Arthur M. Anderson*, a U.S. Steel ore carrier, had joined the 729-foot iron boat *Edmund Fitzgerald* the day before, as the two ships were departing the western end of the 379-mile-wide lake.

With gale warnings flying from the Duluth (Minnesota) Coast Guard station's storm mast, Capt. Jesse "Bernie" Cooper, master of the *Anderson,* and Capt. Ernest M. McSorley of the *Fitzgerald,* had conferred by radiotelephone and agreed to take their vessels along the "northern track" of the lake.

The route Cooper and McSorley had selected—hugging the Canadian shoreline at the top of the lake—was longer and not routinely chosen by ship's masters guiding their vessels between Duluth and the locks at Sault Ste. Marie (pronounced "Soo Saint Marie"), Michigan. But the path had the advantage of a wind-blunting effect to the strong northerly winds sweeping down over the Canadian land mass, while the normal southern route placed ships in the teeth of winds which had built up force and speed as they moved over the flat, wide expanse of the lake.

The *Fitzgerald*—faster of the two ships—had drawn steadily ahead of the *Anderson,* and by midafternoon, November 10, was about seventeen miles in the lead. The storm, which had raged about them throughout the day, was continuing to intensify with intermittent rain and snow and visibility at times near zero.

While the trip across the lake had been increasingly rough, it had been, for the most part, uneventful—until 3:30 in the rapidly darkening afternoon.

"I have experienced some topside damage," Captain McSorley radioed the *Anderson.* "I have a fence rail laid down, two vents lost or damaged, I am taking on water and have a list."

The vents were eight-inch-wide covered openings leading to the ship's ballast tanks. With these gone, the tanks were open to small amounts of water coming over the *Fitzgerald*'s decks.

"Do you have your pumps going?" Captain Cooper asked.

"Yes, both of them."

McSorley then advised Cooper that he was "checking down" (slowing his ship) to allow the *Anderson* to catch up.

Cooper felt no immediate apprehension for the safety of the *Fitzgerald*; the huge ore boat had four seven-thousand-gallon-per-minute ballast pumps and two two-thousand-gallon-per-minute auxiliary pumps available. The minimal quantity of water coming through the open vents could easily be controlled by any two of these pumps. Still, the list . . .

The two ships were steaming on a southeasterly heading, running for the calmer waters of Whitefish Bay at the eastern end of Superior, approximately seventy-five miles to the south.

"Could you stay by me until I get down?" McSorley inquired.

Cooper said he could.

Then at 4:10 P.M. (1610 hours) McSorley radioed that both of his radar antennae had been carried away. He was now "blind" in the blowing snow and growing darkness; he would need navigational assistance. Cooper was temporarily out of the wheelhouse, but First Mate Morgan Clark quickly assured McSorley that the *Anderson* would provide radar plots to help guide *Fitzgerald* into Whitefish Bay.

By 7:00 P.M. (1900 hours) the *Anderson* had drawn to within nine miles of the *Fitzgerald*; the men in the wheelhouse could easily identify the "blip" on the radar screen that was the *Fitz.*

But at 7:10 a furious snow squall struck, leaving the center of the radar screen, as Captain Cooper would later describe it, "just a white blob." The *Fitzgerald* disappeared into the blob.

About five minutes later, First Mate Morgan Clark radioed Captain McSorley to advise him that an upbound ship had been spotted some nine miles ahead of *Fitzgerald*. Clark told McSorley that the *Fitzgerald* would clear the approaching vessel, and then, as an afterthought, Clark asked, "Oh, by the way, how are you making out with your problems?"

The reply was a noncommittal "We are holding our own."

At 7:25 the snow squall abruptly ceased, and visibility greatly improved. But the *Anderson*'s wheelhouse watch could find no sign of the *Fitzgerald*—either visually or on radar.

Cooper, Clark, and Wheelsman Robert L. May strained to see ahead, trying to spot the *Fitzgerald*'s lights.

The storm was now at its peak, and the lake was heaving mountainous waves upward, tossing them over the freighter's stern and rolling them along the deck to crash into the superstructure at the bow. The winds clawed at her, trying to swing her broadside to the gale, where they could vent their full force against the *Anderson*'s side and possibly capsize her. Bob May fought the wheel, struggling to keep the ship from moving to the starboard into a trough of the waves.

The wheelhouse shook from the fury of the wind gusts, windows rattled and banged, and a fine mist of water spritzed through tiny cracks in door and window frames. Outside, the winds had reached hurricane velocity, snatching the white tops from the gray-brown waves and hurling the spray against the windows, making it difficult to see through the glass.

Suddenly, May thought he saw a pair of lights—one red and one white—off the port bow. He studied them for about a minute before deciding that the red light was a radio antenna light, probably from Coppermine Point on the Canadian shore. And when he attempted to point out the white light to the captain and first mate, neither man was able to see it. Within a few minutes Bob May, too, was unable to see the light any longer.

Soon First Mate Clark could see lights dead ahead. These proved to be those of three upbound saltwater vessels: the *Nanfri*, the *Benfri*, and the *Avafors*, which were heading into Lake Superior from Whitefish Bay. The closest was about seventeen miles away, and this puzzled Morgan Clark. The *Fitzgerald* should be half that distance; yet her lights were not visible.

Clark voiced his bewilderment to Captain Cooper, who was also becoming perplexed over their inability to locate the *Fitzgerald*.

"He may have had a power blackout," Cooper suggested. "Look for a silhouette."

Meanwhile, he attempted to reach Captain McSorley by radio. There was no response. He called one of the upbound ships, but again there was no answer to his call. Perhaps his radio wasn't getting out.

"*William Ford,* this is the *Anderson.* Can you pick me up?"

The ore carrier *William Clay Ford* was anchored in Whitefish Bay, waiting for the storm to blow itself out. They could hear the *Anderson* "loud and clear."

Had the *Fitzgerald* somehow made it into the bay? Cooper asked the *Ford*.

The *Ford* replied in the negative; they could not see the *Fitzgerald* visually or on radar.

First Mate Clark thought that he spotted the missing ship on one of *Anderson*'s two radar screens: a blip was showing up at a point on the lake about where the *Fitzgerald* should be. But after several sweeps of the radar scanner, the apparent target faded away, only to return several sweeps later and then disappear again. It was a false return.

Clark attempted to adjust the radar set while Captain Cooper called Capt. Albert Jacovetti, a Great Lakes pilot aboard the Swedish saltwater freighter *Nanfri*.

"Do you have the *Fitzgerald* on your radar?"

"No, we are getting a great deal of sea return." (The radar beam was bouncing from the towering waves and returning as a fuzzy image.) "It is difficult to identify targets," Jacovetti replied. "We have you on the screen but we cannot pick up *Fitzgerald*."

"Can you see her lights?" Cooper asked.

"No, we cannot see her lights."

Morgan Clark tinkered with the radar, cutting the gain control down until the scope displayed only solid targets—there were three of them: the *Nanfri*, the *Benfri*, and the *Avafors*. The *Fitzgerald* had vanished!

The atmosphere in the *Anderson*'s wheelhouse, tense because of the fury of the storm, now became palpable. A feeling of horror gripped the men on watch: a sinking, icy depression that tightened the throat, choking off any immediate attempt to speak of the unspeakable, to even think of the unthinkable. They had spoken to the *Fitzgerald* only minutes before. There had been no call of distress—"We are holding our own," McSorley had said.

Morgan Clark, a tinge of approaching panic fluttering in his voice, made repeated radio calls to the *Fitzgerald*—all but pleading for a response. Only a ragged hiss seeped from the speaker.

Bernie Cooper felt a burning in the pit of his stomach, his pulse throbbed in his temples, and perspiration began to bead on his forehead. He mentally shook his head in disbelief; there had to be an acceptable explanation for what was happening now.

Morgan Clark looked down and, in the dim light of the wheelhouse, saw his fingers trembling wildly.

"It was the strangest feeling I've ever had," Clark would later recall. "Everything told us that the *Fitz* had gone down: the radar couldn't pick her up, there was no answer when we called her on the radio, and no matter how hard we looked, we couldn't spot her lights. Yet we couldn't believe it; she *couldn't* be gone."

At about 7:39, Cooper called Soo Control—the Coast Guard station at Sault Ste. Marie—using Channel 16, the emergency frequency. Cooper was told to switch to Channel 12, to keep Channel 16 free. But when Cooper called on 12 he received no reply. It was fifteen minutes later when he reestablished contact with the Coast Guard and informed the radio operator that he had lost contact with the *Fitzgerald,* that he was unable to pick her up on radio, and could not spot her visually or on radar. The Coast Guard seemed unconcerned at this point, asking that Cooper keep an eye out for a sixteen-foot outboard that had been reported missing in the area.

Cooper was stunned. He had called to voice his fears for a 729-foot ore freighter and was being asked, instead, to look for a sixteen-footer. At 8:32 he again radioed the Soo.

"I am very concerned with the welfare of the steamer *Edmund Fitzgerald,*" Cooper announced forcefully. "He was right in front of us, experiencing a little difficulty. He was taking on a small amount of water and none of the upbound ships have passed him. I can see no lights as before, and I don't have him on radar. I just hope he didn't take a nose dive."

*   *   *

Shortly after 10:30 P.M. on this November evening, Gerard Spears sat in his home in Toledo, Ohio, drowsily half-watching a "Dean Martin Roast" of motorcyclist-stuntman Evel Knievel, which was being televised on Channel 13. Spears had spent many years aboard the Great Lakes iron boats. Many of his closest friends still worked the boats; one of his sons was crewing an ore boat.

Jerry had left the lakes following the deaths of his wife and then a few years later his oldest son, preferring the somewhat more stable life of a truck driver.

As he sat, dozing, something on television attracted his attention and he sat upright, now wide awake. At the bottom of the television screen ran a news bulletin: an ore freighter had been reported missing and was feared sunk during a fierce storm on Lake Superior.

The bulletin would have caused Spears, as a former sailor,

to feel the sudden tug of fear that all mariners experience when the word goes out that a ship is in trouble. But Spears had added reason to worry: his son, Tim, had shipped out aboard the *Armco*—an ore freighter—a few days earlier and was headed for Superior. The bulletin had not identified the stricken ship. Could it be Tim's?

Almost immediately the phone at the Spears home began ringing as friends and relations—having themselves seen the television bulletin—anxiously called to ask if Jerry had additional information.

In other homes around Toledo, other people were frightened and seeking answers to nagging questions. Toledo is a Great Lakes port city, with facilities to dock and unload the ocean-going ships coming down the St. Lawrence Seaway bringing goods from nations around the globe. Many sailors made their homes in the Toledo area—including seven members of the *Fitzgerald*'s crew. Telephones jangled mercilessly as the frenetic quest for news swelled: was it true? . . . had a ship gone down? . . . what ship was it? . . . what about the crew—had anyone heard about the men—were they safe? . . .

The questions continued unsatisfied until eleven o'clock, when the local radio and television news broadcasts at last provided some of the answers: the missing ship had been identified as the ore carrier *Edmund Fitzgerald*, she had apparently sunk, a search by Coast Guard vessels and aircraft—assisted by several commercial ships in the area—was underway. No word was available at that time regarding the twenty-nine-man crew.

To friends and families of men who were known to be aboard other ships, the identification came as a blessed relief, dampened by the dreadful knowledge that this feeling of happy release would not be shared by the wives and children, the mothers and fathers, the brothers and sisters, the sweethearts, and the friends of the men of the *Edmund Fitzgerald*.

"Superior never gives up her dead" was an established *truth* well known to all who have ever sent loved ones out on the unforgiving and malevolent lake, and it rang like a chilling tocsin as through the long, anguished night news continued to filter into the homes around Toledo and Cleveland and Ashtabula and North Olmsted, Ohio; and in Bradenton and Clearwater, Florida; and in Duluth; and in Superior, Wisconsin; and in Canogha Park, California. And the news was all bad.

Calls to the shipping company that operated the *Fitzgerald* provided little comfort to the families of the crewmen, whose future lives, in the early hours, seemed to be hinging on the caprice of an unfeeling and uncaring news media.

"We have no information. . . . There is nothing to worry about; the ship is probably anchored in some sheltered spot. . . . We will be in contact with you when there is something definite to report. . . . There is nothing definite at this time. . . ."

They knew better.

The Coast Guard was no more liberal with the information it had when beseeched by those with the greatest vested interest in the activities occurring on Lake Superior this stormy night.

When definitive statements did begin reaching the families of the crew, the hideous news was most often transmitted in one of two ways: by radio or television news broadcast or by telephone.

Irmengard Kalmon, wife of the *Fitzgerald*'s second cook, was in the bedroom of their Washburn, Wisconsin, home when her seventeen-year-old daughter walked in.

"They just said on TV that Dad's ship is missing," the high school senior told her mother.

Helen Bindon, wife of the ship's first assistant engineer, learned the next morning when her sister-in-law telephoned the Bindon's Fairport Harbor, Ohio, residence to say that a Cleveland radio station had reported the sinking of the *Fitzgerald*. In nearby Berea, Ohio, Wilmer Holl, brother of Chief Engineer George J. Holl, received a telephone call from his daughter, who had heard the news on a Windsor, Ontario, radio station. Delores Ulrich, stepdaughter of Capt. Ernest M. McSorley, answered the telephone in her Toledo home; it was her mother-in-law, who, in a tremulous voice that puzzled

Delores, asked to speak to her son. Delores got the word a few minutes later when her husband, his face suddenly gone ashen, hung up the telephone.

In far-flung corners of the nation, relays clicked and circuits were opened to permit minuscule impulses of electricity to flash with the speed of light, activating telephone bells and buzzers which were followed by somber, choking voices whose utterances carried the same message: the *Fitzgerald* had vanished.

A few passed quiet nights in their beds, not to learn of the tragedy until the next morning.

At 5:00 A.M. on November 11, Brooksie Rafferty, wife of Robert C. Rafferty—the temporary cook who had been on the *Fitzgerald* for the past month—turned on her radio to hear the news broadcast reporting the loss of the ore boat. The report brought only mild concern to Mrs. Rafferty, whose resolute faith in the impregnable strength of the huge ship made the possibility of her foundering unthinkable. Brooksie felt confident that the *Fitz* was quietly languishing in some safe harbor, waiting for the storm to wane. There had been many occasions when ships on which Bob had sailed had been missing for several days in heavy fog or in impenetrable ice. This was another such instance, Brooksie felt sure. But her blind faith in the ship's safety was shattered later that morning when she turned on the television and heard a news commentator on the "Today" show announce with flat finality that the ore carrier *Edmund Fitzgerald* had sunk and that "an extensive air-sea search of the area had failed to find any survivors . . . no bodies have been recovered."

Ruth Hudson, mother of *Fitzgerald* Deckhand Bruce Lee Hudson, was driving into Cleveland on her way to work that morning, the car radio tuned to a local station. The cold, mechanical news report came like a hammer blow; Ruth later could not remember how she got back home.

Richard Orgel, a St. Lawrence Seaway tugboat captain, also heard a radio news report of the sinking and experienced the same shiver of dread Gerard Spears had felt the night before. Orgel, who three years earlier had served as third mate under

McSorley aboard the *Fitzgerald*, vividly recalled a stormy November night in 1972 when the ship, buffeted by gale-strength winds, seemed to be reacting erratically. As McSorley prepared to leave the wheelhouse for his cabin, he turned to Orgel and said ominously, "Oh, this thing, this sometimes scares me."

*   *   *

A spiritless, overcast dawn was breaking over Lake Superior, November 11, as Capt. Jesse "Bernie" Cooper of the *Anderson*, sagging with exhaustion and emotionally shaken, gazed out at the heaving, windswept lake and shook his head. In his thirty years on the lakes, Cooper had been witness to many storms and had lived through frequent periods of "heavy weather." But never had he seen a storm on the Great Lakes like the one that was now blowing itself out. Like a gigantic but invisible beast with its jugular cut, it had thrown itself down on the lake and had thrashed about madly as its life slowly drained away. Now, with a final shudder and a last gasp, it was dying. And in its death throes the storm had claimed a 729-foot-long freighter and killed twenty-nine men.

In 1958, when the *Fitzgerald* had splashed into the Great Lakes Engineering Work's launching basin, she had been the largest vessel ever to be dropped onto Great Lakes waters. Now, seventeen years later, she became the largest vessel ever to sink beneath them. And she had done so with such suddenness that the men on watch in her pilothouse had not the time to alert other ships in the area of her deadly peril.

A few hours earlier, having braved the furious storm to return to where the *Fitzgerald* had last been detected, the *Anderson* spotted the wreckage of one of the *Fitzgerald*'s lifeboats, so badly mangled that it looked as if it had been bitten in two by a ferocious sea monster.

Now, as he stood on the wing of the bridge, still trying to accept the reality of the loss of the *Fitzgerald* and her entire crew, a single word echoed and reechoed in Bernie Cooper's thoughts: *How?*

CHAPTER 2

"Nothing Is Certain"

Saturday, November 8, 1975.

High over the eastern slopes of the Rocky Mountains in New Mexico the low-pressure system churned, feeding a warm front then centered over Oklahoma. The low—with its counterclockwise circulation—sucked hot, moisture-laden air across west-central Texas from the Gulf of Mexico. The warm front was rapidly building towering cumulonimbus clouds, stretching upward to over fifty thousand feet. Each of these huge clouds was a potential storm factory; pulling the moist air from the surface—from plowed fields and from rocky terrain and even from paved roads—it carried the air far up into the clouds until it reached the saturation point, where it condensed, forming waterdrops which then began falling back through the clouds. As the waterdrops fell they produced friction, which then generated heat. The heat warmed the surrounding air, which then began to rise, pulling the waterdrops back toward the top of the clouds. This, in turn,

13

dragged additional moisture far up in the clouds, pumping more fuel into the growing system.

The low-pressure cell over New Mexico then joined with a low-pressure disturbance located over Ontario, forming a trough along which the warm front began to slide, moving to the northeast. If the warm front were to meet cooler, drier air along its path, the result would be a storm, with precipitation in the form of rain or snow. Such a meeting would also produce winds, the intensity of which would depend upon the difference in the temperatures of the two systems. However, as long as the warm front continued to move unrestricted by cooler air masses, it would steadily grow in strength. And on this Saturday, November 8, 1975, there was no concentration of cold air of sufficient size to halt the warm front's growth; it continued to lap up the hot air as it headed northward at twenty-five miles per hour. Like a forest fire left unchecked, it raged as it went, increasing its strength, feeding on the fuel in its path.

Far to the northwest, in the Canadian province of Alberta, a strong low-pressure cell had spawned a massive cold front which, on this same Saturday, was pumping cold, dry Arctic air down across the north-central United States. This system, which was strong enough to trigger the warm front moving up from Oklahoma, was rapidly heading east. If these two weather systems should meet, a fierce storm would result. And they would meet. On Monday, November 10, they would come together over Lake Superior.

*   *   *

Twenty-eight-year-old Richard Bishop had his own storm brewing on that Saturday in November. He was pacing nervously around his Duluth apartment, annoyed and frustrated after a month away from his job with a severe case of bleeding ulcers. The medical treatment he'd received had seemed to be working—at least until today. He'd felt good—better than he had in over a year—with no further stomach problems in two weeks. His physician had checked him at midweek and pronounced him sufficiently improved to return to work, "as long as you have no further pain." Bishop happily notified his employer that he would be back on the job Sunday, November 9. But now he wasn't so sure. A searing pain had begun early this morning and was slowly growing.

Like an animal who sensed an approaching storm and wandered about, aimlessly looking for a place to escape what he knew was coming, Bishop paced the room, certain that the burning deep in his stomach would grow until it became an agonizing inferno, inflaming his insides and leaving him writhing on his bed.

By midafternoon, Bishop had decided that he would not be going back to work the following day as he had planned and regretfully informed his employer—the Columbia Transportation Division of Oglebay-Norton Company—that it would be necessary for him to see his doctor before reporting for duty. He was first cook, assigned to an ore freighter operated by the company. The freighter was the *Edmund Fitzgerald,* and Richard Bishop's decision not to return aboard her the following day saved his life.

* * *

As the *Fitzgerald*'s first cook was coming to his fateful decision, the man who was to die in his place was busily cleaning the huge stainless steel table in the spacious galley aboard the big ship. He was tidying up between feedings as the ore boat plowed through a light chop on Lake Superior, heading down to the Duluth-Superior port facility where they were scheduled to load taconite pellets consigned to the Great Lakes Steel Company's complex near Detroit.

Sixty-two-year-old Robert Charles Rafferty had been a ship's cook and steward for more than thirty years. A big man, weighing close to two hundred pounds and standing just under six feet, he was the picture of what a ship's cook should look like.

Bob had spent half his life at sea and had been seven times

around the world on a variety of vessels. A perceptive, well-read man, he had overcome an unhappy childhood. Born in East Toledo in 1913 with a congenital malady which left him totally bald throughout his adolescence, he bore the brunt of years of cruel humiliation and ridicule administered by his contemporaries. He did not have a reasonable head of hair until his early twenties, and even then the hair grew so slowly that Bob once kiddingly remarked that he was considering applying to the television quiz show "I've Got a Secret" as a man who had never had a haircut. Orphaned at age thirteen, he had grown up in a Masonic Home and had won a partial scholarship in chemistry at Oberlin College in Ohio. But the depression years made continuing his education at that time impractical, and so Bob Rafferty gravitated to the sea, shipping out on his first cruise in 1931.

In 1948 Rafferty became interested in a twenty-two-year-old widow from Knoxville, Tennessee, named Brooksie, who had been corresponding with Bob's roommate in Toledo.

"The fella was a brother of a girl I worked with," Brooksie recalled. "We began writing to each other and dating whenever he was in town. One day Bob got hold of a letter I had written to this guy, and began writing to me himself. Then, the next thing I knew, Bob showed up in Knoxville."

After a modest courtship, Bob and Brooksie were married.

Brooksie brought her two-year-old son, Randall, to live with the newlyweds in Toledo.

"Since my first husband had died, rather than my having been divorced, Bob did not adopt Randy, but insisted that the boy keep his father's name. But in every other way, Randy was like his own son."

When Randy, then a member of the U.S. Air Force, mentioned to Rafferty that he would be making periodic trips to Vietnam, Bob immediately signed up for ocean duty on the Pacific run to have an opportunity of seeing his son as often as possible. "They had a bet between them as to who would get to Vietnam first," Rafferty's wife remembers.

But Bob made it to the Far East only twice, and on both

occasions he and Randall missed connections and did not see each other.

Bob was a loving, doting father, both to Randy and his natural daughter, Pamela. "I can remember him spanking us only once," Pam recalls. "He was napping when Randy and I began fighting. Dad came down and spanked us both with a toilet brush."

"He wasn't a strict disciplinarian," Randy insists. "In fact, he was really a soft touch."

Randy also remembers his stepfather as a highly intelligent man. "He was far more intellectual than I am; the boats did more harm to him than good, intellectually."

But Bob Rafferty loved his job and the ships on which he worked. ("If I threw water on the house and shook it, maybe he would stay home more," Brooksie had once jokingly remarked.) He was an excellent cook among cooks who are noted for their culinary talents, and he was particularly proud of the cakes, pies, and tasty breads he created in the well-equipped boat galleys.

Yet while he took great pleasure in his work, his devotion to his family made the long months away from them all the more prolonged, and constantly tore at him. His children had not only grown up, they had grown away, and the years he could use to stem his regret at having lost something precious were rapidly passing him by. He and his beloved Brooksie were in the twilight of their lives. It was time to concentrate on the mellow years they could yet spend together—to lavish in the joy of grandchildren, of holidays together as a family, of peaceful walks and quiet conversation—closing out their years bathing in the relaxing warmth of one another's nearness. It was time to think of retirement.

It would not be easy for him; he had worked all his life, and idleness was an assault on his patience. He knew that in the stillness of warm summer nights stretching out in front of him, there would be times when he would pause and listen intently for the low roll of a ship's whistle on the Maumee River, and in these moments he would feel the stubborn tug of more than thirty years of sailing away. And there would be the incessant memories. The diaphanous faces of a thousand shipmates would drift through limitless reverie. The ghosts of a hundred ships would steam away in the gloom of his melancholy dreams. The dull throb of a hundred decks would reverberate in endless nights of fitful sleep.

No, it would not be easy for him. But easy or not, this would be his last year on the iron boats.

To prepare himself for the day when he would finally turn his back on the lure of the Great Lakes, Bob Rafferty had forsaken his customary practice of signing on with a single ship at the beginning of the season and staying with it throughout the year. Instead, he had worked 1975 as a "temporary," taking berths on an interim basis, filling in for cooks and stewards on vacation or off their ships for personal reasons. This had allowed him more time at home with his family and had permitted him to skip an occasional trip to test his newly acquired determination to learn the art of idleness.

A month earlier he had been assigned to the *Edmund Fitzgerald* to fill in for her first cook, who had been taken off the boat with a severe case of bleeding ulcers. Rafferty was delighted at the opportunity to work aboard the flagship of the Oglebay-Norton fleet. The ship was well known and admired by practically all of the mariners on the Great Lakes. Bob loved the huge, modern galley with its stainless steel tables and equipment, and particularly her excellent ovens— perfect for baking bread.

"He was like a little kid with a new toy," his family said of his reaction to learning of the assignment.

But something had happened.

As the ship steamed toward Superior-Duluth, Bob Rafferty was anxious to be off the *Edmund Fitzgerald*.

His daughter, Pamela Johnson, was due to present Bob with his fourth grandchild, and he wanted very much to be at home when the happy event occurred.

But there was another more disturbing and totally irrational reason for wanting to be away from the *Fitzgerald*. After three decades at sea unconcerned with the possible threats to his life posed by the vagaries of nature, Robert Charles Rafferty had suddenly become afraid.

Not a superstitious man, he had never taken stock in omens of any kind. Yet for the past nine days Rafferty had been plagued by a disturbing premonition. It first struck him on October 31—Halloween—during his last visit to his Toledo home.

"He seemed bothered by something and spent an unusual amount of time with me, talking about the upcoming Michigan–Ohio State football game. We always watched it on TV together," Randy would later recall. "But this time he said that I would have to watch it without him. I didn't understand."

Then, just as he was preparing to leave to report back to the ship, Rafferty—never a demonstrative individual—suddenly threw his arms around Randy and placed a tender kiss on his stepson's cheek.

"I was twenty-eight years old, and for him to have done that was very surprising; I can't remember him having done that since I was a little kid."

The *Fitzgerald* sailed from Toledo on the final day of October 1975, steaming to Silver Bay, Minnesota, where they loaded taconite pellets for Ashtabula. From Ashtabula the ship headed north again, this time bound for Superior, Wisconsin.

Throughout the voyage, Rafferty had been unable to shake the feeling of imminent calamity threatening the *Fitzgerald*. His normal effusive demeanor gave way to a raw, somber mood which was only briefly relieved when he was informed— at Silver Bay—that the regular cook might return to duty when the ship called at Superior on November 8.

"Get off this ship as soon as you can," he had blurted to a crewman.

As the *Fitz* moved smoothly past Isle Royale in calm seas on that Saturday, November 8, Rafferty's dismal perspective began to lift slightly. He would leave the ship as soon as she docked and he was assured that Dick Bishop would, indeed, be returning to duty. He would then catch the first flight out of Duluth for Toledo. If the ship made Superior early enough, he might be in his home that very night.

He sought out First Mate John McCarthy, who he had seen a few minutes earlier in the officer's dining room, to ask when they would be making port.

"Sorry, Bob," McCarthy said, sipping from a large coffee mug. "Bishop notified Cleveland that his ulcer was acting up again. I forgot to let you know: you'll be staying with us for a while."

Rafferty shrugged, masking the bitter disappointment he felt, and walked back into the spacious galley. Moving to the open door leading to the fantail, he gazed out at the ship's wake, looking at—but not seeing—the gulls following the ship, dropping to pause occasionally on the gentle swell of the lake.

The *Fitz* was scheduled to take the Superior load of taconite to the Great Lakes Steel complex at Zug Island, near Detroit. From there the orders were to proceed directly back north, this time to Superior, Wisconsin, where they were to load taconite for Toledo. Bob took small comfort in the fact that he would have a few hours at home while the ship was being unloaded in Ohio. Then it was back for one more load at Silver Bay, which would close out the shipping season for the *Fitzgerald*. If Bishop did not report back to duty during this season, Bob would stay aboard the boat until it was secured for the winter, probably at Toledo. It meant that he would be able to have Brooksie and Randy aboard for Thanksgiving dinner. This pleasant thought brightened his mood and sent him rushing to his quarters to begin working on a Thanksgiving menu.

*   *   *

In the modest mobile home off Consaul Avenue in Toledo, Brooksie Rafferty also busied herself on that pleasant November Saturday, tidying up the living room of the home she and Bob had purchased the year before because it was close to the boat docks.

As she moved about the room dusting and straightening the furniture, her eyes fell upon the picture postcard Bob had mailed from Silver Bay.

The face of the card bore a full-color photograph of the rocky shoals along the Lake Superior shoreline. On the back was a brief, handwritten message which said simply: "May be home by Nov. 8. However, nothing is certain."

CHAPTER 3

"She Was for Homesteading"

Sunday, November 9, 1975.

It would be a nice day. The temperature had been unseasonably warm for northern Wisconsin during the past several days. What snow that had been on the ground had disappeared; the thin coating of ice in the rivers and streams had melted.

As Clarence Edward Dennis drove on to U.S. Highway 2 near his home in Maple and headed west, he luxuriated in the thought that working outside today would be almost pleasant. Ed (he hated his given first name) was employed as a boat loader with Burlington Northern Company, operating the machinery that directed raw iron ore or taconite pellets—coming from the once-rich mines along the Mesabi Range in northeastern Minnesota—into the holds of the huge freighters that called throughout the shipping season at the docks lining the sheltered harbor between Superior, Wisconsin, and Duluth.

Dennis had spent sixteen of his thirty-four years' service with Burlington Northern as a loader and had grown accustomed to, if not happy with, the frigid winds that whip across Lake Superior from early November until late spring. Working high atop the loading pockets exposed him to the full force of the icy blast coming off the lake when the winds blew out of the north and made his days a seemingly endless agony during the bitter months. Summers were something else; they made the horrors of winter bearable. The bright, warm sun and gentle breezes—plus the added feeling of freedom afforded to those who labor in the outdoors—were benefits bought and paid for during the bone-chilling, teeth-rattling months. It was a trade-off that men like Ed Dennis made willingly, a bargain struck with Mother Nature that occasionally earned a bonus—an unexpected and welcome largess—a break from the tedium of uninterrupted heat or cold or rain or drought. Today would bring such a gift.

As the first light of a cloudy dawn filtered over the hilly Wisconsin farmland and a soft puff of southerly air caressed the tall pines and the leafless oaks, maples, and birch trees along his route, Ed Dennis almost smiled. Yes, it would be a nice day.

*   *   *

In the National Weather Service Forecast Office in Chicago, the staff meteorologists on duty at 6:00 A.M., November 9, 1975, were putting the finishing touches on the preliminary forecast for Illinois and the Chicago area. A marine weather forecast would also be prepared in this office, detailing the conditions expected for the next six hours on Lake Michigan and Lake Superior. These forecasts would be broadcast on two special frequencies to all ships on the lakes every five minutes, twenty-four hours a day, seven days a week. Special weather updates or advisories were broadcast whenever conditions on the lakes required. At least one meteorologist trained in marine forecasting was on duty in this weather office at all times.

The Lake Superior forecast which would be released at
10:34 on this Sunday morning would read: "South-southeast
winds, 8 to 16 knots this afternoon, becoming southeast to east
and increasing to 20 to 33 knots tonight and becoming east to
northeast 28 to 38 knots Monday: cloudy, occasional rain
tonight and Monday, waves one to three feet increasing to
three to eight feet on Monday."

The marine forecaster on duty used computer data and
teletype sequence reports supplied to weather service forecast
offices by several hundred official reporting stations throughout the country, plus local and long-distance weather radar
and twice-hourly photos from weather satellites positioned in
stationary orbits over the North American continent. The
marine forecaster also scanned communiqués sent from the
eight Coast Guard stations around Lake Superior as well as
information sent from various commercial vessels which had
been designated by the National Oceanographic and Atmospheric Administration as weather-reporting ships (the *Fitzgerald* was one of forty vessels so designated). Adding this data
to the bits and pieces of meteorological facts constantly
pouring into the weather office, the marine forecaster sought
to synthesize from the myriad of obscure numerals and cryptic
symbols a succinct prophesy of things to come. It was—when
reduced to its simplest denominator—with all the advantages
and advancements in modern technology, largely an exercise
in scientific fortune-telling, a technological tea leaf reading on
which countless lives might depend.

The most significant of the complex measurements and
observations funneling into the Chicago office that morning
was the growing storm system speeding up from the southwest. The National Weather Service Office in Kansas City had
indicated that the system would spawn a "typical November
storm." But to the forecasters in Chicago, this weather cell
had all the characteristics of a "Texas Hook," a storm that is
born of Pacific air which swoops out of the central Rocky
Mountains into Texas and Oklahoma—picking up large
quantities of warm moisture—and then veers to the north,
where it can boil over in violent winter storms over the

Midwest. There was, early on November 9, an uneasiness among the Chicago weathermen that this storm had the potential of becoming something other than "typical."

At 0700 the center of the low-pressure cell was located over south-central Kansas, moving to the northeast with a minimum barometric pressure of 29.53 inches of mercury (reduced to sea level). By one o'clock in the afternoon the storm would have moved over the northeast corner of Kansas, intensifying rapidly as it moved at an average forward speed of thirty-seven knots. At this time its minimum barometric pressure will have dropped to 29.40 inches.

The forecasters, early on Sunday, were predicting that the track of the storm would take it south of Lake Superior. This prediction would later be changed.

*   *   *

As the meteorologists in the Chicago weather office plotted the advancing storm's course, and as Ed Dennis drove the nearly deserted highway leading to Superior, Wisconsin, the steamer *Edmund Fitzgerald* was plowing through calm seas at a steady nineteen knots on a heading of 250 degrees, about fifteen miles northeast of the breakwater dividing the huge lake from the Superior-Duluth ship harbor. Activity aboard the ship was beginning to pick up as members of her crew gathered for breakfast in the two mess rooms located in the after deckhouse. The ship and her crew were about to make their last port of call; less than forty hours from this moment the *Fitzgerald* would lie twisted and broken on the bottom of this lake, just seventeen years after her gala christening.

*   *   *

June 8, 1958, dawned as a warm, hazy, overcast Sunday in southeastern Michigan. Since before 9:00 A.M. a line of automobiles had moved slowly along Great Lakes Avenue in River Rouge, a downriver suburb on the southern fringes of Detroit.

The destination of this vehicular traffic was the drab, sprawling grounds of the Great Lakes Engineering Works—a shipbuilding firm. The people coming here this quiet Sunday morning were to attend the launching of a huge ore freighter.

Identified by its builders as hull number 301—constructed on order from the Northwestern Mutual Life Insurance Company of Milwaukee—the ship had already been chartered, under a long-term lease, to the Columbia Transportation Division of the Oglebay-Norton Company, a transportation and mining firm with headquarters in Cleveland. The lease was scheduled to run until 1983.

Shortly before noon on this June day in 1958, a large crowd—one newspaper estimate gave the size of the gathering as high as ten thousand persons—watched eagerly as the wife of the new ship's namesake, the president and chairman of the board of the vessel's owners, bashed the traditional bottle of champagne against the hull, signaling a spectacular side launching. Dozens of shipyard workers, clinging precariously to a mammoth rolling crane on the opposite side of the launching basin, waved and shouted. With a grinding, screeching moan, she slid down the greased way timbers to splash into the oily black water of the basin, wallowing for several minutes in the backwash of her launching while three members of her construction gang clutched the poop deck railing to steady themselves following the wild ride. Above them, a large American flag flapped from the ship's jack staff.

As horns and whistles loudly declared the birth of this new steamer, those in attendance stood and marveled at her awesome size. At 729 feet she was the longest ship ever to be launched on the Great Lakes, a distinction she would hold for the next thirteen years. With a beam measuring 75 feet and a depth from keelson to spar deck of 39 feet, she was, by the standards of that day, a big ship.

Across her stern, in freshly painted white letters, gleamed her name: *Edmund Fitzgerald.*

The Fitzgerald family had been associated with Great Lakes shipping for generations: Edmund Fitzgerald's grandfather and five great uncles had served as skippers aboard lake steamers. The family felt certain that this new giant would add a worthy and memorable page to the Fitzgerald history.

A conventional "straight decker," the *Fitzgerald* had a rated cargo capacity of 25,891 tons, but with a later increase in allowable tonnage, she would in 1969 set a single trip record for ore freighters of 27,402 tons. Driven by a seven-thousand-horsepower steam turbine engine, she had a top speed, fully loaded, of sixteen knots, making her among the fastest ore boats on the lakes.

Soon nicknamed *"Big Fitz,"* she became the flagship of the Columbia fleet, an honor that rated a special salute when meeting other company ships. Duty aboard her was awarded to the best and most experienced officers. The honor of shaking down the new boat following her commissioning in September 1958 went to Capt. Bert Lambert, a crusty old-timer whose final assignment for Columbia before retiring was to "bring out" the *Fitz.*

With the retirement of Lambert, command of the *Fitzgerald* fell to Capt. Newman C. "Joe" Larsen, a veteran ship's master who, until his retirement following the 1965 shipping season, set annual records for the number of trips completed and total tonnage carried each season.

Larsen's successor was a resolute but colorful sea dog of thirty-four years' experience as ship's master named Peter Pulcer. With twenty-six years' seniority commanding Oglebay-Norton vessels, Pulcer was a man of flamboyant personality given to referring to himself as the "Commodore" of the Columbia fleet because he commanded the company's flagship.

Pulcer "went on the beach" at the end of the 1971 shipping season, turning over command of the *Fitzgerald* to a soft-spoken, unpretentious veteran of forty-four years' sailing experience named Ernest Michael McSorley.

Born in 1913 amid the high bluffs of Ogdensburg, New York—a small upstate village whose most famous native had been Frederic Remington, the noted artist-sculptor of the

American West—McSorley had spent his youthful years roaming the banks of the St. Lawrence River, which flows by the town. It was here that his love for the water had its genesis. A quietly intense boy, he had few interests beyond his dream that someday he would sail as master of a ship. His passion for command was overpowering, yet seldom stated. He, even as a boy, kept his dreams to himself, rarely confiding in anyone.

McSorley began his career on the lakes at the age of eighteen, signing on as a lowly deckhand. In 1938 he came to Columbia as a wheelsman, staying with the company for the rest of his working life. His determination to one day captain his own ship drove him on. He patiently moved up the ladder of command: third mate, second mate, first mate, until in 1951, just before his thirty-eighth birthday, he was appointed master of the 255-foot *Carrollton*—a sand and pig iron carrier—thus becoming the youngest ship master on the Great Lakes at that time.

After one season aboard the *Carrollton*, Captain McSorley served the next three years as master on the *William E. Stifel* and the *Ben. E. Tate*. During the 1955 shipping season he commanded Columbia's *Harry T. Ewing* and spent 1956 aboard the *Robert J. Paisley*. Next came a two-year command on the *J. B. Sensibar* and three years aboard the *W. W. Holloway*. Then it was back to the *Sensibar* for another three seasons before assuming command of the *Joseph H. Frantz* for a four-year tour. In 1970 he was moved over to the *Armco*, one of Columbia's larger and newer ore carriers.

With the beginning of the 1972 shipping season, after thirty-four years' service with Columbia, Capt. Ernest Michael McSorley—whose determination had fired his sometimes slow and painful movement up the chain of success—finally grasped what was for him the golden prize, the quest for which had pushed and prodded him throughout the long difficult years. The mighty *Edmund Fitzgerald* became "his."

No longer the *"Big Fitz"*—the 858-foot *Roger Blough* had become the largest Great Lakes vessel a year earlier—still, she was the company's flagship, with a proud and enviable record of achievement. She was the newest of the more than twenty ships operated by Columbia; she was considered a lucky assignment among the men who regularly worked the iron boats of the Great Lakes.

McSorley loved the boat with the same passion he had shown for his ambition to reach the top of his chosen profession: rejecting midseason vacations, feeling reluctant to be away from the ship for more than a few hours when in port, once refusing to go ashore when ill with pneumonia.

He was a quiet, sober man whose sharp but pleasant features and full head of thick, dark hair gave him the distinguished appearance of a bank president or company executive a full ten years younger than his true age. Never a boisterous man, he wore a quiet gentleness that belied his Irish heredity. He did not fraternize well with his crew; even his officers found him cool and distant, serious and all business. But what he lacked in personal warmth he had more than made up for in an industrywide reputation for competence and skill; he was a gifted virtuoso with the huge, awkward ore boats. McSorley was a man whose crew came to trust and respect him for his willingness to treat them as the professionals they were, rarely intruding into their areas of responsibility, never reminding them unnecessarily of his high office as master of the vessel or of his power with the company.

Beyond his deep and permanent affection for his ship, the only other love to occupy his thoughts was that for his gentle, soft-spoken wife, Nellie.

Their union had produced no offspring, but Nellie was the mother of three children by a previous marriage; McSorley found it difficult to feign the effusive behavior of a stepfather desiring to fill the void left by a natural male parent. Consequently he did not, with one exception, feel close to Nellie's children. The exception was Delores, with whom he developed a close father-daughter relationship, one which gladdened his heart and helped to relieve the gnawing sense of loss at not having produced an heir to his blood.

Nellie had been in poor health for some time by November 1975. On October 31, while in Toledo—where they had made their home—he had visited her at a nursing home in nearby Sylvania, Ohio, where she was recuperating from a slight stroke. Although neither realized it at the time, it was to be their last meeting.

Because of his wife's declining health, McSorley had begun to turn his thoughts to the subject of retirement, to a time when he could at last direct his full concentration and concern to his precious Nellie.

"The *Fitzgerald* was his whole life," Delores would say later of her stepfather. But while he did not always show it, he loved his wife as well, and he had become increasingly conscious of her need for more attention than he could personally provide during the ten months he was away from home each year.

His willing commitment to the woman who shared his life ashore was now being added to the full weight of the years of struggle he had spent to reach his goal, and the years of crushing responsibility to his company, his crew, and his ship had begun to warp his trenchant enthusiasm for the siren call of the open water.

Retirement would not necessarily come at the close of the 1975 season and perhaps not the next, or even the next. But it was an inevitable step he knew he must take before too many more seasons had passed.

Giving up his beloved *Fitz* would be an indescribable agony for him; leaving her for the last time would be tantamount to abandoning a cherished, helpless child. She was everything he had dreamed a good ship would be, and the memory of her would, he knew, haunt him for all the days of his life. There would never be another *Fitz* for him.

Indeed, the *Fitz* was a special ship for all who sailed in her.

"She was for homesteading," is the way a former crew member would later describe her. Once having been assigned to the boat, sailors tended to make every effort to preserve their berths aboard her.

To the landbound observer it is often difficult to understand the mystical veneration lake sailors have for the swollen, bargelike ore boats—"the scows with glandular conditions"—that plod sluggishly over the Great Lakes. Yet there *is* a strange majesty, an isolated grandeur that attracts attention. On Sunday afternoons in summer, the parks and drives along the shoreline—particularly those bordering the Detroit River—are lined with autos occupied by individuals, couples, and entire families who have stopped to watch the massive freighters glide slowly by. On Belle Isle, an island park in the river between Detroit and Windsor, they come by the hundreds to relax and watch the boats as they pass just a few dozen yards away—so close that the men in the wheelhouses or off-duty crewmen, basking on the hatch covers, can easily be seen.

To the men who sail in them, these leviathans of the lake are their places of employment—their offices and shops and plants. They are functioning industrial complexes staffed by men for whom rush hour traffic jams, jammed parking lots, and all the other annoyances and indignities faced by those who labor on shore are unknown. Their daily lives are encapsulated; their ships contain—in addition to their work locations—their living rooms, bedrooms, kitchens, and bathrooms. Within a few yards of each other are places of recreation and relaxation, places of social activity, or places to be alone. To many sailors the ship is the only real home they have ever known; the ports at which the ship calls are the only towns they can identify with.

And by the 1970s, the ore boats had become pleasant, comfortable places in which to live and work. Gone were the days of the infamous "glory-holes," the forecastles into which the crews were crammed: a single compartment that was alternately freezing cold or unbearably hot but always damp, sweaty, and smelly, where narrow, uncomfortable bunks lined the walls and where a long table down the center of the crowded room offered the only place to sit, eat, write, gamble, or simply engage a fellow crewmate in conversation, places that offered little comfort and no privacy.

Aboard ships such as the *Fitzgerald*, each member of the

crew, with but two or three exceptions, had a private room similar in size and layout to a moderately priced room in a good motel. Painted in bright, pleasant colors, the rooms had at least one porthole to allow light to enter, a comfortable bed with innerspring or box mattress, a closet or wardrobe, a writing desk and chair, a dresser, and wall shelves. The floors were tiled, and some rooms had private baths. Those that did not had sinks with hot and cold running water, with a semiprivate shower located down the passageway. The men were encouraged to decorate their rooms in whatever manner or motif suited their personalities, and many brought colorful bedspreads, curtains, and area rugs aboard to give a special touch of homeyness to their quarters. Most had their own radios or televisions—reception quality was dependent upon the location of the ship—or stereo or tape players.

The *Fitzgerald*, like other ore boats, was divided into three basic sections. The forward, or maneuvering section, consisted of the dunnage deck, main deck forward, spar deck forward, forecastle deck, and Texas deck. These five deck levels contained storage and machinery areas; windlass and anchor engines; quarters for the captain, mates, wheelsmen, and deckhands; guest staterooms; and a passenger lounge, captain's office, wheelhouse, and chart room.

The after, or engineering section (sometimes referred to as the propulsion section), included the engine room, operating deck, main deck aft, spar deck aft, and poop deck. In these spaces were the machinery to drive and power the ship; quarters for the engineering officers, engine room crew, cooks, and stewards; a large, fully equipped galley, pantry, and food storage sections; separate crew's and officer's dining rooms; a small machine shop; fire-fighting equipment; and laundry facilities for the crew. Both forward and after sections of the *Fitzgerald* had crew lounges which contained a television set, refrigerator, tables and chairs for letter writing or playing cards, easy chairs and a couch, and an electric coffee maker. Coffee and snacks were available twenty-four hours a day.

Between the fore and aft sections was the cargo hold—a

huge warehouse measuring approximately five hundred feet in length, almost fifty feet across, and thirty feet deep. Twenty-one hatches provided openings into the hold through which the material to be transported by the ship could be loaded.

The men aboard worked in three shifts, or "watches," of four hours followed by eight hours off duty. The men on the first watch came on duty at midnight and worked until 4:00 A.M. They were then off watch until noon. The second watch worked from 4:00 A.M. until 8:00, and the third watch stood from 8:00 until noon, when the first watch reported back on duty.

The watches were set at the beginning of the shipping season and were determined by seniority, with those having the longest service aboard the boat getting first choice of the watches.

The shipping season on the Great Lakes began, as a general rule, in March or April—when the ice on the lakes had broken up—and continued until late November or early December, with a few ships operating into January, ice conditions permitting. In the 1960s and early 1970s, attempts were made to keep the lakes open to shipping on a year-round basis. Most shipping ceased, however, when the frigid winds from Canada closed the lakes to all but the Coast Guard icebreakers and those who chose to crawl slowly behind them. The majority of ships "wintered up," and their crews went ashore until the soft winds of spring once again opened the lakes for business.

The nonofficer crewmen aboard the ore boats were represented, for collective bargaining purposes, by the United Steel Workers of America, and wages for these crew members were structured as part of the union's contract with the shipping companies.

In 1975 a crewman aboard the *Fitzgerald* received a base pay of $5.63 an hour for a forty-hour workweek. Since the ship operated on a seven-day week, a crew member earned an additional twenty-four hours in pay based on time and a half for every hour over the initial forty, totaling $360.32 per week in gross income. In addition, he was given a periodic cost-of-living adjustment. Added to this was a bonus of ten percent of his gross earnings if he stayed with the boat until December 20, and fifteen percent if the crewman remained aboard after the twentieth of December. An annual bonus of between $50 and $200 (depending on length of service with Oglebay-Norton) was also paid.

With room and board supplied by the ship owner, an unmarried crew member, if frugal, could end the season with savings in excess of $15,000. Even for the married sailor supporting a family and buying a home, the wages he could earn during a season on the boats was not bad for ten months' work in the mid-1970s.

As the *Fitzgerald* steamed through the breakwater, heading for the Burlington Northern loading docks, the major problem for the crew would be not how much they would earn for the year. Without knowing it, they were facing the problem of how to spend the last hours of their lives.

CHAPTER 4

"He Was a Good Friendly Guy"

Ed Dennis swung his 1974 Buick off Second Street in Superior and into the Burlington Northern employees' parking lot. Locking the car and heading toward the one-hundred-foot-high ore dock number 1, he could see a ship sliding up the quarter-mile-long quay. The stack markings—a large yellow *C* affixed to a red star—told him the boat belonged to Columbia Transportation Company. Number 1 dock was Ed's; he would be loading this boat today.

He took the elevator to the top of the dock, walked into the employees' locker-lunchroom, and checked in with the time-keeper. It was 7:00 A.M. Although he was not scheduled to begin work until 7:30, Dennis made it a practice of arriving at least a half hour early each morning.

As Dennis pulled on the pair of coveralls he would wear that day, Donald Amys, BN general foreman, strolled into the room, a book with a dirty brown cover tucked under his arm. Ed recognized it as the "boat book," a volume in which was

37

kept a running record of the ore or taconite pellets loaded from number 1 dock into the freighters calling at Burlington Northern.

As Dennis and Amys exchanged greetings, the foreman flipped open the book to a page headed "National Pellets."

"This boat just came in; the night shift left it for you," Amys said with a wry grin, handing the open book to Ed. On the second line of the open page, written in pencil, he read the words "E. Fitzgerald—11/9." Below this were printed columns of numerals signifying pocket numbers in the loading dock. Next to each pocket number the number of tons of ore pellets in each pocket had been pencilled in.

"Don't remember ever loading *Fitzgerald* before," Dennis commented.

"I was just up on the deck, checking the pockets. She's a straight decker; you shouldn't have any problems. Besides, it's a nice day; even the mate should be in a good humor," Amys said before moving on through the room.

At 7:27, Ed stepped out of the door and up a short flight of stairs to the large deck at the top of the loading dock. Moving to the east side, he leaned over the railing and looked down at the ore boat, her starboard side secured to the wharf. In large white letters, painted across the front of her after deckhouse, was her name: *Edmund Fitzgerald*.

Looking the ship over, Dennis could not remember having seen her before. In fact he probably had, but not recently. The *Fitzgerald* called only on infrequent occasions. She usually loaded fifty miles north of Superior at Silver Bay. During the 1975 shipping season, the *Fitz* had called at Burlington Northern just four times, and not at all in 1974.

Scanning the spar deck of the ore boat, Dennis noted a short, stocky man walking along the starboard side of the deck, watching as the large mobile hatch crane rolled on its tracks over number 17 hatch—the four hatch covers toward the stern had already been removed and placed on the deck in the spaces between the hatch coamings—as a four-man deck crew prepared to fasten the steel cables, dangling below the crane, to the eyebolts at each corner of the seven-ton hatch cover. The man, Dennis concluded, would be the boat's first mate—the officer usually supervising the loading operation.

"We've got two-six-one-one-six for you," Ed shouted down to the mate, reading the total tonnage scheduled to be loaded on board the boat from the shipping order that called for 26,116 long tons of taconite pellets. He also informed the mate that the loading pockets contained loads of 300- and 100-ton increments.

"Fine," the mate shouted back and waved. "We're ready to load any time."

This one seemed friendly, Dennis thought. Many first mates were inclined to be less than cordial. "Some of them are real crabby," Dennis would later comment. "They can screech at you pretty loud. But this guy was real nice."

On the loading deck, spaced every twelve feet, were pairs of levers. These operated the 187 loading chutes on the east side of the dock—one set of levers for each chute—raising or lowering the chutes to stop or start the flow of pellets into the cargo hold of the ship.

Dennis moved to chute number 84, which lined up over hatch number 21—the most after hatch on the *Fitzgerald*—glanced back to the ship's deck, and began pulling the levers. One lever operated the clutch mechanism that caused the chute to rise; the brake controlled the lowering of the chute. A foot pedal also controlled the brake, allowing the loader to stop and hold the chute in any position desired without holding the lever. It was vital to the loading process that the ship be in a level position when fully loaded, and the loader could—by raising and lowering the chutes in the proper manner—fully control where the stream of pellets went in the hold. To assist both first mate and the loader in positioning the load, two sets of "trim lights" were provided. One set of lights—a red, a green, and a white—were located high on the stack at the rear of the ship. An identical set of three lights was fastened, horizontally, to the radar mast atop the wheelhouse. The lights were carefully monitored during loading by both the mate and the loader. A red light meant the ship was tilting to the left (port side); a green light indicated a starboard list. A white light told them the boat was level.

Dennis lowered the chute of pocket number 84 down to 21 hatch, braking to slow the chute until it gently came to rest on the raised coaming of the hatch.

"The mates don't like it if the chute hits the coaming hard, so you don't do it," Dennis remembers.

> The system of hatch coamings, gaskets, covers and clamps installed on *Fitzgerald* required continuing maintenance and repair, both from routine wear because of the frequent removal and replacement of the covers and *from damage which regularly occurred during cargo transfer* . . . a general item to repair hatch covers and coamings had been included in the work list for the winter lay-up which *Fitzgerald* was approaching when it was lost. It is concluded that the system of cargo hatch coamings, gaskets, covers and clamps which was installed on *Fitzgerald* and the manner in which this system was maintained did not provide an effective means of preventing the penetration of water into the ship in any given sea condition, as required by Coast Guard regulations . . . —Department of Transportation, Coast Guard Marine Casualty Report (USCG 16732/64216), page 93.

A "tripper," usually a Burlington Northern employee, worked on the deck of the loading ship, opening the doors of the chute to allow the pellets to flow out of the pocket. On November 9, 1975, Elmer Koski was Ed Dennis's tripper.

Once the chute was opened, the contents of the pocket were allowed to completely empty into the ship, with a slight raising or lowering of the chute to direct the flow of pellets.

Through the first few hours of loading, the *Fitzgerald* took a "straight run" of pellets, all twenty-one hatches over the boat's three cargo holds taking one pocket each of three hundred tons. The ship was then shifted, moving back toward the far end of the dock to align the hatches with the next series of full ore pockets. Five or six additional three-hundred-ton pockets were emptied into the after hold to lower the stern of the ship. This done, the mate shouted to Dennis that he was going to stop loading to "pump out"—to empty the ballast tanks which ran along both sides and the bottom of the ship. The tanks had been partially filled with lake water on the trip up to keep the empty boat more stable and riding more smoothly in the swells. Now this water must be removed to prevent the ship from settling too low in the water.

This procedure would take about an hour, Dennis knew, so he and Koski moved into the employees' lunchroom for coffee and sandwiches.

"That mate is a real character," Koski commented as he and Dennis settled themselves for lunch. "He was jokin' and laughin' the whole time out there."

"He sure ain't like a lot of them that come in here," Dennis agreed. "This one seems like a jolly guy, all right."

* * *

He was born John Henkle McCarthy, July 14, 1913, in Pittsburgh, the first of four sons and two daughters born to John Lychester McCarthy and Ruth Henkle McCarthy. A devout Irish Catholic family, the McCarthy children—John, William, James, Robert, Mary, and Sally—were educated in parish schools and spent liberal amounts of time quietly praying in church.

Jack inherited a robust Irish sense of humor, a zestful love for competition, and a gentle, sensitive appreciation of literature. He loved to write—once winning two tickets to a local movie theater as first prize in an essay contest held in connection with the release of the motion picture *My Son, My Son*—and seriously considered someday becoming a writer.

Intensely interested in sports as a youth, Jack could never quite match his athletic abilities with his enthusiasm.

"He was no outdoorsman, by any means," his brother Bill

recalls. "He loved to play sandlot baseball but could never make the high school teams."

Although he got on well with his contemporaries, Jack never achieved leadership status among the neighborhood crowd.

Because he tended to be smaller in height and build than the other boys his age, he was frequently the victim of physical abuse at the hands of the boys in the neighborhood. But he refused to use his slight physique as an excuse to run from trouble.

Bill, a year behind him in school, recalls a day when Jack—an eighth grader—took on the school bully.

"Dutch Murphy had been calling him 'four eyes' because Jack had to wear glasses. One day after school I heard that Jack was meeting Dutch at an empty garage two blocks from the school. It was the usual spot the kids picked to have fistfights.

"As soon as I heard, I took off running for the garage, thinking that Jack would surely get himself killed trying to fight Dutch Murphy."

When Bill, breathless from running, arrived at the garage and pushed his way through the crowd of onlookers, he was stunned at the sight that greeted him.

"There was Dutch, flat on his back on the ground, with Jack standing over him, holding his broken hand."

He had beaten the school bully, an act of courage and determination that earned him the respect of his younger brothers, the kids in the neighborhood, and Dutch Murphy himself.

An individual, growing from adolescence into manhood, brings certain traits with him—traits that are destined to remain an integral part of his personality and character throughout his life. With Jack McCarthy it was his puckish Irish humor. Laughter washed over him like an irresistible flood through all his worldly days; it poured from him in an uninterrupted gusher of mirth.

"I don't miss the paychecks or the fancy house or any of the other things he gave us," his wife of thirty-three years would answer when asked what she missed most about her lost husband. "I miss the laughter."

Shortly after his graduation from Central Catholic High School in 1932, Jack and the family moved from Pittsburgh. Jack's father, who had owned a small building firm, had been forced out of business when the Great Depression of the 1930s strangled the economy and plunged the nation into a financial abyss. The McCarthys settled in Lakewood, Ohio—a suburb of Cleveland—where the elder McCarthy found work as a laborer with a construction company that was engaged in building a number of grocery stores.

Young Jack, to help the family, took a job as a soda jerk at Marshall's Drug Store, at Ninth and Euclid in Cleveland. One of his daily customers was Cleveland Cliffs Iron Company's marine director, A. E. R. Schnieder. The company operated a fleet of lake boats, and Jack seized on his burgeoning friendship with the executive to try to enhance his job possibilities.

"If you ever have an opening on one of your boats, give me a call," was a statement Jack served up as regularly as the coffee Schnieder came in for.

Jobs on the boats in the thirties were very difficult to come by—even for the most experienced lake sailors. But true to his irrepressible sense of optimism that everything is possible, he pestered Schnieder ceaselessly.

Finally one day in October 1935, Schnieder strolled into Marshall's and announced to the delighted young McCarthy: "If you can be in Ashtabula by seven o'clock tonight, you've got a job as a deckhand."

Jack immediately quit the soda fountain job, grabbed what clothes he had at home, and caught the first bus for the fifty-five-mile trip east to the Ohio port city on Lake Erie; there he joined the crew of Cleveland Cliffs bulk carrier *Yosemite.*

The family found Jack's newfound career a source of extreme humor.

"Jack was just not mechanically inclined," brother Jim chuckles when remembering the early days of Jack's life at sea.

"The idea of him having to contend with a deckhand's job, not knowing one end of a paint scraper from the other, was real funny."

Bill had ferreted out his own job aboard a lake freighter a year earlier. He worried about his older brother's tendency toward ungainliness and would call the tug office in any port where his own ship docked to determine if Jack's boat might also be there.

"The first time our paths crossed was the year after he went on the boats. I was in South Chicago and found out that Jack's ship was at Chicago's Navy Pier. It was about six o'clock in the evening when I got up there, and what do I find but Jack sitting on number 1 hatch, surrounded by kerosene lanterns—we didn't have electricity throughout the ship in those days—and there he was, with all these lamps around him, cleaning them up and trimming the wicks, looking just like a lost soul."

Jack maintained close contact with the family during these years, writing long, interesting letters.

"He was sometimes prosaic and sometimes verbose when he was trying to get a particular thought across. But usually, his letters were very well written, beautifully written," Jim remembers. "He wrote some of the most beautiful letters anyone could write."

"I always got at least one letter a year from Jack—on my birthday," Bill recalls. "I still have all of them. They were beautiful, funny, touching letters."

The McCarthys sent three of their four sons to sea: Bill and Jim became saltwater sailors when World War II came, and Jack was assigned to the Coast Guard, remaining on the Great Lakes.

While Bill and Jim were commissioned as officers after completing marine academy training, Jack worked his way up the command chain and was awarded his master's papers in the early 1940s.

At about the same time he began spending a great deal of his winter lay-up time at the home of a Cleveland Cliffs shipmate, Gabriel Liedtag. And while Jack was very fond of his friend Gabe, the major reason for his frequent visits to the Liedtag household was Mary Catherine Liedtag, Gabe's pretty sister. Soon the twenty-seven-year-old, happy-go-lucky Irishman had become hopelessly smitten, and in 1942, some eighteen months after their first date, John Henkle McCarthy and Mary Catherine Liedtag were married.

That same year Jack moved over to Oglebay-Norton's Columbia Transportation Division, where he began moving up in responsibility and prestige.

Patiently working his way through the Columbia fleet aboard big and small freighters such as the *G. A. Tomlinson* and the *Sensibar*—where he first met Ernest McSorley—Jack was finally given his own command—the *Joseph H. Frantz*, once the company's flagship.

McCarthy's fortune seemed to be prospering. He and Mary were blessed with four healthy children, John, Mary Catherine, Elizabeth, and Daniel; the family moved into a new home in suburban Cleveland; and Jack was being given a variety of commands.

Then in 1956, while master of the small self-unloader *Ben E. Tate*, Jack sailed out of Sandusky Bay into Lake Erie and unexplainably went the wrong way—taking the South Passage amidst a group of small islands rather than going into the deeper area of the shallow lake—putting his ship on the rocks off Catawba Island and tearing the bottom out of her. The damage to the ship was estimated at two hundred thousand dollars and resulted in Jack being "put on the beach." It was several months before it was decided whether he would ever again sail for Columbia—in any capacity.

A close personal friend, Father Nelson Callahan, Jack's parish priest, saw him that summer of trial and vividly recalls Jack's state of mind after the accident.

"I ran into him at Higbee's Department Store in Cleveland one day that summer. He was very upset and embarrassed—and worried. He was certain that he would never be allowed aboard a ship again, that his career on the lakes was finished forever. He had a family to support, and he didn't know what else he could do . . . the lakes were all he knew."

But Jack McCarthy was much too valuable to the company to be condemned to a bitter life of never-ending self-reproach on shore. Oglebay-Norton knew this and, following the Coast Guard hearing into the *Tate*'s grounding, sent him back to sea once more—but not as ship's master.

He sailed as first mate aboard several Columbia ships, finally settling on the *Armco* in 1970. The *Armco*'s commander was Ernest Michael McSorley. The two men—only a few months apart in age—soon became more than captain and first mate; they became a close, smooth-working team, and they became dear friends who for the next five years would sail the lakes together and ultimately would stand side by side when their ship would take them to the bottom of Lake Superior.

When McSorley was given command of the *Fitzgerald* in 1972, it came as no surprise to anyone who knew and understood the two men that Mac should ask McCarthy to come along as first mate.

The *Fitz* was a fitting place for the two men to be; she was the company's flagship, one of the most recognized and admired of all iron boats, a sturdy, reliable, comfortable ship manned by the best sailors on the Great Lakes.

For Jack McCarthy, the *Fitzgerald* was a proper and honorable vessel in which to close out his years at sea—a haven in which to enjoy the final stanzas of the sonnet of his career. He was nearing the sixth decade of his life; he had more than thirty years with Oglebay-Norton; and with the new pension program offered by the company, Jack could retire at full benefits.

"I'd be crazy to keep going," he repeatedly told Mary Catherine. "I could spend more time at home if I retired."

The fact was he felt lost ashore and there was no longer a compelling reason to spend a great deal of time at home. The kids had grown and were beginning to move away; he had lost the opportunity to share their formative years—a fact he deeply regretted and frequently bemoaned. They had been, to a large extent, fatherless during the years when a father was vitally important to them. Jack was painfully aware of this throughout the children's adolescent years. "Get them the best sports equipment you can buy," he had told Mary when the boys had indicated an interest in Little League activities. "It's good insurance; it'll keep them off the streets." He loved his family deeply, and, although he may never have fully realized it, they returned that love in full measure.

But with the inevitable approach of retirement, Jack McCarthy was faced with the dilemma of how he would spend these "golden years."

Jack had few outside interests beyond his life on the lake boats; he did not enjoy the sports activities men his age were normally restricted to, such as golf or bowling. He wasn't a painter or photographer, and he was admittedly inept at gardening or repairs around the house. Mary had always tended to such mundane domestic chores; she was the plumber, the electrician, the carpenter, and the grounds keeper in the McCarthy household.

"I gave Mary her usual pliers and screwdriver this Christmas," he would jokingly tell his friends.

He and Mary had enjoyed travel in the years before the children began coming, and Jack thought that they might spend some of his retirement seeing those places in the world not bordering on the Great Lakes.

Almost from the time he came aboard the *Fitzgerald* as first mate, Jack had spent increasing amounts of time thinking about "throwing in the towel"; he and McSorley discussed their mutual fear of, and distaste for, a day that would have no thrill to it. They were both constantly reminded that their days on the lakes were numbered, that the spectacular sunsets, the sting of a fresh breeze smarting against the face, and the blackness of the sky and the water on quiet nights were all finite.

As a young man he had answered the call of the crashing surf, had left the land and the family that he loved. And somewhere along the long years, that lad had disappeared and had been replaced by the man who loved the sea and his ship and his crew, and who was forced to divide this love with a wife and children and home ashore, and was never certain that the division was equitable to those ashore.

Perhaps after one more season he could finally begin to correct the injustice Mary and the kids had suffered. Perhaps then, when the throbbing engines and the smell of paint and oil no longer drugged his senses and clutched him in a hopeless addiction, he would leave the boats forever without having to fear the threat of looking back, never again to feel the guilt at having to say to Mary, as he had too many times before: "Just one more year."

As for Mary, she knew the boats and the lakes for the demanding rivals they were. And while she could not fully bury the envy she often felt because of the claim they held on him, she had learned to come to terms with it, to pay the incredible price a sailor's wife must pay, living without her man through a full three-quarters of every year; she had learned to accept the burdens that were foisted on her trying to maintain a home and raise a family, alone. She had managed and had preserved that special effervescence that gave many the impression that it had all come easy, that it had not required the remarkable reserve of strength and determination that was all that kept her going in times of loneliness and times of crisis; she, and only she, had had to face and deal with the crushing assaults of an often unsympathetic and unforgiving world.

Jack had never known—she had not wanted him to know—of the nights when she had been afraid, had felt helpless and had cried into her pillow, wondering how she could ever manage to keep the family together with her husband away so much of the time.

Mary was aware of the cruel struggle Jack was waging within himself—torn between his passion for the lakes and his devotion to his family—and she was equally aware that it was a conflict he had to suffer by himself. Whether he chose to come ashore permanently or continued sailing the ore boats, he would feel a restless longing to be doing that which he had denied himself.

If only the choice were out of his hands, then perhaps a life on the beach would be much easier for him to accept; then perhaps Mary could, at long last, drive away the nagging vexation she felt toward the call of the sea to which Jack had for so many years harkened, a call she could never hear nor fully understand. Then, perhaps, they could find it possible to truly share a full, satisfying life together. There could yet be many years left to them, years when he would never have to leave her side, when she might be the focus of all his days, and the days would all be bright and happy.

* * *

Ed Dennis heard the one long and one short blast of a ship's whistle, placed the thermos in his lunch box, and closed the cover; the *Fitzgerald*'s first mate was signaling him that the water ballast had been pumped out and loading could continue.

Once back on the deck of the loading dock, Dennis moved quickly to complete the process of emptying the taconite pellets into the hold of the ship; pockets were emptied, and the boat was shifted to line up with full pockets, which were emptied in precise order according to the mate's wishes.

As the pellets flowed into the hold, the mate was checking the ship's draft—how deep in the water it was settling as the weight of the taconite was added to that of the ship— communicating by walkie-talkie with members of the crew stationed fore, aft, and amidships, observing draft marks on the hull and rudder. It was a practice among ship's masters and mates to have slightly more weight in the after portion of the boat to keep the stern down and to give the propeller—or "wheel"—a bigger bite in the water.

"I've got two hundred-ton pockets left," Dennis shouted down to McCarthy when the loading was almost complete. "Where do you want them?"

"We'll shift the boat to take them in the center," McCarthy

called back, pointing toward the hatches amidships.

At approximately 1:15 P.M. (1315 hours) central standard time (CST), the last pocket of taconite pellets was emptied into number 11 hatch. During the loading process the ship's fuel tanks had been topped off with 50,013 gallons of No. 6 fuel oil, delivered from a fuel barge under contract to Marine Fueling, Inc.

As soon as the loading had been completed, McCarthy called for the draft readings fore and aft—the midships readings had been taken for his own information while loading—and jotted them down in a notebook he carried. These readings would later be transcribed into the ship's deck log. A copy would also be sent up to Dennis on the loading dock to be inserted into his boat book.

"Bow shows twenty-seven feet, two inches," the crewman on the dock at the forward end of the ship radioed.

"The draft at the rudder is twenty-seven feet, six inches," the man at the stern radioed.

These readings were important. They would be checked by the Coast Guard when the *Fitzgerald* passed through the Soo Locks, McCarthy knew.

As with oceangoing ships, all merchant vessels engaged in voyages on the Great Lakes are regulated in terms of the amount of cargo they are permitted to carry on any given trip. Such restrictions are governed by Coast Guard Load Line Regulations. Each ship is issued a Load Line Certificate, spelling out the cargo loading limits for that vessel. The limits are based on the minimum required "freeboard" allotted to the ship, freeboard being the distance between the waterline of the ship when loaded and the level of the ship's main cargo or spar deck. This freeboard requirement varies with the four periods in the shipping season and has been altered several times over the years—primarily in response to pressure by shipowners seeking greater cargo capacities for their ships.

In 1958, when the *Fitzgerald* was commissioned, her minimum required freeboard had been determined to be 11 feet, 4½ inches during operation in the spring; 12 feet, ½ inch in the summer; 13 feet, ¾ inch in the fall months; and 14 feet, 3½ inches during winter operations.

During the succeeding fifteen years the freeboard requirement was reduced four separate times until, in 1973, the *Fitzgerald's* load lines had been established at 10 feet, 5½ inches in the spring; 11 feet 2 inches for the summer and the fall months; and 11 feet, 6 inches for the winter months.

The effect of this load line reduction was to permit the *Fitzgerald*—during the most perilous season of the year on the Great Lakes—to carry several hundred tons more cargo than had been considered safe for the boat when she was built.

At 1:20 P.M. CST, as the last of the twenty-one hatch covers was replaced, the *Fitzgerald* prepared to get under way.

The process of securing the hatches required that, once the fourteen-thousand-pound cover had been positioned over the hatch coaming—a vertical steel rim, extending around the outer edges of the hatch opening and standing twenty-four inches above the spar deck level—the cover then be secured by sixty-eight manually positioned Kestner clamps, which were double pivot, adjustable tension clamps, arranged on two-foot centers around the coaming. Each Kestner clamp had an adjustment bolt which, when swung into place, applied pressure on a concave-shaped "button" located on the hatch cover at a point which corresponded with each clamp. Adjusting the bolts increased or decreased the force required to position the clamps and determined the deflection of the hatch cover and the compression gasket—running around the underside of the cover—and the tightness of the closure. Each hatch cover measured 54 feet in length and 11 feet, 7 inches wide and was formed by $5/16$-inch stiffened steel.

A three-foot-long, two-pronged clamp wrench was employed to snap each clamp into place; the clamping process took two men approximately thirty minutes.

It was First Mate McCarthy's responsibility to personally check the clamps to insure that they were properly secured. In bad weather, strong winds could peel an improperly secured hatch cover away as easily as if it were paper, and heavy boarding seas could gain access to the cargo hold. The ship's

life and the lives of her crew depended to a large degree on
these clamps and the manner in which they had been positioned.

> . . . In the opinion of the Marine Board, if the clamps had
> been properly fastened, any damage, disruption or disloca-
> tion of the hatch covers would have resulted in damage to
> or distortion of the clamps. But the underwater survey
> showed that only a few of the clamps were damaged. It is
> concluded that these clamps were the only ones, of those
> seen, which were properly fastened to the covers and that
> there were too few of these and too many unfastened or
> loosely fastened clamps to provide an effective closure of the
> hatches . . . —Department of Transporation, Coast Guard
> Marine Casualty Report (USCG 16732/64216) page 94.

*   *   *

On several Duluth area golf courses the unusually pleasant
weather had attracted dozens of inveterate golfers who had
seized this opportunity to get in one last round before the
snow and ice could close the courses down.

Along the lakeshore in Duluth and Superior, motorists, on
their way to or from Sunday church services, had paused to
breathe in the fresh lake air and to steep themselves in the
warm, moist, springlike weather.

In Proctor, Minnesota, Dick Bishop was slowly awakening
from a disturbed, fitful sleep. His stomach pains had persisted
spasmodically throughout the night, making sleep all but
impossible.

At 1:52 P.M. the *Fitzgerald* steamed through the breakwater
and into Lake Superior. Standing on the deck of the Burlington Northern loading dock, Ed Dennis watched the ship
slowly disappear. He smiled as he remembered the jolly first
mate, who, as the boat backed out of the quay, waved gaily
and shouted to Dennis and Koski "So long boys, good luck!"

"He was a good friendly guy," Dennis said to Koski as they
turned and headed down the stairs to the lunchroom. "I won't
soon forget that one."

CHAPTER 5

"That Damned Computer"

The engine room telegraph clanged twice; the pointers moved from *SLOW* to *FULL AHEAD.*

"Give me ninety turns, Ollie," a voice on the intercom requested.

The engine room was an orchestrated cacophony of roaring fires, whining turbines, throbbing propeller shaft, and hissing boilers, making it necessary for Third Assistant Engineer Oliver Joseph Champeau to shout his response.

"Ninety turns."

Outside his office, on the deck immediately above, Chief Engineer George John Holl stood, looking down at Champeau as he turned the spokes of the engine throttle until the tachometer read ninety revolutions per minute.

The throttle controlling the forward motion of the ship looked like the chrome-plated helm of an expensive yacht with its gleaming wheel and highly polished spokes. Immediately above the wheel was an equally shiny console on which were clustered the engine operating gauges. On the panel was a plate which had been etched with a single word: *AHEAD*. Three feet to Champeau's right was an identical chrome wheel and set of gauges whose etched plate stated *ASTERN*.

An assortment of meters, gauges, and display lights was clustered in a large console to Champeau's left. It gave an instantaneous readout, in a pageant of multicolored lights, that advised the third assistant engineer of the condition of the automatic, computerized pneumatic combustion and feedwater control system, which managed the process of turning water to steam.

This complicated collection of space age hardware is known technically as the Bailey Meter Digital System, Type 762. It is designed to perfectly blend the fuel, air, and water which then results in the steam required to power the turbine engine. And Chief Engineer George Holl hated it with a fiery passion. He refused to refer to it as anything but "that damned computer."

"That damned computer, with its electric brain, went bad again," he frequently complained in his letters to his brother Wilmer.

There is some question as to whether the computer was as unreliable as Holl pictured it in his letters and statements to those at home. But there is no dispute over the dislike many ship's engineers had for the automated system. To the older men, who remembered the days of the "black gangs" and the coal-fired furnaces of the iron boats, this "electric brain" had taken away their full control over the machinery that drove their ships and had made them little more than "meter readers." It also meant fewer men in the engine rooms. So complete was the system's control that a two-man engine room watch—an engineering officer and an oiler—was all that was necessary to operate the propulsion machinery. Two additional crewmen were on duty between 7:30 A.M. and 3:30 P.M. An engineering officer and a wiper performed general maintenance work on the engine, electric generating system, pumps, and other machinery necessary to the operation of the boat.

Holl's mistrust of the Bailey System was his only complaint about the *Fitzgerald*. Unlike many other ship's officers and crew, chief engineers tended not to move from boat to boat out of sudden caprice, and George Holl was one of that monogamous breed. He had been only the second chief engineer to serve on the *Fitz*, taking over for the chief who had "brought her out," Wendle Freeman, when he retired in 1971.

The *Fitzgerald* had originally been built as a coal burner, and, to Holl's eventual sorrow, one of his first duties as chief engineer during the winter lay-up of 1971–72 was to oversee the removal of her coal furnace and the installation of oil-burning equipment. Not that he had anything against oil—as a matter of fact, he preferred it to the dirty, dusty alternative fossil fuel. But along with the oil-fired furnace had come the "damned computer." Holl had not liked it when the system first intruded on his domain, and his confidence in the mass of sensors, transistors, relays, and flashing lights had not improved very much during the intervening four years.

A short man—just five feet seven—his 180 pounds made him appear stockier than he actually was. Born in 1915, the youngest of five boys, he had grown up on a small farm in the mountains of western Pennsylvania amid the little villages with the pleasingly odd names of Slate Lick, Buffalo Creek, Dock Hollow, and Kittanning.

George's mother had died when he was eleven months old, his father when George was five. The Holl boys had been raised by a maiden aunt, eking out a meager existence on the small family farm. After graduating from high school in Butler, Pennsylvania, George drifted through a series of unspectacular and unsatisfying jobs. When World War II came along, George enlisted in the merchant marine to avoid being drafted in the army. He made two Atlantic crossings during the days of the much-feared German U-boats, which were exacting a bloody toll on Allied shipping during the early days of the war. Next followed several trips to Venezuela aboard oil tankers. In 1943 he was assigned to the Great

Lakes, sailing the ore boats that were bringing vital iron ore from the ranges in Minnesota and Michigan down the lakes to the throbbing steel plants of the Midwest.

Starting as an oiler—squirting drops of oil on the huge bearings of the reciprocating steam engines—down in the searing, soggy bowels of the ship, he slowly worked his way up through the ranks, serving on a dozen different boats after the war, taking the examinations for a higher rating as quickly as he could adequately prepare for them.

He considered the *Fitzgerald* as the ultimate engineering command—in spite of its automated system—and was intensely proud and protective of the boat.

He was married in his early twenties; his marriage quickly disintegrated, ending in a divorce that tainted his interest in matrimony and left him a bachelor for the rest of his days.

Denied a family of his own, Holl lavished his paternal instincts upon the children of his brothers—particularly Wilmer's son, Roger, and daughter, Lois, who he seemed to view as the children he had never had.

George and his nephew Roger became especially close over the years, their mutual interest in woodworking eventually flowering into a pact to go into business together once George had retired, which he planned to do in one or two years.

His personality was enigmatic; on the one hand quiet and self-contained, but suddenly bursting forth in fits of practical joking.

"He once rigged a fake tarantula spider on a string in the ship's dining room so that it suddenly dropped down just as the men were beginning their meal. It scared the hell out of all of them," Roger recalls.

"One time he sewed up all the pockets on Roger's carpenter's apron," Lois remembers. "He also liked to empty the powdered cream from their containers and substitute it with instant potatoes."

This dichotomy of character was all the more puzzling when viewed against the sincere concern he demonstrated toward the personal problems of his men. He is remembered by many who served under him as understanding, sympathetic, and generous. His competency as a maritime engineer earned him the respect and trust of Captain McSorley, with whom Holl enjoyed an excellent relationship.

"He and McSorley were very close friends," Wilmer states. "They were like two peas in a pod; to both of them, the boat was the main thing in life."

The two men shared one other mutual certainty in life: the *Fitz* was the most unsinkable ship on the Great Lakes. They would bet their lives on it.

*   *   *

Unlike the *Fitzgerald*'s chief engineer, Thomas Bentsen had no mistrust for the Bailey System. In fact, he considered it a perfectly reliable and worthwhile adjunct to the apparatus filling the three decks which made up the propulsion section of the boat.

At twenty-three, Bentsen had been sailing for just two years and had been aboard the *Fitzgerald* only six months. A 1973 graduate of the Great Lakes Maritime Academy (GLMA) in Traverse City, Michigan, he needed additional "time in service" credits to complete the prerequisite requirements before writing for his third assistant engineer's license.

His presence on the *Fitz* was largely the product of coincidence. Having crewed ships of the Cleveland Cliffs Iron Company fleet, Tom had gotten off the boats early in the 1975 season to attend the wedding of his father who—divorced from Tom's mother years earlier—was remarrying. Following the wedding, Tom was unable to secure a berth back aboard one of the Cliff's boats and had to register with the union hiring hall, asking to be placed on the first available vessel. His mother underwent cancer surgery in April, and Tom stayed at her St. Joseph, Michigan, home during her convalescence. Finally, in May, he was offered a berth as an oiler aboard the Columbia boat *Edmund Fitzgerald*.

Like his presence on the *Fitz*, Bentsen's involvement in

Great Lakes shipping was somewhat coincidental.

Born on January 10, 1952, in La Porte, Indiana, his family had moved to Chicago when he was two years old and then a year later moved to St. Joseph on the opposite side of Lake Michigan.

Throughout his early years in this lakeside community of eleven thousand, he had not been lured by the absorbing immensity of the huge lake; he resisted his father's blandishments to join him fishing on the lake, and he had no compulsion to join his friends in small boating excursions over Lake Michigan's turgid waters.

Tom developed an interest in music during his teen years. "He played the bass fiddle," his mother, Florence Bentsen, remembers. "He had good hands for it." Later, his musical interests would shift to the guitar.

A good-looking boy—he stopped growing upon reaching six feet, one inch—with blue-green eyes, dishwater blond hair, and a slim build, his youth was largely unremarkable.

"He was an obedient boy, although he did occasionally get into mischief," his mother says. "He tried 'pot' but knew that it was no good."

After graduating from St. Joseph High School in 1970—where he had played an unpretentious game of varsity football—Bentsen, not knowing what else to do with his life and in seeming contradiction to his early indifference to the lakes, enrolled in the maritime engineer's program at Great Lakes Maritime Academy.

The academy, affiliated with Northwestern Michigan College in Traverse City, specialized in a three-year associate of applied science degree program, which qualified successful graduates for examination by the U.S. Coast Guard for either first class Great Lakes pilot licenses or third assistant engineer (steam and motor vessel) licenses.

While at GLMA, Tom met and fell in love with pretty Cynthia Gagnier, a Northwestern Michigan College student. Tom and Cyndy planned to marry, but first there was the matter of the needed credits that stood in the way of his third assistant's license and the opportunity to make the starting salary of twenty-five thousand dollars a year that an engineering officer could make on the iron boats. One final trip and he would have those credits and would no longer have to work as an oiler or a wiper; he would be a ship's officer, and he would enjoy the added benefits, privileges, and prestige that always accompany rank.

Before his twenty-fourth birthday, he hoped, he would be "somebody." He would then be able to think seriously of a home and family of his own—a *complete* family that would provide his children with a secure and stable home life with a full-time father—the things he had longed for as a small boy, the product of a broken, disrupted home.

Perhaps as a subconscious desire to add some degree of permanency to his life, he became an impulsive collector, choosing older objects such as badges, drinking mugs, an old ship's horn, a tattered ship's flag—things that, in his view, had some lasting meaning.

He maintained a close relationship with his mother and his younger brother Bruce, telephoning home whenever he reached a port of call, letting them know where he was and that he was all right.

On September 22, 1975—Bruce's seventeenth birthday—Tom called from East Chicago, Indiana; the *Fitzgerald* was unloading taconite at Inland Steel. During the conversation he abruptly asked that Florence and Bruce drive the seventy miles from St. Joe to the Indiana port to spend the evening with him.

"It was already nine o'clock at night, and I hesitated because the area around the harbor isn't a good place for a woman to be," Florence recalls.

"Mom, it's Bruce's birthday. Why don't you come down?"

Her car broke down halfway, and when she and Bruce finally reached East Chicago, they went to the wrong steel mill. Tom, learning that they were at the docks across Indiana Harbor, grabbed a taxi and set out to meet them, unaware that his mother and brother were now on their way to the correct location. They passed each other midway between the two points, consuming more valuable time.

When at length the three got together, it had gotten quite late—too late to go out to dinner, and to add to the disappointments of the evening, the security guard at the gate refused to allow Mrs. Bentsen and Bruce to enter, even though Tom had arranged with First Mate McCarthy to permit them to tour the boat.

Standing in the parking lot—their evening together now in scattered shreds—they said good-bye.

"He looked so tired, so depressed," Florence said, fighting against the tears that always come when she remembers that night, the last time she was to see her son. "He didn't want us to go."

*   *   *

Captain McSorley paced silently between the wheelsman's platform and the engine telegraph and radar pedestals at the front of the pilothouse. The window at the center had been lowered a few inches, giving access to a chill breeze.

Stopping in midstride, as if a stray thought had intruded on his meditations, he turned to First Mate McCarthy.

"Jack, are all the hatch clamps dogged?"

McCarthy looked back, a quizzical expression spreading over his broad Irish face.

"Of course they are, Mac. I checked them all; they're secure," he replied, wondering why McSorley would ask the question. Company orders required each clamp, on every hatch, to be fastened during the stormy months of fall and winter. "The tank vents are all screwed down, too."

McSorley had been preoccupied of late with the poor health of his wife, Nellie, McCarthy knew. He had left the ship while she was being loaded in Superior to call Nellie.

"I wish you could come up to Detroit and meet me so we could spend some time together," he had said after explaining that the *Fitz* would turn around and head back for a load at Silver Bay before heading to Toledo on the next-to-last trip of the season.

There was a weariness in his voice that Nellie had never

heard when he was talking about his ship or sailing her.

"I'll be glad when it's over," he said abstrusely.

"I will, too, dear," Nellie replied, puzzled at this extraordinary statement from the man she knew to love the lakes with a passion that rivaled his devotion to her. "I will, too."

*   *   *

At 3:30 P.M. CST the 767-foot U.S. Steel ore carrier *Arthur M. Anderson* steamed out of Two Harbors, Minnesota, approximately twenty-five miles north of Superior-Duluth, having loaded taconite pellets for the giant steel-making complex at Gary, Indiana. In the chart room, directly behind the wheelhouse, a pipe wedged between his teeth, stood Capt. Jesse "Bernie" Cooper, a soft-spoken North Carolinian with thirty-eight years of sailing experience.

He was gazing down at Lake Survey Chart No. 9—a map of Lake Superior that, in addition to depicting the geographic details of the lake, also indicated various depth readings across its expanse. Cooper was plotting his course out into the lake. Using a plotter-protractor, he set a course line of seventy-seven degrees, which would take the *Anderson* to Devils Island in the Apostle Island group at the tip of Michigan's Keweenaw Peninsula.

At 3:39 the Weather Service broadcast announced the raising of gale warnings on the lake, forecasting winds of thirty-four to thirty-eight knots. A "fringe gale," Cooper called it, not unusual at this time of year.

Looking out the chart room windows, Cooper could see, about fifteen miles astern and to the starboard, an ore boat, obviously having come out of the Duluth area. Grabbing the radiotelephone handset, he called the boat.

"W4805, *Arthur M. Anderson* to the vessel northbound abeam Knife River. Do you read me?"

"*Anderson*, this is the *Edmund Fitzgerald*. Over."

"This is the *Anderson*. Have you picked up the gale warnings the Weather Service just posted? Over."

"This is the *Fitzgerald*, ah, roger."

"I'm thinking I will take the northern track; get to the north shore for shelter in case it really starts to blow. Over."

"I've been thinking the same thing. I'm steering sixty-five degrees for Isle Royale."

Might as well run across the lake together, Cooper thought. It's better to have company any time of the year, but particularly when the weather got heavy.

The winds were east by north at thirty-one knots as the *Anderson* "rounded the corner" off Devils Island, coming to a heading of sixty-five degrees and putting the bow of the ship almost directly into the fresh breeze.

*   *   *

The storm was intensifying rapidly as it passed over east-central Iowa. By seven o'clock on that November Sunday, it would have a minimum barometric pressure of 29.33 inches—a drop of .07 inches in just six hours. As the weather cell crept toward Lake Superior, winds on the lake were picking up; a slight chop was developing, and an occasional gust sent up on the *Fitzgerald*'s spar deck a frothy spray that streamed along the hatch coamings, eventually finding its way to the scuppers, where it was carried back to the lake surface. No water was finding its way under the hatch covers and into the cargo hold—not yet.

*   *   *

In Superior, Wisconsin, Doreen Cundy, wife of Ransom Edward Cundy, a *Fitzgerald* watchman, was clearing the dinner dishes in their comfortable mobile home.

Ransom—Doreen called him "Ray"—had arrived home that morning in time for breakfast, bringing with him Fred Beetcher, a porter on the *Fitz* who had a mobile home located in the same mobile home park as the Cundys.

The tall, almost gangling fifty-three-year-old Cundy (six feet, two inches and 189 pounds) and the short, stocky fifty-six-year-old Beetcher (five feet, six inches and 165 pounds) were inseparable friends, spending their free time on and off the ship together.

"They looked like 'Mutt and Jeff,'" Doreen remembers, referring to an old comic strip pair—one very tall and the other very short.

Cundy was one of the most popular men aboard the *Fitzgerald*; his irrepressible good humor made him the frequent target of playful leg-pulling by his shipmates, who delighted in teasing him about his almost totally bald head, calling him "skinhead" and "Handsome Ransom."

Born in Michigan's Upper Peninsula mining town of Houghton on April 16, 1922, the son of an ore miner, Ransom had spent practically all of his life on the Great Lakes, leaving the area only to serve a two-year stint as a gun crewman with the merchant marine near the end of the war. He had sailed the lakes for fifteen years, all of which was spent as a watchman in the employ of Oglebay-Norton. He had served aboard the *Armco,* the *Reserve,* and the *Davidson.*

In 1968, while the *Davidson* was unloading in Lackawanna, New York—a suburb of Buffalo—Cundy had spotted an attractive woman crew member standing on the deck of the *Sir Dennis Lowson* of the Canadian Algoma line. Ransom had waved to her, and, to his delight, the pretty cook had smiled and waved back.

The next evening, the woman accompanied two other female crew members to a bar near the docks. Ransom was in the tavern at the time and spotted her, came over, and introduced himself.

He and Doreen then began a nine-month-long mail correspondence, culminating in their marriage on August 8, 1969, having had but a single date—the night they first met in the Lackawanna bar.

Doreen had a nine-year-old daughter, Dorlean, by a previous marriage. Ransom, also previously married, was the father of two daughters: Jeanette, twenty-two, and Cheryl, seventeen.

Doreen left the boats after the wedding, setting up a home for Ray in Superior. Doreen was the perfect sailor's wife. Having herself worked aboard the boats, she was well-prepared for the long absences of her husband, making the most of their time together during his brief visits home throughout the season and the months when ice covered the lakes and sealed the ships in winter lay-up.

To those who knew the pair, Ransom seemed to have lucked out, to have found a life that would run smoothly and easily. It did not appear that "Handsome Ransom" had much to worry about.

But one dark night in 1974, a moody young man seized a gun and shot his twenty-seven-year-old wife to death before turning it on himself. The woman was Jeanette Beth Miller, Ransom's older daughter and the mother of his two- and three-year-old grandchildren.

The tragedy sent Cundy into a yearlong period of unremitting grief and frustration.

"It was a very bad year for Ray," Doreen says. "He almost went crazy."

But the human psyche does not often permit total despair, and by the autumn of 1975 Cundy had renounced, as much as was possible for him, the melancholy he had so bitterly suffered; he seemed to be more his former self.

"Life goes on; it has to," he had conceded to a close friend.

The close friend was Freddy Beetcher, who had lived his own tragedian experience. Freddy was a widower whose wife had died when their only child, a boy named Eugene, was still an infant.

Working as a porter on the lake boats was all Beetcher knew, and being away so much of the year necessitated leaving the boy to grow up in a succession of foster homes. The boy loved his father with an intensity that was surprising, given the circumstances of having been virtually abandoned by his only surviving parent. But Gene seemed to sense when still very young that it hadn't been his dad's choice, that staying with the boats offered the best possibilities for providing the boy with a better life during his early years; he hoped for the day—when Gene had grown—when they could somehow be together permanently.

The loss of his wife and the subsequent need to give up his son profoundly affected Freddy's life. The lonely life of a sailor became lonelier still for a man who had no one to come home to. The happy chatter of his shipmates talking of families ashore, of days spent together, of winters traveling with each other, of parties and holidays, of times full of joy and sharing—none of which he could be a party to—became unbearable for Frederick Beetcher. He became increasingly reclusive aboard ship and took to spending long, miserable hours ashore in dismal dockside taverns, alone and friendless.

His drinking became more than a crutch to help him through the bitter times of a meaningless and unfulfilled life; it became a quest for oblivion, where pain could not find him, where loneliness and emptiness would have no significance.

"He was a good worker, but he had this drinking problem," a ship's steward remembers. "He did his work, all right, except for an instance or two when he had been drinking on the job."

But then a blossoming friendship with Ransom Cundy, added to the realization that his son was approaching an age when he would be able to move into a home that Fred would provide—to be there when Beetcher came into port or was home during winter lay-ups—to become his "family," gave him a fresh outlook and made it possible for him to master his use of alcohol. His personality brightened; he became more genial and more sociable than acquaintances had ever known him to be.

As if to compensate for the years of estrangement from the men in the crew, Freddy became insatiably concerned about the solace of his shipmates, overly generous, and anxious to give whatever was needed or even wanted.

He brought this newly discovered interest and compassion to the black anguish of his dear friend Ransom Cundy. The quiet understanding he gave to Cundy helped him eventually come out of his own caustic purgatory, and in so doing, the friendship was permanently cemented.

*   *   *

At 12:15 P.M., November 9, a warm, beautiful Sunday, Doreen, Ray, and Freddy drove up to the gate at Burlington Northern; the two men climbed out of the car, said good-bye to Doreen, and began walking toward the *Edmund Fitzgerald.*

"I sat in the car and watched them go through the gate, their bundles under their arms, talking, happy—they were really happy—like nothing was wrong. There was no premonition of any kind. They just walked away—like Mutt and Jeff. Whenever I go by that gate I still see them. I see them so clear."

*   *   *

By eight o'clock Sunday evening the watches had been set: the four-to-eight watch had signed off to the eight-to-twelve group. First Mate McCarthy had turned the bridge over to Second Mate James A. Pratt, of Lakewood, Ohio.

"Steer six-five true," McCarthy had relayed the course to Pratt. "Winds are thirty-five knots from the northeast. We're going for the northern track because of the gale warnings they put up. The ship ahead is the *Arthur Anderson*; she's heading north, too."

Taking over the helm was Wheelsman John David Simmons, of Ashland, Wisconsin.

"Going to donate some more money to the boys' poker game tonight, Red?" Simmons asked Wheelsman Eugene William O'Brien, who was just going off watch.

"Naw, tonight I'm going to clean them all out," O'Brien said with a wide grin. "I've just been suckering them all this time."

Each night the men off watch gathered in the crew's recreation room in the after deckhouse for a running game of poker. O'Brien's statement that he was going to clean the other players out was little more than bombast; the games were almost always nickel-dime limits, and rarely would a player lose more than a few dollars during an evening.

Those not interested in card games had gone to their rooms—the *Fitzgerald* was still close enough to Duluth for the men to be able to pick up WDIO, Channel 10, on their television sets. Others tuned in FM radio stations or played stereo tape decks. Some read; others wrote letters or slept.

Second Cook Allen George Kalmon mixed dough for bread and breakfast rolls as the last of the crew strolled out of the dining rooms following the evening feeding. Porters Freddy Beetcher and Nolan Frank Church mopped floors and straightened the chairs in the officer's dining room. Off the galley, in his room, Bob Rafferty sat in an armchair, his feet propped up on the bed, a cup of coffee in one hand and an open book in the other.

In his spacious stateroom on the Texas deck, below the wheelhouse, Captain McSorley lay stretched on his bed, eyes closed, listening to the wind beating against the bulkhead just outside his cabin. The pitch was increasing to a high-toned whistle, indicating a growth in wind strength. Occasionally he heard the splash of wind-whipped spray against the portholes: the seas were building.

CHAPTER 6

"When I Go Out the Whole World's Going to Know about It"

By 10:39 P.M. the marine forecaster in Chicago had revised his projection for Lake Superior, predicting: "Easterly winds 32 to 42 knots becoming southwesterly Monday morning, and west to southwest 35 to 45 knots Monday afternoon, rain and thunderstorms, waves 5 to 10 feet increasing to 8 to 15 feet Monday."

> Wave heights in National Weather Service forecasts refer to the distance from peak to trough and are "significant wave height." Significant wave height is a statistical evaluation, roughly equivalent to the average height of the highest one-third of the waves. The actual distance from peak to trough of the highest wave could be as much as twice the "significant wave height."—Department of Transportation Coast Guard Marine Casualty Report (USCG 16732/64216), page 19.

The storm continued to intensify. At 0100 (1:00 A.M.) on Monday its center would pass over central Wisconsin. At that time it would have a minimum barometric pressure of 29.24 inches and would be moving northeast at twenty-nine knots.

This "typical November storm" had become a monster, moving ponderously but unerringly toward Lake Superior, ready to unleash its accumulated fury. Deep inside the towering storm clouds the air churned, mixing snow and rain in a potent brew of mischief, complete with brilliant shards of lightning.

In North Olmsted, Ohio, Odis and Ruth Hudson were preparing to retire for the night. It had been a beautiful, warm Sunday, so untypical for November that they had been lured outdoors to tend to a number of yard chores they had assumed would have to wait for the following spring. Kelly, the German shepherd owned by their son, Bruce, had used the opportunity to frolic happily under the Hudsons' watchful eyes.

In Ashtabula it had been a similar summerlike day with afternoon temperatures climbing into the seventies. William and Betty Peckol also used the unexpected balmy weather to putter in the yard at their attractive Ridge Street home. Their thoughts on this quiet Sunday in November drifted occasionally to the coming Thanksgiving Day celebration, when the family would gather for the traditional feast, and the house would be filled with the laughter and excited chatter of the seven Peckol children. There would, almost certainly, be the lilting warble of clarinet music supplied by their talented son Karl, who would be preparing for a trip to Arizona following the hectic sailing season on the lakes.

And in Canogha Park, California—where this Sunday had been pretty much like every other day in the year in terms of the temperatures—Mr. and Mrs. Aaron Weiss spent a quiet, uneventful day. They, too, were thinking ahead. Their son David was expected home later in the month for a short visit between fall and winter terms at the Great Lakes Maritime Academy, where he was in his final year as a maritime cadet.

Dave planned to bring a friend home with him: a crewmate from the ore freighter he had sailed during the past several months, fulfilling the academy's requirement that cadets serve a minimum 270 sailing days during the three-year curriculum as observers aboard commercial vessels on the Great Lakes. The friend was Bruce Hudson, and the ship on which he, Dave, and Karl Peckol were serving was the *Edmund Fitzgerald.*

These three families, like the twenty-six other families of *Fitzgerald's* crew, would be hard pressed in later times to remember the fine details of November 9, 1975. There had been little about this day to etch it indelibly apart from other days in their otherwise ordinary lives. This day would have taken its place in the composite of all other days and weeks and months that blend events into a vaporous montage of unrelated comings and goings that have no consequence by themselves. They would have no such difficulty recalling the minutiae of the days that were to immediately follow. All will vividly remember November 10.

*   *   *

The three had gathered after dinner to play stereo tapes, to talk and laugh, and to discuss their futures; they came to speak with mock seriousness of the role each imagined for himself in the mysterious scheme of life, in a world that had become complex and hostile to the young.

They had come together because they were young and easily felt the tingle of excitement that the full lives before them could yet offer. And because, although they quickly had learned to assimilate shipboard life among the older, wizened men of the *Fitzgerald's* crew, there still existed a sufficient generation gap to cause them to want occasionally to be off by themselves, to depart for an hour or two from the world of yesterdays, and to luxuriate in the effusive vision of a world of tomorrows.

The three—Bruce Lee Hudson, twenty-two, David Elliot

Weiss, twenty-one, and Karl Anthony Peckol, twenty—were among six aboard *Fitzgerald* who were in their twenties. Two others were in their thirties, six were in their forties, ten men were in their fifties, and five—including the captain and first mate—had passed their sixtieth year.

The men who sailed aboard the *Fitzgerald*—like all men who have gone to sea—did so for a wide-ranging variety of reasons almost as numerous as the number of men. Some had genuinely answered the seductive call of the rolling lakes, but to most, "working" the boats was just that: a job of work. Most of the men were not sailors in the traditional sense; they were, instead, hourly waged, blue-collar workers whose place of employment happened to be afloat. Many sought out these jobs because their skills—or lack of them—could not command the wage scales on land that were afforded the men who sailed the lakes. For some, it was an opportunity to save money—their room and board were provided at no charge for nine months of the year. To others, working the iron boats offered an extended vacation between shipping seasons and allowed them more free time for travel or other recreational pleasures not possible in a factory job on shore. Still others came to the lakes to escape an unpleasant life on the land or to run from a disastrous marriage. And there were those who found life on the lakes calming and providing a tranquil atmosphere in which to find themselves, to sort out the bits and pieces of their tattered lives and to attempt to reconnect them before rejoining a bewildering, unyielding world. Many found the boats a temporary haven where they might bide their time for a season or two while they decided what they wanted to do with the rest of their lives.

For Bruce Hudson, biding his time was a major influence that caused him to be attracted to the lake boats. He had, from the time he was a small boy, been fascinated with the enormous ore boats he had observed from the Lake Erie shore near his home in North Olmsted. Yet sailing away in them had not seemed to be one of his compelling ambitions as a child.

Born September 10, 1953, in Lakewood, Bruce was to be the only child of Odis and Ruth Hudson. His parents had come from West Virginia to the Cleveland area, where Odis found work in one of the General Motors plants that dot the state.

The family had moved to North Olmsted when Bruce was ten, and he spent his adolescent years in a stable, loving home that was strongly imbued in a Christian ethic of morality and commitment to love of God and fellowman. Bruce became a member of the United Methodist Church of North Olmsted youth group, attending regular retreats under the direction of Rev. Mark Collier. He joined the Boy Scout troop sponsored by the church, rising to the highest rank attainable—Eagle Scout. Later, he served as a church usher, sang in the choir, and volunteered his free time as a young adult working with and counseling the younger members of the youth group.

An early interest in music led him to become a member of the North Olmsted High School marching band, where he played trombone. This love of music prompted him to take up the guitar in the years following his graduation from high school in 1972.

After a year at the Ohio State University Agricultural School in Wooster, Ohio, he spent a year as a construction worker in Atlanta.

In 1974 he returned to Ohio, bringing with him a female German shepherd named Kelly, found by Bruce one cold, rainy day, sick and starving. The dog became hopelessly devoted to Bruce, needing to be tranquilized whenever Hudson went out of town.

Looking for a job after his return from Georgia, Bruce recalled that a high school classmate and friend was the son of an Oglebay-Norton official, Sidney Spinner. Calling on the fleet engineer, Hudson succeeded in obtaining a berth as an oiler aboard Columbia's bulk carrier *Ashland*. He remained aboard as shipkeeper during the 1974–75 winter lay-up, and in April 1975 was offered a deckhand berth on the company's flagship, the *Edmund Fitzgerald*, a position he considered to be an advancement.

"He was very excited about serving on the *Fitzgerald*," Ruth Hudson recalls. "He spent a lot of time decorating his quarters; he had a TV, a stereo, even a small refrigerator in the room. It was very nicely decorated."

But while he used the money he made on the boats to acquire many of life's luxuries—he also bought a 1974 Dodge Challenger and a Kawasaki motorcycle—he was far from rapacious with his "wealth."

"He left signed personal checks at home and told us to just fill in the checks and cash them if we needed any money," Mrs. Hudson remembers.

When the *Fitzgerald* called at Toledo on October 31, Bruce made a hurried trip home to collect his car. He and shipmate Dave Weiss were planning to drive to California as soon as the season had concluded, and since the *Fitz* would be wintered-up in Toledo, Bruce wanted the car there, where he and Dave could retrieve it with a minimum amount of wasted time; Weiss had to be in class at the Maritime Academy early in January. The abbreviated visit in October was to be the last time Bruce Hudson would be home.

From Toledo, the *Fitzgerald* went to Silver Bay, where it loaded taconite pellets for Ashtabula.

"He called us from Ashtabula on November 5," Ruth says regretfully. "He wanted me to drive over and pick him up."

But Odis, who was still recuperating from major surgery, was not feeling well enough to accompany Mrs. Hudson, and she didn't know the dock area in Ashtabula well. She told Bruce that she would attempt to locate a friend to ride with her. However, when he called back she had to inform him that she hadn't been able to find anyone to go with her and would not be making the trip; he would have to stay with his ship.

"I've always felt bad about not going after him that last time. But it just didn't seem practical then; it would have been close to midnight when we arrived back in North Olmsted, and I would have had to leave about six the next morning to get him back at the ship by eight."

But there was another reason that influenced her decision

not to go after him that evening. Ruth knew that Bruce wanted to come home in order to have an opportunity to ride his motorcycle for a few hours. Ruth feared the machine.

"As a mother I had worried that he would get hurt on that thing."

"Ma, don't worry. I'm not going to get killed on that motorcycle," he had told her. "When I go out the whole world's going to know about it."

*   *   *

The increasing throb of the ship's engine and the mounting seas crashing into the bow set up a vibration that interfered with the stereo tape music, driving the three out of the ten-by-seventeen-foot room Hudson and Weiss shared.

From the door of their room, Hudson, Weiss, and Peckol walked the few steps around the corner to the open doorway leading to the portside tunnel—a 520-foot passageway below deck—connecting the forward and after sections of the boat. Electric lights, positioned every twelve feet along the window-less corridor, glistened from the polished surface of the deck.

As they strolled briskly along, their laughter echoing metali-cally from the bulkheads, the trio could feel the twisting and springing of the deck as the long ship corkscrewed in the growing sea.

Calling attention to the movement, Weiss commented, "If we're going to have to run in a storm, it's better to be loaded heavy. If we were in ballast, we'd really be pitching around."

The ore boats, heading north empty, filled their ballast tanks with water to provide some added strength to the long cargo holds. In stormy seas, fully loaded cargo spaces kept the ship deeper in the water and gave a smoother ride. The ballast tanks, located along the sides and bottom of the ship, permit-ted a ship's master to create a degree of stability in bad weather by pumping water into the tanks and thereby increas-ing the ship's weight. A large ore boat, unloaded and unbal-lasted, could be capsized or twisted in two when the November storms struck the Great Lakes.

At the end of the tunnel, Hudson, Weiss, and Peckol turned left and then went up a flight of stairs, which brought them out on the spar deck. Through a door and down a narrow hall lined with the crew's luggage lockers they went, a jog to the right, past Third Assistant Engineer Ollie Champeau's quarters, a jog to the left at Porter Freddy Beetcher's door, and then another thirty-five feet farther down the hall to a stairway situated against the wall of the after crew's recreation room. The laughter and shouts of the evening's poker game penetrated the wall and overwhelmed the whining throb of the turbines in the engine room below their feet. Peckol, now in the lead, turned and looked quizzically at the other two. Each shook his head in the negative—no poker tonight. Climbing the stairs took them to the poop deck level of the after deckhouse, a turn to the right brought them into the crew's mess room.

Along one wall of the thirteen-by-twenty-foot room stood a long counter on which had been placed platters heaped with several kinds of cold meats, five or six different cheeses, some salad, dishes of leftover desserts, containers of milk, hot chocolate, chocolate milk, tea, and the ever-present coffee urn. Running down the center of the room was a single mess table surrounded by backless stools, which were fastened to the deck on swing arms that could be folded under the table to facilitate sweeping and mopping.

Several members of the crew were seated around the table that night, drinking coffee and chatting.

Chief Engineer George Holl, forsaking the empty officer's dining room, was engaged in a discussion of past storms with Watchman Bill Spengler and Maintenance Man Tom Borgeson, while two younger members of the crew listened attentively.

Hudson, Weiss, and Peckol made sandwiches and seated themselves to listen.

". . . Superior is the stormiest in the late fall, but it's the safest for the iron boats," Holl was saying. "There's more deep water maneuvering room up here. The lower lakes are more treacherous because they're shallower. And Michigan and Huron are really bad in northerly winds because the winds sweep down the whole length of them and let the waves build high. The *Bradley* and the *Morrell* broke apart in those waves; two survived the *Bradley* sinking; only one lived to tell about the *Morrell's* last minutes. I knew guys on both those boats—they didn't make it. . . ."

Karl Peckol listed with halfhearted interest, finally drifting away into thoughts of his own.

"If you're on the boats for three years, it'll get in your blood and you'll never leave them," Karl had been told by several longtime lake sailors. He had vowed that it wouldn't happen to him.

Karl Anthony Peckol, six feet tall with a slim build and younger in appearance than his brief twenty years, did not plan to make the boats his life's career. Known as a very analytical type who carefully researched a question before reaching a decision, he had concluded that his future security would best be served if built upon a college education, and that a few seasons on the lakes offered the speediest means of saving the money needed to pay for that education. But now in his second year, he had begun to fear that he was becoming too comfortable in this life, that sailing had gotten into his blood.

The sixth of William and Elinor (Betty) Peckol's seven children, Karl was the youngest of four boys.

"He was everybody's favorite brother," Betty Peckol states, recalling his role as family peacemaker, settling the childish arguments of his brothers and sisters.

Demonstrating an early talent for music, Karl became a gifted clarinetist at Ashtabula High School and was chosen as that city's lone representative to the All Ohio State Band convention held in Columbus in 1972. It was at this convention that Karl became enamored with the colorful, highly competent Ohio State University marching band, and, after his customary practice of carefully studying a move before deciding to make it, he happily announced to his family his intention to attend the university at Columbus.

Ashtabula, located on Lake Erie midway between Cleveland

and Erie, Pennsylvania, is a busy Great Lakes port city of twenty-five thousand residents. Karl had long been familiar with the ponderous freighters which nuzzled against the wharves during the warm-weather months.

He had always been intrigued by the men he saw moving to and from the hulkish boats; they didn't fit the image of tough, hard-drinking, brawling sailors depicted in movies and on television. The older men often appeared to be balding and overweight, giving the appearance of sedentary living on too much good food and too little physically taxing labor. The younger ones blended with their land-based contemporaries, wearing their hair long and opting for the tight jeans, the beads, and the cowboy boots and hats favored by the youth of the early 1970s. It seemed enigmatic to Karl that the two diverse groups could somehow coalesce into an efficient, functioning ship's crew, working and living together in seeming harmony. His musical training had developed in him a deep appreciation for congruity among groups and heightened his interest in lake sailing as a means to fund his college education.

After graduation in 1973, Karl secured a berth aboard Columbia Transporation's self-unloader *Sensibar*. His obvious intelligence and keen interest in his work attracted attention, and in the summer of 1975, he was sent to Cleveland for a brief watchman's training course. In July, to his great delight, he was assigned to the newest and best boat in the Columbia fleet, the *Edmund Fitzgerald*.

He quickly made friends with the older crewmen as well as the five men his own age.

"His letters were always happy, full of jokes; he liked to poke fun at the life on the boats," his mother recalls. "He never exhibited any fear of the lakes."

Asked on one occasion about being afraid, he had responded curtly, "I couldn't live like that, worrying about something happening; it could happen in any job."

But Betty Peckol was not convinced. She had talked to the only survivor of the *Daniel J. Morrell*, a 603-foot ore boat that had broken apart and sunk during a furious storm on Lake

Huron in 1966. She knew the dangers her son faced; she was aware of the constant threat that was posed to all men who flounced and flaunted their presumptuous invulnerability in the face of a capricious nature.

"I just wasn't too happy about him going on the boats."

*   *   *

While Karl Peckol was preoccupied with his own reverie, Dave Weiss was paying close attention to what the *Fitzgerald*'s chief engineer had to say about the storms of Lake Superior.

Weiss planned to make sailing these waters his life's work, and he was intensely interested in the recollections and specific knowledge of the men who had spent more years challenging the lakes than he had been alive.

To those who had known Weiss in his formative adolescent years, this dedication to and hunger for advice and direction from a senior would have been incredible.

Born David Elliot Weiss on Friday the thirteenth in November 1953, he seemed destined for a luckless, troubled future.

"Dave just didn't seem to know where he was going," it had been said of him. "He couldn't apply himself."

Born in Paterson, New Jersey, he had spent but one year in school before the family moved to southern California, where there was a succession of moves—from Vestida to Canogha Park to Agoura—and a number of different schools, new people to meet, new friends to make. He had difficulty concentrating on schoolwork, and his grades reflected this problem.

At Huges Junior High School in Canogha Park, his grades had fallen so far that he could not officially graduate.

"They let him go on to high school anyway," his mother remembers. "I guess they were just anxious to get rid of him."

At Canogha Park High School his problems continued; he was experimenting with drugs and proving to be "troublesome." Another change resulted, this time to Agoura High, where he managed to settle down enough to become a member of the football team and, eventually, to graduate.

"Dave wasn't a bad kid; he just fooled around too much," a friend insists.

He had considered joining the navy, perhaps to fill a subconscious need to go off somewhere and attempt to find himself, to understand himself. Instead he became a wanderer, traveling to Colorado, where an acquaintance's family lived. He sought to become a dog trainer but soon became disenchanted with the idea.

A friend visited him in Colorado and suggested that Dave move to Michigan with him, where the two could work on the family farm. Dave quickly agreed—yet another move.

While living in Michigan, Weiss heard of the newly created Great Lakes Maritime Academy at Traverse City. He became intrigued with the possibilities of becoming a ship's officer: to travel, to gain respect—respect of others, but certainly respect for himself—and to be paid well for it.

He called his parents in California.

"I think this is what I've been looking for," he told his mother. "I think I can do well there."

And he did.

"We were so pleased. He'd settled down, his grades were very good, his instructors liked him, and he made a lot of friends at the academy."

After three years Dave was nearing graduation; the time aboard the *Fitzgerald* would be completed after the close of the shipping season, then it would be back to classes after a short visit home. He would be ready to read for his Great Lakes pilot license in March.

It had taken him a long time to find himself—his twenty-second birthday would occur just four days from this November 9. A whole new life stretched out before him, and what a handsome young officer he would be: blond with curly hair, deep blue eyes, a well-muscled body on his five-foot-eight-inch frame.

Sitting in the crew's mess, listening as George Holl talked in somber tones of stormy days from the past, Cadet David

Elliot Weiss was feeling good about himself. The "trouble-some" kid from Canogha Park had justified the intrinsic faith his parents had in him, that parental certainty that "he will turn out all right." He had been aware of a dark promise shading his early life: as a Friday the thirteenth baby he was predestined for calamity. People had mentioned it to him, as if putting him on notice that there would be little in life for him to look forward to—that perhaps his personality prob-lems, his difficulties in school, and his tendency to show small interest in the valued ethics of serious study, hard work, and morality were all the result of the terrible jinx that follows those who were untimely enough to choose such an afflicted day to make an entrance into this world.

"Bullshit!"

He had proven them wrong; there was no jinx, and serious study, hard work, and morality were not just a touchstone used to prove to someone else how perfect you are. His three years at the academy were proof enough that he was capable of all three of those endowments and a great many more. All the better that he had been able to make something of himself with the so-called jinx hanging in his face like a carrot in front of a donkey, as a reason to chase in circles, never going where he wanted. He had ignored the carrot many had wanted him to chase; he had not used the stupid jinx as an excuse to give up on himself. And if it were all true—if he did have some ominous cloud poised over his head—he wouldn't let it make that much difference; he would still want to keep trying to prove to himself that he was somebody, that David Weiss was *somebody!*

*   *   *

At 0100 the *Edmund Fitzgerald,* as a designated weather-reporting vessel, radioed its scheduled report, detailing the conditions observed at its present location.

The *Fitz* at 1:00 A.M. was twenty-three miles south of Isle Royale's Siskiwit Bay and thirty-eight miles west of Eagle Harbor on Michigan's Keweenaw Peninsula.

A heavy rain dropped visibility on the lake to between two and four miles. Waves were then ten feet high, and the winds were north-northeast at fifty-two knots (sixty miles per hour).

In the Chicago office of the National Weather Service, the marine forecaster took the *Fitzgerald*'s position report and added the information to the other data coming in from additional ships on the lake, weather satellite photos, and sequence reports from other Weather Service offices. Working steadily, he prepared a "Special Weather Bulletin" that would be broadcast on radio frequencies 162.55 megahertz and 162.40 megahertz at 0200 eastern standard time (EST): "Change gale warnings to storm warnings immediately."

*   *   *

In the after deckhouse crew's recreation room, the poker game had broken up. Wheelsman Red O'Brien, scheduled to report for the four-to-eight watch, headed for his spar deck cabin forward, not having "cleaned" the other players, as he had jokingly bragged he would do. But he hadn't been cleaned out himself, either; he was about two dollars ahead.

"Wait until tomorrow night," he warned the others as he left the recreation room.

On the deck above, Hudson, Weiss, and Peckol were also making their way back forward, still reflecting on the evening's conversation, which had gone from a discussion of past storms on the Great Lakes to an examination into the safety of the *Fitzgerald* in a severe storm such as the one that was now beginning to lash the ship.

"This ship could stand any blow that has ever hit Superior," George Holl said confidently.

"But what if it did break up? Would we have enough time to launch the lifeboats?" Hudson had asked.

Holl pursed his lips and shook his head.

"If we were about to go down in heavy weather, no one's getting off in one of those damned boats. As far as I'm concerned, I'd just crawl in my bunk and pull the blankets over my head."

*   *   *

Considerable testimony was received from both licensed and unlicensed Great Lakes Merchant Mariners concerning the use of primary lifesaving equipment. Without exception, the witnesses expressed considerable doubt that lifeboats could have been successfully launched by the crew of the vessel under the weather conditions which existed at the time *Fitzgerald* was lost. . . . Drills, in good weather, at the dock, show that a conventional lifeboat could not be launched in less than ten minutes and testimony indicated that as much as thirty minutes might be required to launch a lifeboat in a seaway. Most witnesses expressed more confidence in the inflatable life rafts than in the lifeboats, although very few of them had ever seen a life raft inflated or launched. . . . —Department of Transportation, Coast Guard Marine Casualty Report (USCG 16732/64216), page 66.

Lifeboat drills . . . on the *Fitzgerald* . . . were not held on a weekly basis as required by (Coast Guard) regulations. . . . —Department of Transportation, Coast Guard Marine Casualty Report (USCG 16732/64216), page 99.

Q. How often were fire and boat drills carried out when you were on the *Fitzgerald?*
A. They weren't.
Q. They were not?
A. No, sir.
Q. No fire drills, no boat drills?
A. No sir.
—Testimony of Charles H. Lindberg, former *Fitzgerald* crew member, before the Coast Guard Marine Board of Investigation, pp. 2724–25.

CHAPTER 7

"Ships Gone Missing"

From the surface of the moon an astronaut, gazing back at the earth, finds them the most instantly recognizable feature on the North American continent. They comprise the largest inland body of water on the globe. They have been called the world's "eighth sea," and their bottom is littered with the wreckage of six thousand ships. They are the Great Lakes.

The gouging, scraping, and dredging of the five lakes began about one million years ago during the Pleistocene Epoch, when four great glacial ages spread over the upper Middle West. The process which formed the Great Lakes has never ended—it continues today. And the ninety-five thousand square miles of water, storing heat all summer, become their own weather factories when the cold polar air in autumn drifts over them, absorbing the heat on the surface in an upward explosion that is replaced with cold, driving winds—the gales of November.

The storms on the Great Lakes erupt with a vicious

suddenness that, prior to the introduction of radio communication and modern weather forecasting, frequently caught mariners unprepared, seizing their fragile vessels in a hopeless grip, wrenching and twisting them in mountainous waves striking more swiftly and more frequently than any ocean crest. It is a seafarer's aphorism that saltwater sailors, viewing the lakes as inland ponds, gain a devout respect for the Great Lakes once having survived a "heavy blow" on one of them. It is not unusual for experienced ocean sailors to become violently seasick in lake waves that have a different, more disturbing motion than those of the earth's seas.

Even more disquieting are the differences in the manner each of the lakes reacts in a storm.

Superior, with its barren, cheerless rocky coastline and its killing cold water, is nonetheless preferred by seasoned skippers in a storm because it affords more maneuvering space than any of the other lakes.

Lake Michigan and Lake Huron claim the lion's share of wrecks in the storms that sweep down their length, piling towering, crushing waves that have thundered out of the wretched black of night to smash to the bottom a hapless ship and her screaming crew.

But it is Lake Erie, the shallowest of all the Great Lakes, that stabs the sailor's heart with icy fear. For even on a beautiful summer day, when the surface appears as hard and polished as a spacious mirror, a sudden squall can churn those shallow waters into a savage madness that can hammer and smash and suck the unprepared vessel below the maelstrom to later vomit bodies and bits of wreckage along its verdant shoreline.

The first recorded loss of a commercial vessel and her crew on the Great Lakes was also the first recorded attempt to carry a cargo over these uncertain waters.

In 1678, at the direction of French explorer René Robert Cavelier, Sieur de La Salle, the Franciscan friar Louis Hennepin established the first shipyard on the Great Lakes for the purpose of building a cargo ship to carry the furs from the western French territories of Lake Superior and Lake Michigan to the eastern end of Lake Erie, where they could then be shipped from the Lake Ontario side of Niagara on to the St. Lawrence.

The shipyard was constructed on the east bank of Cayuga Creek in present-day Buffalo, New York, at a spot now named LaSalle Park, in honor of the once-favored son of France.

The Seneca Indians watched in uneasy awe as the huge ribs of the giant "canoe" rose and the ship began to take form. She was sixty feet long, weighed between forty-five and sixty tons, and had five cannons mounted below her main deck. Her two square sails were ornamented with the fleur-de-lis, her prow with the armorial griffin—the fabled animal with the body of a lion and the head and wings of an eagle—the crest of the house of Louis de Buade, Comte de Palluau de Frontenac.

She was christened the *Griffon* as the blessing of God was pronounced over her bow, and the men sang the Te Deum and fired a salute from her guns. The Indians watched unbelievingly and then got drunk on French brandy.

She was towed out into Lake Erie, and on the morning of August 7, 1679, she sailed west, bearing trinkets for trading along the way.

The trip across Erie was serene, and La Salle, resplendent in a ceremonial cloak and plumed hat, stood at the rail marveling at the lush green, abundant game, and wild fruit lining the shore.

North through *détroit* ("*the straight,*" which would later give the Motor City its name) the *Griffon* sailed, La Salle still commenting on the beauty of "this fertile and pleasant" waterway.

On August 12 the ship moved out of the river into a small lake. It was Saint Clare's Day, and La Salle named the non-Great Lake in honor of the abbess of Assisi.

Adverse winds required that the crew move onshore and pull the *Griffon* through what is now the St. Clair River and into the fast-flowing funnel at the site of present-day Port Huron, Michigan, the gateway to Lake Huron.

The second day on Huron dawned with the sky hazed in high, cirrus clouds, the perverse harbinger of malevolent weather.

The storm struck late in the day, first a squall blowing with a sudden anger out of the northwest, slamming into the *Griffon* head-on and catching her master and crew unwarned. The ship was mauled viciously by the raking winds while the men aboard, helpless against the unfamiliar peculiarities of the storm, fell, exhausted, to their knees, hurling their prayers to the wind, calling out to a merciful God to deliver them from extinction. In a characteristically human attempt to bargain with a seemingly wrathful Jehovah, many in the crew joined in a common vow to make Saint Anthony of Padua the patron saint of this embryonic voyage on the lakes and to build a chapel in his honor, if only the wind and waves were stilled.

Only M. Lucas, the vessel's pilot and an experienced ocean navigator, demurred at divine entreaty, choosing instead to curse and revile La Salle for having brought him to this humiliating end in a "nasty lake" rather than an honorable death on a noble sea.

The storm, as Great Lakes sailors have come to expect, ceased as quickly as it had begun, and the *Griffon*, with her worn and wondering crew, sailed in idyllic weather up the lake and into the Straits of Mackinac—their frantic promises to Saint Anthony unanimously forgotten.

The *Griffon* put into Saint Ignace, where La Salle went ashore to kneel and quietly pray over the spot, under the floor of the crude log chapel, where lay the bones of Jacques Marquette, the Jesuit missionary who had founded a mission at the site eight years before.

A week later, La Salle sailed the *Griffon* into Lake Michigan and down the west shore to Green Bay, where he made contact with his advance party, who had been sent months earlier to select and purchase the finest beaver, mink, and muskrat pelts the Indian and French trappers could supply.

On September 18, 1679, the *Griffon,* loaded with a fortune in furs, sailed out of Green Bay, headed back for Niagara.

La Salle, infected with exploration fever, had decided to remain behind with a small party and go looking for the headwaters of the Mississippi River.

As he watched his ship disappear below the eastern horizon, a smile of satisfaction crossed his thick Gaulish lips. He had gambled heavily on this venture, borrowing against his property at 40 percent interest. But, he thought as the *Griffon* sailed away, it had been worth the risk. He had won! Or so he thought.

Back again into Lake Huron the ship and her still disgruntled pilot, Lucas, went. And again they were pounced upon by a violent storm. It is not known whether or not the crew attempted to renew their unfulfilled contract with Saint Anthony. What is known is that the *Griffon,* her crew, and all their valuable cargo vanished without a trace. To this day the hulk remains the quest of countless divers and historians.

There are those, however, who claim the ship still wanders the lakes, a freshwater *Flying Dutchman,* condemned to sail forever, never making port, and skippered by a man who eternally curses La Salle for bringing him to "this nasty lake."

And there are those who will tell you that, during the howling winds of a Great Lakes storm, they hear the anguished cries of sailors in distress, shouting a word which sounds like *Mayday* but in fact is the French *m'aidez* ("Help me!").

*   *   *

When the month of November comes to the Great Lakes, shipmasters begin anxiously searching the skies. It is axiomatic among Great Lakes mariners that with the eleventh month will come the storms and gales, and so, too, the cold, ice-making temperatures from the north. Then it will be but a matter of weeks before the lakes will start to congeal, to curdle in a white mass that begins first along the Superior shoreline, smearing outward, feasting on the open water, growing thick and swelling closer to the center with every frigid, wind-scourged day, until it meets and joins with the ice from other parts of the lake in a copulative union that will last for three long months.

Time becomes vital when November crawls upon the lakes. Each additional load picked up and delivered means added revenues in the shipowner's treasury, added prestige, a good report in the shipmaster's personnel file, a few more dollars in the crew members' pockets, and a happier Christmas. And so they throw the dice "one more time," gaming with nature. Usually they win the throw. But the stakes in this game are immense, and when they lose, the price is often excessive. "Getting in a few more trips" has cost the life of many a whimpering sailor.

The price paid in men and ships during the 1913 November storm is the highest nature has ever exacted. It has been termed "the worst storm to ever strike the lakes."

It began November 7, a Friday.

In Lake Superior the passenger vessel *Hamonic* was heading for the locks at Sault Ste. Marie. One of the few passenger ships still operating on the lakes, she was a study in opulence at a time when fortunes had only begun to experience the sting of the Sixteenth Amendment—the income tax—and money was still employed lavishly to stimulate pleasure.

A cruise ship, the *Hamonic*—one of three sisters—boasted all the comforts of life ashore: a barber shop, a beauty salon, banquet rooms, a snack bar, observation rooms, and an elegant ballroom.

Making the final cruise of the season, her cabins were largely unfilled.

During the late afternoon of the seventh, her pilothouse windows were smashed in upon the bridge watch by a sudden, crushing wind that seemed to grasp the black-hulled, white-decked vessel and shake it like a rag doll.

Standing in the shards of the front windows and the debris of the wooden frames, the captain called for crewmen with axes to chop away the remaining rubbish. Then, with the gale blowing through the wreckage of the *Hamonic*'s bridge, he and his wheelsman battled the rapidly mounting waves, fighting to get the ship into Whitefish Bay, where she could be run aground before going to the bottom.

At about the same time, the steamer *Cornell*, some fifty miles to the west of Whitefish Bay, was badly mauled by the winds, sustaining serious damage. Again, the captain and crew fought savagely to keep the ship afloat throughout the night, making for Whitefish.

Across the land the storm generated heavy snows, driven by blizzard-force winds. A recently constructed breakwater in Milwaukee was reduced to rubble by the force of the waves coming off Lake Michigan. A park in Chicago had its buildings leveled and its equipment swept away by the storm. In Michigan and Ontario, telephone service was knocked out in many areas. Train schedules were abandoned, roads were drifted closed—a twenty-two-inch snowfall in Cleveland shut the city down—hundreds were stranded. Hundreds of thousands of dollars in damage resulted from the four-day rampage by nature.

On Lake Huron, the ships were to suffer the full brunt of the cyclonic winds and the mountainous seas. Eight ships and 178 men would vanish in these writhing waters.

On Saturday, November 8, Milton Smith, assistant engineer aboard the 524-foot ore boat *Charles S. Price,* came to a fateful decision: he would leave the ship there in Cleveland.

"You're crazy, lad," Chief Engineer John Groundwater said when Smith asked for his time. "The ship will be tied up for the winter in a few weeks; you'll collect your bonus on top of your pay."

But Smith would hear none of it; something was nagging at him, telling him to get off the ship now, while the leaving was good. He packed his gear and headed for his home in Port Huron. Left behind on his bunk was Saturday's edition of a Cleveland newspaper. It was turned to the page which carried the weather forecast.

"Nov. 8: Snow or rain and colder Saturday, with west to southwest winds. Sunday, unsettled."

On the same day, young John Thompson was wrestling with his own problem: why hadn't he notified his parents in Hamilton, Ontario, that he had switched ships and was no longer aboard the *James C. Carruthers?*

He had made the switch suddenly and unexpectedly, leaving the giant 550-foot grain carrier—the largest and newest of the Canadian fleet—for a smaller, less comfortable vessel. Perhaps he was afraid his father would ridicule his decision to leave the best ship of the fleet for a less attractive berth.

While the *Carruthers* was downbound from Fort William on Lake Superior with 340,000 bushels of wheat, Thompson was on Lake Ontario, headed for Toronto.

He would, he decided, call his parents from Toronto—maybe.

Throughout the day and into Saturday night the storm continued to build as it swept down from the north, spreading over Superior all the way down to Erie, with Lake Huron as its focal point. And still the freighters moved out into the lakes, leaving secure harbors with a firm sense of confidence, to challenge the forces of nature.

On Sunday morning the *Charles S. Price* moved past Marine City in the St. Clair River headed toward Lake Huron.

Second Mate Howard Mackley was on the bridge; he had been there for over an hour, even though his watch was not scheduled to take over for another three hours. He was there for a special reason, and he watched carefully as the huge boat glided slowly by the homes and cottages that lined the river, so close that residents standing in their yards could easily see the men in the wheelhouse and could be heard distinctly by men on deck on a windless day.

At last he saw what he had been looking for. Grabbing the lanyard hanging from the pilothouse overhead, he gave it one two-second pull, releasing a blast from the ship's whistle. A pretty young woman standing on a small dock waved excitedly. The woman was Mackley's wife, and he made it a regular practice to signal her whenever the ship passed their riverfront home.

Capt. A. C. May, master of the 550-foot *H. B. Hawgood,* was also in the St. Clair River, sailing north into Lake Huron.

At about noon on Sunday, May spotted the *Price* just north of Sand Beach. He noted that the *Price* was laboring in increasingly heavy seas. He also found that the wind had shifted to the northwest and was rapidly increasing—it registered between sixty and seventy-two knots on his ship's anemometer. That was enough to convince May that it would be prudent to bring the *Hawgood* about and steam back to Port Huron. As he pointed the boat south he saw the *Regina,* a 269-foot Canadian packet freighter, plowing up the lake, seemingly unconcerned with the worsening weather. About three hours later May sighted the 524-foot *Isaac M. Scott,* bound for Milwaukee.

May was the last to see the two vessels. Both sailed into eternity on the storm-tossed lake, taking all hands with them.

A total of eighteen ships grappled with the storm on Lake Huron all through Sunday and into the early hours of Monday. The storm grew worse on Monday, as the wind-driven lake built waves of thirty-five feet and higher and sent them against ships in rapid succession. By Tuesday all eighteen ships had been wrecked; eight of the best boats sank, drowning all their crews.

On Monday morning a tugboat captain spotted the bow of a freighter, bottom up in the water, about twenty miles north of Port Huron, her stern completely submerged. It was the *Charles S. Price.*

On Tuesday the first of the bodies began washing up on the Canadian shoreline. Singly and by twos and threes they drifted in, as if coming to be present at some grisly muster, shrouded in life jackets bearing the names of "ships gone missing." The *Wexford, Argus, John A. McGean, Hydrus, Isaac M. Scott, Regina, James C. Carruthers,* and *Charles S. Price;* they all had sent representatives to the shore to announce to everyone that they had foundered, that their crews were all dead. Stiff, bloated, and battered, their heads capped in ice, they floated in, rolled and pitched by the combers crashing on the beach up and down the Canadian side near the southern end of Huron. They came draped over life preservers, they came wrapped in each other's arms, they came frozen together in clusters. All week long they came, to be collected by area farmers, loaded on wagons, and driven along snow-clogged roads to small villages where, in combination furniture store–funeral homes, they were stretched out on the floor and covered with blankets to await friends or relatives to come and claim them.

The young wife of Howard Mackley, the *Price*'s second mate who had tooted the ship's whistle to her, came to the villages to quietly pass along the rows of silent bodies, looking in vain for her husband. His body was never found.

Milton Smith, the assistant engineer who had spontaneously left the *Price* in Cleveland, came, too, requested to do so by the shipowners because he knew them all so well. The first body he identified was that of Chief Engineer John Groundwater, the old friend who had plaintively urged him to stay aboard for a few more weeks.

"Are you certain this man came from the *Charles Price*?" a provincial official asked Smith.

"Of course I'm certain," Smith had responded angrily.

"Then why has he got a *Regina* life preserver wrapped around him?"

It was a question no one alive could answer. The question remains unanswered to this day.

Another who came to view the corpses was the father of John Thompson. Young Thompson had not gotten around to advising his parents that he had left the *Carruthers,* and they had assumed that their son had gone down with the ship.

The elder Thompson found a body that, while it had sustained a considerable battering, bore a striking resemblance to his son. A scar on the body like one his son had and the tatooed initials *J.T.* confirmed for him the sorrowful fact that his son was dead.

Meanwhile, John Thompson, safe in Toronto, had the eerie

experience of reading a newspaper account of the loss of the ships and the deaths of so many men—including himself. Rushing home, he found a coffin in the family parlor and preparations under way for his own funeral.

The body occupying the coffin was never identified. It was buried with four other unclaimed corpses in the cemetery at Goderich, Ontario, under a marker bearing a carved anchor and the following inscription: "A memorial to the unidentified seamen whose lives were lost in the Great Lakes disaster of November 9th, 1913." On the opposite side of the marker is carved but a single word: *SAILORS.*

There was, amid the terror, the panic, and the confusion, evidence of at least one act of bravery, self-sacrifice, and kindness. The body of a Mrs. Walker, stewardess aboard the *Argus,* washed ashore wearing the heavy coat of the ship's engineer and the life jacket belonging to Capt. Paul Gutch. When Gutch's body drifted onto the beach it was without a life preserver.

In 1957 a historical marker was erected at Port Sanilac, Michigan, overlooking the lake that had taken the largest single toll of mariners in Great Lakes history. The marker reads:

THE GREAT STORM
OF 1913

Sudden tragedy struck the Great Lakes on November 9, 1913, when a storm, whose equal veteran sailors could not recall, left in its wake death and destruction. The grim toll was 235 seamen drowned, ten ships sunk, and more than twenty others driven ashore. Here on Lake Huron all 178 crewmen on the eight ships claimed by its waters were lost. For sixteen terrible hours gales of cyclonic fury made man and his machines helpless.

*   *   *

It would be twenty-seven years before a storm with the destructive potential of the Lake Huron storm would again

strike the Great Lakes. And while the loss of life would not
begin to rival the 235 deaths resulting from the 1913 storm,
the Armistice Day Storm of 1940 was to become known for its
incredible fury, its hurricane winds, and towering waves that
were, in the minds of sailors who weathered both, more
furious than those of 1913.

The autumn of 1940 had been one of the most pleasant in
memory, with mild sunny days and little rain or wind.
Sunday, November 10, was an especial bonus to the midwest-
erners who seized the opportunity to spend the day outdoors,
to take a quiet drive in the country or a pleasant walk in the
woods.

As the delightful weather was being savored throughout the
lakes region, an intense low-pressure system was racing across
the northern tier of states.

Two days earlier, the system had thundered off the Pacific
Ocean. Its cyclonic winds had rushed upon the state of
Washington, blasting into the Tacoma Narrows Bridge, causing it to sway ominously and finally to collapse into the gorge
below.

At about the same time, another low-pressure system came
skidding down the eastern slopes of the Rocky Mountains.
Moving over the southern Great Plains, it pulled warm, moist
air up from the Gulf of Mexico and the southern Mississippi
valley, before swinging northeast toward the Great Lakes.

As they approached one another, the two massive systems
generated a counterclockwise circulation of the warm air
trapped between, promoting a gigantic storm system which
covered thousands of square miles.

As darkness neared, ships were pounding along in quiet
seas, caressed by gentle breezes.

Rounding the tip of Michigan's mitten the following
morning, at the point where Huron and Michigan converge,
the 420-foot Interlake Steamship Company bulk carrier *William B. Davock* was headed for South Chicago with a load of
coal. Sixty miles astern was the Canadian freighter *Anna C.
Minch,* loaded with grain from Fort William, Ontario, bound
for Chicago.

As he cleared Grays Reef and steered south-southwest to pass Beaver Island to the east and set up for the Manitou Passage, Capt. Charles W. Allen of the *Davock* was heard on the radiotelephone commenting on the beautiful, mild November weather.

At about ten o'clock in the morning on this Armistice Day, those who were to participate in the parade through Chicago's Loop were beginning to assemble. There was to be a silent observance precisely at 11:00 A.M. followed by a few brief tributes to the fallen heroes of World War I.

A similar ritual was scheduled for Joliet, Illinois, southwest of Chicago. But an explosive avalanche of frigid wind swept down on the waiting crowd, pelting them with hail and airborne debris and sending them fleeing for shelter. Store windows were shattered, trees were plucked from the ground and hurled against cars and buildings.

The storm covered the forty miles to Chicago in just fifteen minutes. Roofs were torn from buildings, shingles scattered like confetti, chimneys crumbled and fell or burst from the force of the wind and flew like cannon shot. A ten-story-high advertising sign at Randolph and the Outer Drive, which had cost over $175,000 to construct, was reduced in minutes to a useless pile of rubble and twisted steel.

A radio station transmitting tower in Gary, Indiana, was snapped in two by the rampaging storm. The station's call letters, ironically, were WIND.

The level of Lake Michigan at Chicago dropped almost five feet from the force of the wind pressing upon the water and pushing out ever-heightening waves.

Capt. Harley O. Norton of the *New Haven Sacony* looked at the midnight weather forecast and wondered. The forecast called for strong northeast winds on the eleventh. His years of experience on the lakes told him that southeast winds rarely spawned northeast gales. But since the ship was headed for Muskegon, Michigan, Norton hauled the *New Haven Sacony* close in to the east shore of the lake to take advantage of the lee, should the forecast prove correct. He could always swing out into the deeper water if it became necessary.

Two hours ahead of Norton was the 253-foot *Novadoc* with a load of coke for Lake Superior. Her captain, too, had opted to run in close to the Michigan shoreline.

By early afternoon the wind had swung around and was coming out of the northwest. Captain Norton knew what was about to happen and swung the *New Haven Sacony* around to port, into the wind and the storm which was advancing on him with black, threatening clouds that rolled and boiled as they moved forward. Capt. Donald Steip of the *Novadoc*, ahead and to the north, had been caught suddenly by the wind and rising seas; already close in to shore—just a few hundred yards out—the *Novadoc* was in peril.

At Ludington, Michigan, Capt. A. E. Christoffersen ordered the watch out of the Coast Guard tower, fearing imminent collapse. It mattered little; visibility was so poor that nothing could be seen anyway.

At about 11:00 P.M., two large car ferries, the *City of Flint* and the *NO. 21*, attempting to dock, were having trouble. The *NO. 21* was driven against the wharf pilings and couldn't move, and the *City of Flint* missed the entrance piers altogether and was pushed broadside to the beach by the force of the wind and waves. Thirty-foot waves began to pound and batter her, forcing her skipper to order the sea cocks opened, allowing the ship to settle to the sand bottom.

The seas exploded against her starboard side, sending spray flying in the air and over her masthead. But the *City of Flint* was able to continue making steam to provide heat and light for her forty-eight crew members and four passengers.

Twenty miles to the south, at Little Sable Point, the *Novadoc* could resist the quartering seas no longer; she was hurled aground, her hull beginning almost immediately to falter. As snow and sleet lashed at her, the *Novadoc*'s lights blinked several times and then went out for good.

William Krewell, the lighthouse keeper at Little Sable Point, observed the ship's grounding and knew of the danger to her crew. He notified the Ludington Coast Guard station, then ran to the beach opposite the *Novadoc* and began signaling with a flashlight. He received no response from the stricken vessel.

All up and down the lake, reports were coming in of incredible waves of thirty-five feet and higher, building more quickly than even the most seasoned veterans of those waters could ever recall. The waves were being driven by winds that had been reported at one hundred miles per hour in some places on the lake. There were reports from a dozen locations around Lake Michigan of ships in trouble: the *Sinaloa,* steam lines broken, no power, thrown against the reefs at Wisconsin's Porte Des Morts—"Death's Door"; the *Frank J. Peterson,* driven ashore on Saint Helena Island in the Straits of Mackinac; nearby the *Conneaut* reported she was grounded with her bottom torn, rudder carried away, her propeller stripped; the *Frank Billings,* dangerously close to the rocks at Grays Reef, reported her pilothouse windows blown in, her helmsman injured, and her forward quarters partially flooded.

To the south, the tanker *Justine C. Allen,* outbound from Indiana Harbor, reported a broken rudder cable and was in danger of being swept aground.

The tankers *Mercury* and *Crudoil* and the fishing tugs *Indian* and *Richard H.* were all overdue and feared lost.

At daybreak, beach watchers south of Grand Haven, Michigan, found parts of a shattered lifeboat, oars, doors, and the top of the pilothouse, all belonging to the *New Haven Sacony.* To those retrieving the shattered pieces of the vessel, there was no doubt that she had broken into a thousand parts and was scattered all over the southern end of the lake or resting on the bottom.

As a matter of fact, while the beach watchers collected rubble, the *New Haven Sacony*—at least what was left of her—was crawling toward Chicago, looking more like an iceberg than a ship. Her captain would later tell of the huge waves that rolled in seemingly endless succession over her, carrying away her lifeboats, deck gear, ventilators, and railing. A wave smashed in the pilothouse windows, carrying out the compass, lake charts, a chair. A monster wave then carried away the pilothouse itself, leaving Captain Norton and the wheelsman standing there, only the wheel stand remaining. Drenched and freezing cold, they nevertheless managed to keep the vessel out of the troughs and sailing ahead.

The tankers *Crudoil* and *Mercury* both survived the storm to limp into port.

Both fishing tugs, *Indian* and *Richard H.*, were thrown on the shore and wrecked, but their crews survived.

After thirty-six hours without food or heat, seventeen members of the *Novadoc* crew were finally taken off by the fishing tug *Three Brothers*. The *Novadoc*'s cook, Joe Shane, and his helper, Philip Flavin, had been swept overboard when they attempted to dash from the after deckhouse forward to join other members of the crew.

On Tuesday afternoon, November 12, the first bodies from Interlake Steamship Company's *William B. Davock* began washing ashore near Ludington. Twelve miles south, at Pentwater, Michigan, the men of the Canadian freighter *Anna C. Minch* were also coming in amid the shattered debris of furniture, cabin doors, and unused life preservers, all mixed with the swollen grain from her cargo hold.

The *Minch* had broken in two before going down about a mile south of Pentwater. The *Davock* was found in May 1972 in 204 feet of water, off Big Sable Point, north of Ludington. She was upside down, her rudder hard to port, as if she had been struggling to get out of a trough but had been rolled over by one or more gigantic waves with no time to announce her plight.

A total of fifty-eight men died on the lakes in the terrible blow of 1940. But as it turned out, they were not the only victims of the storm.

The unseasonably mild weather before the violent storm hit had lured a large number of duck hunters out to the inland lakes and the marshes in the area. They had come unprepared for the severe change in the temperature, dressing for the conditions that had prevailed the week earlier. Fifty of them froze to death in their blinds and small boats before they could be rescued.

*   *   *

On the sunny Sunday afternoon in 1958, when the *Edmund Fitgerald* slid into its launching basin to become the largest ship ever to be launched on the Great Lakes, her name joined a long list of ships to claim that title—a list that stretched back over almost three hundred years. In 1927, when she was christened at Lorain, Ohio, the title was passed to the 640-foot bulk freighter *Carl D. Bradley*. And like the *Fitzgerald,* the *Bradley* began almost immediately setting records. By the summer of 1929, the *Bradley* had set the record for the largest single cargo ever carried on the Great Lakes: 18,114 tons of limestone.

In November of 1958—just two months after the *Fitzgerald's* first cargo trip—the *Bradley,* thirty-one years old, was in her prime as a lake boat and was still considered among the giants of the Great Lakes. But as young as she may have been, she was also beginning to show the ravages of her fast, hard life. The owner, U.S. Steel Corporation, had decided the *Bradley* was due for a new $800,000 cargo hold and planned to have the ship fitted out at the end of the '58 season.

In point of fact, the *Bradley's* skipper, Capt. Roland Bryan, believed his ship was overdue for repairs.

"The hull is not good," he had said in a letter to a friend, Ken Faweet. To another friend, Bryan had written: "This boat is getting pretty ripe for too much weather. I'll be glad when they get her fixed up."

There had been reports by men in the *Bradley's* crew that the ship had "rust pouring from her hold" and that the ballast tanks leaked constantly. There were also weakened and missing rivets in one ballast tank's interior wall, discovered during a Coast Guard inspection early in 1958. But bolts had been installed in place of the rivets, and the Coast Guard certified the ship as seaworthy, as did the Lloyds Register of Shipping Inspection Service.

On Monday, November 17, the *Bradley* unloaded her cargo of limestone in Indiana and at 6:30 P.M. turned back into Lake Michigan and started for home: Rogers City, Michigan, a thirty-hour sail away. It was scheduled as the last trip of the season.

Of the thirty-five men aboard the *Bradley*, twenty-six were residents of Rogers City, six were from the Northern Michigan area, and three from out of state.

The weather had been deteriorating for the past two days, with strengthening winds and building seas, but there appeared no reason for concern as the *Bradley*, now with nine thousand tons of water in her ballast to give her stability, plowed through a moderate whitecapped lake, followed by a southwest wind.

Early Tuesday morning gale warnings were posted for Lake Michigan, sending many ships to safe harbor. But the *Bradley* steamed ahead; most large freighters, used to sailing through heavy weather, do not fear the gales, having confidence in their ship's ability to withstand a little pounding. Besides, this was the final trip of the year and the crew was anxious to be home.

As dusk approached, the *Brad* was swinging more to an easterly heading as Captain Bryan prepared to thread his way through the passage north of Beaver Island and into the Straits of Mackinac.

At 5:15 P.M., Bryan radioed the Bradley Transportation Line, a division of U.S. Steel Company, at Rogers City, advising that he expected to have the ship in at about 2:00 A.M.

In the crew's mess, a simple dinner of hamburgers, french fries, cold tomatoes, peaches, and cake was being served. With the boat only a few hours from home, the entire crew was in an almost festive mood.

The wind had increased to fifty-seven knots (sixty-five miles per hour), and the seas were between twenty and thirty feet high. In these heavy seas the *Bradley*, with only water ballast to keep her rigid, was twisting and bending like a huge snake. Down below, the stresses on the hull were causing rivets to shear off, popping them like bullets from a rifle, and with each lost rivet the hull grew weaker.

At 5:31 P.M., as Captain Bryan stood in the wheelhouse discussing the passage through the Beaver Island archipelago with First Mate Elmer Fleming, a sudden and unusual thud was heard, causing the two officers to look back along the spar deck.

Two-thirds of the way down the deck, illuminated by a string of weather lights running down the center, the men saw the aft section of the ship sag downward.

"She's starting to break apart!" Bryan shouted, leaping to the engine telegraph and moving the levers to *ALL STOP*. He then sounded the general alarm, alerting the crew to the emergency.

Within half a minute a second thud came, and the boat appeared to be humping midships as the stern sagged further.

First Mate Fleming, at the captain's order, grabbed the radiophone and shouted: "Mayday! Mayday! Mayday! This is the *Carl D. Bradley*. Our position is approximately twelve miles southwest of Gull Island. We are in serious trouble."

Captain Bryan was on the ship's intercom system advising the crew: "Run, grab life jackets. Get your life jackets."

"The ship is breaking up in heavy seas," Fleming was broadcasting to a stunned audience of Coast Guard stations and other ships on the lake. "We're breaking up. We're going to sink. We're going down."

Bryan now reached for the ship's whistle and gave the "abandon ship" signal—seven short blasts followed by one long.

A fourth thud came and the *Bradley* jumped, sagged once more, and then split in two. Fleming, giving the Mayday call again, stopped in midsentence. It was no longer of any use; the power cables had been severed, the lights and the radio went dead. Radio transmission had halted at exactly 5:45 P.M.

Throughout the two sections of the rapidly sinking vessel, the crew scrambled to get out. Several men attempted to launch the starboard lifeboat on the after section, but the now stern-high deck prevented them from getting it away.

As the forward section began to roll over, the men out on deck were thrown into the frigid, heaving lake. Captain Bryan remained in the wheelhouse. At almost the same moment, the stern half of the boat dived below the surface, her boilers exploding as the icy waters poured in. The *Carl D. Bradley* was gone—the largest ship ever to be lost on the Great Lakes.

The majority of the crew had jumped or been thrown into the water, and most managed to don life jackets. But the pounding waves and the freezing wind rapidly sucked the life-giving warmth from their bodies. The water temperature was thirty-six degrees; the air temperature was in the twenties.

As the forward section had gone down, the forty-two-year-old First Mate Elmer Fleming and Frank Mays, a twenty-six-year-old watchman, had been thrown into the water almost on top of the ship's only life raft—a series of empty oil drums topped with an eight-by-ten-foot section of timbers. Crawling aboard, they attempted to reach a hand to other crew members, but the thrashing waters carried them away.

After fruitless attempts at grabbing those struggling in the water, Fleming and Mays managed to bring Gary Strzelecki, a twenty-one-year-old watchman, and twenty-five-year-old Dennis Meredith, a deckhand, onto the raft.

Four miles away, the 250-foot German freighter *Christian Sartori*, under the command of Captain Muller, a former U-boat officer, had heard Fleming's radio distress call and had informed the Coast Guard that he was heading for the scene. Heading into the stiff wind and the oncoming waves, the *Sartori* took two hours to travel the four miles.

Meanwhile, at the Charlevoix, Michigan, Coast Guard station, forty-eight miles from the spot where the *Bradley* had gone down, a 36-foot power launch, manned by three men, put out into the fury of the storm. After an hour of fighting the mountainous seas the boat was recalled, and the 180-foot

Coast Guard cutter, *Sundew*, a combination buoy tender–ice breaker, set out from the harbor. The *Sundew*'s sister ship, the *Hollyhock*, from Sturgeon Bay, Wisconsin, had been on the way to the scene of the *Bradley*'s sinking since the first distress message; the two vessels arrived in the area at about eleven o'clock and joined the *Sartori* in the crisscross search for survivors. A Coast Guard aircraft from Traverse City also joined the search, dropping flares over the area to assist the surface vessels.

On the pitching life raft, four men clung together, trying to coax out a mutual warmth from their sodden, trembling bodies. In the early hours, First Mate Fleming had fired the flares he found in the raft's survival kit, saving the last until a rescue vessel was actually sighted. When a ship did approach through the blackness of the stormy night, the flare failed to fire.

Countless times through the night the waves flicked the bobbing raft out of the water, turning it completely over and throwing the men into the lake, forcing them to struggle for their lives to get back and drag themselves aboard again. After one capsizing, twenty-five-year-old deckhand Dennis Meredith failed to return. And just before dawn, Gary Strzelecki, the twenty-one-year-old watchman who had labored valiantly to keep everyone's spirits high throughout the long and wretched night, let his own spirit flag, drifting into a rambling state of semiconsciousness and then shock. He slipped from the raft and was gone, in spite of the efforts of Fleming and Mays to save him.

Mays became very frightened when he noted that ice had begun to form in his hair and had encrusted his jacket.

"I prayed every minute of the time," he said later. "I felt that, if we were still on the raft by morning, someone would surely find us."

Finally, at daylight, twenty miles and fourteen hours from where the *Carl D. Bradley* had gone down, the cutter *Sundew* picked them out of the water.

The two men refused the offer to fly them by helicopter

back to the hospital. Instead, they asked to remain aboard while the search for their shipmates continued. But no other survivors were found; of the thirty-five men aboard when the ship started back up the lake, thirty-three, including her fifty-two-year-old skipper, failed to make port. In Rogers City, fifty-five children were left fatherless. Eighteen bodies were recovered; the other fifteen—including the eighteen-year-old son of Alex Selke, who had gone aboard the *Bradley* to save money for college—were claimed forever by the tempestuous lake that will not be tamed.

At a joint funeral for the recovered bodies, held in Rogers City and attended by Protestants and Catholics alike, Monsignor Womicki, bishop of Saginaw, Michigan, voiced the thought that burned in the hearts of all who were there: "While reaching for the stars and moon, we have not yet mastered our elements of air, water, and fire."

*   *   *

Eight years later more children would be left without fathers; more funeral services would be held for those who had been aboard a ship that had "gone missing" on the Great Lakes. This time Lake Huron would be the one to again assess a grisly fee against those who dared trespass her waters when the gales of November threatened.

*   *   *

Dennis Hale lay in his bunk trying to sleep amid the cacophony of banging anchors, crashing chains, bumping metal drums, and rattling tools, all coming from the windlass room on the opposite side of his stateroom wall. The clamor was caused by a howling storm which raged around his ship, the 660-foot ore freighter *Daniel J. Morrell,* as it struggled northward in Lake Huron. The screaming winds and tumultuous waves were oscillating the ship in a multidirectional plunge through the seas that promised to set everything loose and flying through the air.

It was late November 1966, and Hale, twenty-six years old, would be happy to see this shipping season end—damned happy.

The six-foot, 230-pound father of four was candidly unenthusiastic about his job as a Great Lakes sailor. He disliked the long periods away from home, and he had a nervous respect for the awesome storms that sometimes struck the lakes—such as the one that was then denying him sleep. But in his third year as a deck watchman aboard the *Morrell*, Hale was equally honest in admitting that the pay was far better than he could earn as an Ashtabula, Ohio, hotel cook.

Still, there were times when he seriously thought he would be better off to chuck the job—money and all—and go back "on the beach."

This last week had been one of those times.

It began on Wednesday as the *Morrell* was returning from Taconite Harbor, Minnesota, with a load of iron ore on what supposedly had been the final trip of the 1966 shipping season. The *Morrell*'s master, Capt. Arthur J. Crawley, informed the crew that Cleveland headquarters had radioed that an additional trip to Lake Superior and back would be required to fulfill the company's tonnage commitments. The news had come as a severe disappointment to Hale and most of the other thirty-two men aboard.

They had arrived at the Bethlehem Steel Corporation (the owner of the *Morrell*) dock at Lackawanna, New York, late on Saturday, November 26, 1966. Two other vessels were waiting their turn at the unloading dock. Hale estimated that it would be at least twenty-four hours before the *Morrell* was unloaded and ready for the return to Taconite Harbor—more than enough time for him to drive the 115 miles to his home in Ashtabula for a few hours with his family, particularly since his Buick station wagon was parked nearby, kept there because Lackawanna was their usual unloading port. A fellow shipmate, watchman John Groh, rode with him as far as the Harbor Creek, Pennsylvania, exit on Interstate 90. Hale and Groh agreed to meet at the same place for the return to Lackawanna the following evening.

But when the two arrived at the dock Sunday night, they were chagrined to discover that the *Morrell* had departed an hour earlier.

Contacting Captain Crawley by ship-to-shore radio, they made arrangements to rejoin the ore boat in Windsor, Ontario, the next day, when the *Morrell* stopped to take on coal.

Hale and Groh sped back to Ashtabula, where Dennis imposed upon a friend to drive the two seamen to Detroit.

At seven the next morning the two weary sailors finally crawled aboard their ship.

The Weather Bureau, at noon on the twenty-eighth, was forecasting gale warnings with northeasterly winds at thirty-four to forty knots the following twelve hours, with snow, or snow and rain, for the next twenty-four hours.

The *Morrell*'s sister ship, the *Edward Y. Townsend,* under the command of Thomas J. Connelly, a veteran of twenty-seven years on the lakes, had followed the *Morrell* up the lake from Lackawanna. The two skippers stayed in radio contact as the ships moved north through Lake St. Clair, the St. Clair River, and into Lake Huron, the *Morrell* a bit more than twenty miles in the lead.

Through the evening the captains conferred as the conditions on Huron steadily worsened. At one point, about ten o'clock in the evening, Connelly considered turning about and returning to Port Huron, but he changed his mind after considering the danger of falling into a trough in the growing seas and not being able to get out again. The two shipmasters discussed heaving-to in the shelter of Thunder Bay.

Dennis Hale had gone off duty at 8:00 P.M. After a hot meal in the after deckhouse crew's mess, he had returned to his room in the fo'c'sle, read for a while, and at about 9:30 climbed into his bunk, stripped to his underwear.

At about eleven o'clock, Crawley called Connelly. But the *Townsend*'s skipper had his hands full at the moment; his ship was blowing around, broadside to the wind, and Connelly was busy trying to muscle the vessel back on course.

"I'll call you back," Connelly had said tersely.

Shortly after midnight on November 29, Connelly, having successfully regained control of his ship, called Crawley. The *Morrell*'s skipper confided that a similar experience had befallen his vessel. The winds at this time were northerly at sixty-five miles an hour, and the seas were twenty feet.

Crawley signed off with a hopeful "Good luck." It was the last contact the *Townsend* would have with the *Morrell*.

Connelly maintained a constant listening watch on Channel 51—the distress frequency—hearing nothing.

Throughout the remainder of the hellish night, Connelly made repeated attempts to raise the *Morrell* on radio, without success. Concluding that the *Morrell* had experienced radio problems—possibly her antenna had been carried away—Connelly felt no concern. It would not be until 12:15 P.M. on the afternoon of November 30—thirty-six hours after the last communication with the *Morrell*—that Bethlehem Steel Company's Cleveland office would notify the Coast Guard that the vessel was overdue at the Soo Locks.

The *Daniel J. Morrell* and the *Edward Y. Townsend* were both sixty years of age, built with a type of steel that had not been used after 1948, when it was discovered to be highly brittle at temperatures below the freezing point—temperatures both vessels experienced on Lake Huron in late November 1966.

Hale, who had finally managed to drift off to sleep despite the terrible din, was awakened at about 2:00 A.M. by a new sound, different than that emanating from the windlass room. This had an explosive, banging quality that Hale felt as well as heard. He lay in the darkness of his room, wondering about the nature of the noise. Within a minute of the first crashing sound there came a second, louder, jarring one. At the same instant, the books on a shelf over his bed came tumbling down. Hale reached up and flipped the switch on his bunk light, but nothing happened. As he clicked the switch several times, trying to get the light to work, he was startled by the loud clanging of the general alarm bells. Jumping out of bed, he grabbed a life jacket and dashed into the corridor. No lights burned there, either. At the watertight door leading to the spar deck he bumped into Watchman Albert Whoeme, who had arrived an instant before. Whoeme undogged the metal door and peered out.

"Oh, my God!" Whoeme shouted. "Get your life jacket!" Hale glanced around Whoeme. The lights at the stern were burning brightly, but they stopped about halfway forward. The aft section of the ship appeared to be higher than the forward end.

Hale dashed back to his darkened room, searching for his trousers and shoes—he was wearing only a pair of undershorts—but in the blackness of the rolling, pitching room he was able to locate only his heavy woolen pea jacket.

Back on the spar deck, Hale found the forward crew gathered around the life raft, all in various stages of dress, none fully prepared for the severe conditions. Hale himself was standing barefoot in a pile of slushy snow.

Getting aft to the lifeboats was impossible. The *Morrell* was being torn apart at hatch 11; the tortured screaming of tearing metal plates, the showering sparks from severed electrical cables, and the geysering clouds from broken steam lines all attested to that fact.

The life raft, around which the thirteen shivering men from the forward section stood, was a pontoon type with a wood-slat floor and wooden sides. It was heavy, but capable of being thrown overboard. But the men decided that the simplest thing would be for all to get inside and wait for the bow section to sink out from under them—it would be but a matter of minutes, they knew.

Into the raft went Captain Crawley; First Mate Philip Kapets; Second Mate Duncan MacLeod; Wheelsmen Henry Rischmiller, Stuart Campbell, and Charles Fosbender; Watchmen Albert Whoeme, Norman Bragg, Larry Davis, and Dennis Hale; Deckhands John Cleary and Arthur Stojeck; and Ernest Marcotta, the *Morell*'s third mate.

With one final screech of pain, the last fragments of steel connecting the two sections of the ship parted. The aft section, still under power, forged ahead, bumping and banging into the helpless fore section, pushing it aside. The bow section slowly slipped around until it had fully reversed its course, and the men on the deck watched in stunned silence as the stern half of the *Morrell* moved past, still making steam and ablaze with light as it churned away into the darkness, leaving them alone in the howling storm. It would only be a matter of time, they knew, before the aft section, taking on water from the gaping hole where the two sections had joined, would slip beneath the waves as even now the forward section was doing.

The men waited for the deck to sink out from beneath them, but a thunderous wave struck the wallowing hulk as it dipped slowly downward and swept men and raft over the side, spiraling down into the freezing lake. Hale came to the surface, gasping against the shock of the extreme cold, within arms' reach of the bobbing raft. By the time he had managed to crawl aboard, Deckhands Stojek and Cleary were already on board. Between the three of them they managed to pull one other into the raft—Charles Fosbender, a wheelsman. None of the others were in sight; they were all that were left.

Fosbender was the only one of the four who was fully clothed—he had finished his watch at midnight and had not yet gone to his cabin when the *Morrell* broke apart.

Hale, going through the raft's emergency kit, found—in addition to a signal pistol, six amber flares, six parachute flares, and a sea anchor—a can of storm oil. He planned to spread the heavy oil over his nearly naked body to help protect it from the cold wind and water. But before he could, one of the others, thinking it was useless, tossed it overboard.

Hale fired the flares, spacing them over several hours. No one saw any of them; the men were alone in one raging corner of Lake Huron.

Through the endless, miserable night they huddled together, trying to keep warm. Before dawn John Cleary and Arthur Stojeck had died, robbed of their precious body heat and their vital will to live.

Through the day of Tuesday, November 29, Fosbender grew steadily weaker, complaining that his lungs were filling with water.

"I told him to crawl near me," Hale said later.

As he did, he raised himself in the raft and shouted that he saw land through a break in the clouds of snow that swirled around them.

Periodically, Fosbender would lift himself up to look, hopefully, for signs of life, of rescue. He saw none.

At about four o'clock in the afternoon, the forty-two-year-old Charles Henry Fosbender turned to Hale and muttered, "Denny, I'm going to throw in the sponge." Without another word, Wheelsman Fosbender turned his face to the side, closed his eyes, and gave up his life.

Through the rest of the day and all of Tuesday night, the six-foot, 230-pound former hotel cook, who never really enjoyed sailing on the lakes, fought a grim and unyielding battle with death. He thought he could see the lights of farmhouses on shore. But his feet were now frozen, and if the raft did beach itself on or near the shore, Hale knew he would never be able to crawl to safety.

He crawled beneath the stiff corpses of his shipmates for some protection and warmth and drifted in and out of consciousness.

During Wednesday afternoon, his feet and one hand now frozen, his hair caked with ice, his body writhing in pain, Dennis Hale suddenly came fully awake. He felt hungry and thirsty and began halfheartedly eating bits of ice that he plucked from his jacket. Suddenly there was someone else with him on the raft—an old man with long, white hair, heavy eyebrows, and a mustache; his complexion was an eerie milk white color, and his eyes were commanding. The elderly apparition grimly warned Hale against eating the ice. Hale dropped into another period of semiconsciousness, and when he awoke he again picked at the icicles on his jacket, putting them in his mouth and chewing them. Again the old man appeared, and, more forcefully this time, lectured Dennis: "I told you not to eat the ice off your coat. It will lower your body temperature and you'll die." Hale drifted once more into a stupor, only slightly aware of his surroundings.

On Wednesday morning the *Townsend,* as instructed by the Cleveland office, docked at Lime Island in the St. Mary's River below the Soo Locks to take on fuel. Captain Connelly still was of the impression that the *Morrell* was somewhere ahead, perhaps experiencing radio difficulties.

Meanwhile, in Cleveland, Chief Dispatcher Arthur Dobson had become increasingly concerned about two of his ships. The reporting station at the Soo had failed to mention the arrival of either the *Morrell* or the *Townsend* on Wednesday morning. He put in a call to the Coast Guard asking for information about either vessel. The Coast Guard located the *Townsend* in the St. Mary's River. The *Morrell,* Dobson was told, could not be found.

At about the time Dobson was making his call to the Soo, the motor vessel *G. G. Post* reported sighting a body floating off Harbor Beach, in Michigan's thumb area. Less than an hour later, the freighter *G. A. Tomlinson* spotted three more bodies and wreckage about four miles north-northeast of where the first body had been seen. All wore life jackets with *Morrell* markings. It now became clear that the *Daniel J. Morrell* would not be arriving at the Soo Locks.

A massive air-sea search was mounted; planes, helicopters, and surface vessels swarmed over the area, with ground parties patrolling the snowy beaches, looking for bodies which may have washed ashore. The *Morrell*'s after life raft was found unoccupied, but with a body trapped beneath.

At about four o'clock Wednesday afternoon, a Coast Guard helicopter sighted a life raft south of Harbor Beach. A crew member, checking the raft with binoculars, informed the pilot that the raft carried four dead bodies—"They're all frozen stiff." The Coast Guard helicopter pilot eased the aircraft down onto the surface of the now relatively calm lake, directly against the quietly undulating raft. Just as the crewman stepped aboard to begin unstacking the bodies, a right arm raised weakly and Dennis Hale lifted his head.

A Coast Guard officer in the helicopter radioed that Hale was "in minor shock but in amazingly good condition." Doctors in Harbor Beach found his body temperature to be 95 degrees—3.6 degrees below normal. Asked how the burly sailor could have survived the grueling ordeal and murderous conditions, one of the examining physicians replied: "He's twenty-six and he didn't panic. But it's still a miracle."

Twenty of the dead *Morrell* crew were eventually recovered from the lake. Eight were never found. A Coast Guard board of investigation concluded that the *Morrell* suffered "brittle fracture" of its hull, caused by prolonged twisting and bending in water whose temperature was sufficiently low to promote the fracturing of the steel. The *Townsend* reported a crack in her deck plates near number 12 hatch that extended down to the shear strake. (Hale recalls the *Morrell* splitting in two at about the same location.) The Coast Guard inspector ordered the ship towed to the nearest shipyard. It was never again permitted to carry cargo, and several years later it was sold to a Spanish scrap company. It broke apart and sank while being towed across the Atlantic Ocean.

Dennis Hale suffered severe frostbite to several toes, but otherwise came away from his ordeal in remarkably good condition, physically. He suffered a greater form of torture as the result of his nightmare on Lake Huron in November 1966. Great Lakes sailors who have survived the disaster of losing their ship and shipmates speak of the "why you syndrome," a malady that manifests itself most painfully when they meet the wives or families of their shipmates who didn't survive. Whether spoken or not, whether real or imagined, these men see in the eyes of the bereaved the unmistakable question, Why you? Why did these few survive instead of their own loved ones?

Hale never went back on the lakes. He works as a machinist

in Ohio, never wanting to discuss his memories or to relive his nightmare.

The day after she was given the news that her husband's body had been recovered from the raft on which Dennis Hale had so miraculously survived, Jan Fosbender received a letter, delivered to their St. Clair, Michigan, home, from her dead husband. It had been dropped to the mail boat *J. W. Wescott* as the *Morrell* was steaming up the Detroit River on the way to her rendezvous with extinction. The letter closed with these words: "If luck is with us, this will be our last trip."

CHAPTER 8

"I'll Never See Him Again"

At 6:30 on the morning of November 10, 1975, the two cooks and two porters were busy in *Edmund Fitzgerald's* galley, preparing for the first influx of crew coming to breakfast. The menu this morning would be eggs (any style), pork sausage (links and patties), pancakes (buttermilk), bacon (Canadian and slab), various kinds of cold cereals, hot breakfast rolls (a large bowl of thick pan gravy was on the table for those who wished to slop it over the rolls), a heaping stack of toast, two juices (orange and grapefruit), coffee, tea, milk, or hot chocolate.

The food aboard the *Fitzgerald*, as with practically every lake boat, was excellent and plentiful.

"They (Great Lakes sailors) are the best-fed men in the world," one ore boat steward insists.

Up on the bridge First Mate Jack McCarthy was preparing to send the morning weather data to the National Weather Service.

At 0700 the *Fitzgerald*'s position was 48°N, 87.8°W. The winds at this location were from the northeast at thirty-five knots, down from the fifty-two knots reported at 0100, due to the ship's proximity to the Canadian shore and to an overall moderation in the storm's activity as its center passed over Marquette, in Michigan's Upper Peninsula. A light rain was falling, and the visibility was two to four miles. Wave heights remained at ten feet, but the *Fitz*, heavily laden with ore pellets, was "working well" in the seas, with little pitching and almost no rolling.

"It wouldn't have rolled an egg off the table."

The *Arthur M. Anderson* was then a few miles astern—the faster *Fitzgerald* had overtaken and passed the U.S. Steel ore carrier at about three that morning.

At 0700 Captain McSorley placed a radiotelephone call from the *Fitzgerald* to Oglebay-Norton's Cleveland office: "Our ETA (estimated time of arrival) at the Soo is indefinite because of the weather," he had said.

Throughout the ship it was "business as usual," or nearly so; there would be no work done above decks due to the spray coming over the rail.

"Have your men work in the windlass room," McCarthy had told Watchman William J. Spengler. "They can do some cleaning and maintenance."

Spengler, fifty-nine, from Toledo, would stand the eight-to-twelve watch and would supervise the work of Thomas D. Borgeson, able-bodied maintenance man, and Deckhands Bruce Hudson, Paul Riippa, and Mark A. Thomas. Cadet Dave Weiss would assist Spengler.

Bill Spengler had come aboard the *Fitzgerald* as a watchman only this year. However, he had sailed on the *Fitz* in previous years as a wheelsman. He looked younger than his fifty-nine years, a well-built man in good physical condition, his full head of hair graying at the temples. He had joined the navy after leaving high school in Archbold, Ohio, becoming a boatswain's mate aboard the battleship *Maryland*. Spengler was aboard the ship on the morning of December 7, 1941, moored alongside the U.S.S. *Oklahoma,* which took a total of five Japanese torpedoes before rolling over. Spengler took over an antiaircraft gun when its gunner was killed, remaining at the weapon until he was injured in one of the two bomb blasts to rock the *Maryland.*

Spengler spent a year in the hospital as the result of his wounds, much of the time in a wheelchair. He began sailing aboard lake boats immediately following his discharge in 1947, working his way up to the wheelsman's job.

After his marriage in 1972 he gave up sailing, moving to California, where he operated a carryout store. After three years "on the beach," he moved his family back to Toledo to work the iron boats once again. In February 1975 he was assigned to the *Fitzgerald,* requesting a watchman's berth because the work of a wheelsman was "too intense."

"He really loved the sailing," his wife Margaret would later say.

Bill Spengler had no plans to retire and had every reason to anticipate a long, long life on this November day; his mother, Maude Spengler, was already ninety years old.

The galley crew would serve breakfast until about 8:30; they were already preparing for lunch.

"Better be ready for a blow," McSorley had advised Bob Rafferty as he was having his own breakfast shortly before seven.

Rafferty ordered Freddy Beetcher to install rolling rods on the galley stoves. The retainers were designed to prevent pots and pans from sliding off the stove tops when the ship was rolling. Just before lunch Beetcher and Nolan F. Church, the other porter, wet each tablecloth to keep dishes, silverware, and condiments from skidding about, a standard precaution in heavy weather. Should conditions become too violent, normal meal preparations would be suspended and sandwiches would be served until the seas moderated.

However, as the last of the breakfast dishes were cleared away, Rafferty decided to go ahead with the menu he had planned earlier: fresh perch, barbecued ribs, home-fried pota-

toes, jello, ice cream, and cherry pie. For dinner there would
be roast pork, broiled chicken, mashed potatoes, hot biscuits
and gravy, pie or ice cream, and maybe some chocolate
pudding.

In a couple of days Rafferty would be home in Toledo,
possibly for good. Perhaps he and Brooksie would travel to
Georgia to see his daughter, Pam, and maybe stay until Pam
had her baby. He had not seen his daughter since March,
when he had traveled to Fort Benning, Georgia, to visit her
and his son-in-law, William Johnson, a career soldier. Pam
recalled later how, as her father was driving away, heading
back to Toledo, she had watched him go. Suddenly a strange,
clammy feeling came over her, a stabbing fear clutched at her,
and she found herself thinking, "I'll never see him again."

*   *   *

Shortly after 8:00 A.M. on November 10, Raymond R.
Waldman, meteorologist in charge of the National Weather
Forecast Office, arrived at O'Hare Office Building Number 2,
on Higgins Road in Rosemont, Illinois, adjacent to Chicago's
sprawling O'Hare International Airport. Room 610, a modest-
sized open area, housed the forecast center. The prominent
feature in the room was a large, semicircular table, around
which sat the three meteorologists and two meteorological
technicians on duty.

Waldman conferred briefly with George Polensky, the super-
visor who had issued the storm warnings earlier that morning.
Waldman, who had spent a quiet weekend at his suburban
Chicago home in Downers Grove, Illinois, was well aware of
the atmospheric eruptions gripping the Midwest; he had been
kept informed by telephone by the men who staffed this office
twenty-four hours a day, seven days a week.

"It's shaping up to be a good-sized storm," Polensky said.
Waldman glanced at the latest data coming in from reporting
stations throughout the nation, nodded agreement, and then,

thinking back over his thirty-three years' experience with Great Lakes weather, said, "We've had worse."

* * *

In Ashland, Wisconsin, Florence Simmons had her hands full. Her youngest daughter, Mrs. Mary Louko, had gone into the hospital the day before to deliver the baby who was to be the ninth grandchild of John and Florence Simmons. Grandma Florence was babysitting the other Louko children.

John had called the previous morning. His ship, the *Edmund Fitzgerald,* was loading taconite in Superior but wouldn't be there long enough for him to make the sixty-five-mile trip east to Ashland. He was somewhat concerned about his daughter, who had the reputation of delivering small babies. Florence told him not to worry—the baby would be just fine, and if it was a boy it would be named Patrick Simmons Louko (the "Simmons" in honor of Grandpa John).

John David Simmons had made a success of a life that had begun with little promise. Born in Bay City, Michigan, on August 25, 1912, he had lived his entire life believing that 1915 was the year of his birth. Because of a defective birth certificate, it was not until his death in the *Fitzgerald* that the error was discovered. "He thought he was sixty," Florence commented later, "but he was really sixty-three. He could have retired in two more years."

Agnes Simmons died when little Johnny was three, leaving the motherless boy to be farmed out among relatives throughout his childhood. His father, a bartender in Ashland, was not able to give John and his sister, Evelyn, the attention growing children must have.

John managed to get a high school education in spite of his uncertain home life, becoming a basketball star at Kelly High School in Ashland. It was said that he was "one of the best this town ever produced."

He went on the lakes in 1937 "because it was a job; things

were pretty tough in those days." He worked first for U.S. Steel, switching to Oglebay-Norton in 1948 after one year ashore "because he wanted to be home more."

In 1940, John began frequenting a restaurant near the Ashland hotel he called home when off the boats. The reason was not the food or the atmosphere; it was a pretty waitress named Florence. On February 10, 1942, John and Florence were married, and for the first time in his memory he had a home that was truly his.

In September of 1958 he was recalled from his wheelsman job on the auto carrier *Howard M. Hanna Jr.* to be one of the three honored men to "wheel" the company's new flagship, *Edmund Fitzgerald,* on her shakedown cruise. The trip from River Rouge, Michigan, to Silver Bay, Minnesota—complete with a number of public figures of the time, company representatives, and other dignitaries, with special catering firms to supply food, drink, and entertainment—was one of the proudest, most exciting experiences of his life.

Simmons was something of a contradiction in his view of his job. "He loved the ship, he loved wheeling it, but he hated sailing," Florence recalls. "He didn't like being away so much of the time; he felt closed in on the boats." As a means of relieving this tendency to be somewhat claustrophobic, Simmons spent hours walking the long spar deck. Five feet, ten inches tall and athletically built, Simmons was in excellent physical condition. He had deep blue eyes and a full head of hair that was almost totally white. He spoke with a dialect that was a mixture of English, French Canadian, and Scandinavian—an accent that is peculiar to the upper Great Lakes region.

He retained the love of basketball that had its origin in his youth and at one time coached the Saint Agnes school team in Ashland.

Simmons was extremely devoted to his captain: "McSorley is a very competent skipper; he is a prince." He also liked and respected First Mate Jack McCarthy. But his closest friend aboard the *Fitzgerald* was Red O'Brien, a dear friend from their days together aboard the *Hanna.*

Eugene William O'Brien—"Red" to his many friends—was known throughout the Columbia fleet as "the lake boat gambler" because of his intense love for any card game, but particularly poker. He could be found every night in the after crew's recreation room, seated at the round table, a stack of nickels, dimes, and quarters in front of him, a can of beer within easy reach. (Company regulations prohibited the possession and/or use of alcoholic beverages of any kind; however, the rule was not strictly enforced as long as no crew member drank while on watch or appeared for duty under the influence. "A lot of the men had their own case of beer," a former Columbia sailor remembers. "They would have a couple when they came off watch or before their supper.")

Red—the nickname derived from a full head of flaming red, curly hair—possessed an irrepressible Irish sense of humor and an untamable enthusiasm for life, which were the hallmarks of his effulgent personality.

"Everyone liked Red O'Brien" is an opinion commonly held by former *Fitzgerald* sailors, wives and mothers of the men who were aboard the boat on her final voyage, Columbia personnel—anyone who knew the fifty-year-old wheelsman.

"Red was the first man you would make friends with when you came aboard the *Fitz*," a sailor who had spent several seasons on the ship recalls. "He would go out of his way to introduce himself to you, and then he would take you around and introduce you to the other guys; he would kind of keep an eye on you, to be sure everything was going all right. He was one hell of a guy."

O'Brien was born in Minneapolis but had spent his childhood in Payette, Idaho. In 1942, at the tender age of sixteen, Red secured his first shipboard employment as a deckhand aboard the Oglebay-Norton vessel *Howard M. Hanna Jr.* It was on the *Hanna,* in 1948, that he began a twenty-seven-year friendship with Johnny Simmons. In 1956, Red married and left the lakes to work at the Libby-Owens-Ford glass plant in Rossford, Ohio. The marriage didn't last, however, and soon after the birth of his only child—a son, John—Red returned to the boats, never to leave them again.

"He adored the boy," friends recall of his relationship with his son. "He spent all of his free time with John, traveling during those times when young John was not in school."

Red made it a point to have his son aboard the ship for no less than one cruise each summer, and John planned to work the boats, at least part-time, as soon as he turned eighteen.

"My dad was going to get me a job on the boats," John states.

Close friends later recalled that O'Brien, who had experienced the fury of several bad storms on Lake Superior, never indicated a fear of the lakes.

"He always looked at the happy side of things," Rev. James C. Southard, associate pastor of St. Hedwig Catholic Church in Toledo, said, recalling his close friendship with the genial wheelsman.

*   *   *

At 9:53 A.M., Captain Cooper of the *Anderson* conferred by radiophone with Captain McSorley.

"The seas are moderating considerably," Cooper said. "I think we could head due east."

McSorley agreed, and the two ships turned to a ninety-degree heading. The *Fitzgerald* was slowly pulling ahead of the *Anderson* and shortly before 10:00 A.M. was about twenty-five miles south of the Slate Islands off the north shore of Lake Superior. The winds were holding out of the north-northeast at twenty-six knots; the seas were down somewhat, with some spray coming over the decks but no "green water."

"Hold this course until you can make for Otter Head with the wind at your stern," McSorley told Second Mate James Pratt. "Stay off about three miles from the Otter Head Light."

McSorley then walked down the single flight of stairs from the chart room just behind the wheelhouse to the forecastle deck. At the bottom of the stairs he turned to the right, went through a door into a narrow corridor, then went to his left two paces to the door leading into his office, a spacious room measuring twelve by fourteen feet. To his left, as he entered the office, was a short hallway which led to his bedroom. Walking to this room, he gazed longingly at the large, comfortable bed. He had not slept well the previous night, having gotten up several times to check on the weather and the condition of the seas. Perhaps a nap before lunch would restore his flagging energy.

Shucking his jacket and kicking off his shoes, he dropped onto the bed. Just before he drifted into a troubled sleep, his thoughts advanced to the time when the last trip of this year was behind him, when he could pull the *Fitz* into winter dockage in Toledo and spend the evenings in his comfortable Bancroft Avenue home, with Nellie there by his side, each taking comfort from the other's presence, a mutual healing that would last through the long, snowy, wind-torn nights of winter. Perhaps when spring came around again they would both have regained enough strength to face another year—*one more year.*

*   *   *

In Fairport Harbor, Ohio, Helen Bindon was puttering around the house when the telephone rang. It was her best friend, Matilda Lipovich.

"Come with me; I want to buy some Christmas candy," Matilda pleaded.

It was a blustery day and turning colder, a reversal of the near-seventy-degree temperatures that had been holding through the weekend in the Cleveland area. But Helen capitulated to her friend's insistent entreaty, agreeing to accompany her on the candy-buying expedition. As they left the shop just after noon, Helen glanced out at Lake Erie, just yards away from where they stood. A howling wind was whipping the lake into a frenzy; the heaving waves were being decapitated, their crowns hurled away in a frothy spray that seemed to fill the air with a swirling white liquid fog. The cold dampness of the blast from the water stung Helen's face and stabbed through her coat. As she looked at the sullen, foreboding sky and the angry, thrashing Erie waters, her thoughts went to her husband, far to the north aboard a ship.

"Oh, Tillie," she said, throwing an arm around her friend's waist, "I hope my Eddie isn't in this storm."

Her Eddie was indeed in this storm.

*   *   *

"Why go?" she had asked him just before he had left that last time.

He had seemed so nervous, pacing around the house; it was clear to her that something was on his mind, but she didn't ask him what it was. She couldn't ask him; he wouldn't tell her if she did. Perhaps, she thought, it was his Uncle Joe.

Joe Kraynik was a grizzled tugboat captain, tough and unyielding, who looked upon hard work as if it were a commission from above, a contract that he had entered into on the day he was born, a pact with his Creator that would not be fulfilled until his life was finished, until the time when he would stand before his God, hold out his callused hands, and say modestly, "It was the best I could do." It was a part of the compact he felt he was a party to that made Joe Kraynik believe he was destined to get only what he had earned from a life of doing the best he could. Edward Francis Bindon knew all too well of his beloved Uncle Joe's philosophy of life, and this knowledge made matters all the more painful for Eddie, for Uncle Joe Kraynik was dying of cancer.

Eddie Bindon, the *Fitzgerald*'s first assistant engineer, had come home when the ship had called at Ashtabula on November 5. Throughout the day he had seemed preoccupied, and Helen had tried to fathom his thoughts. She knew that his uncle was on Eddie's mind; she understood, too, that the *Fitzgerald* was also concerning him. When the ship sailed again, it would mark his last trip aboard her; it would be his final voyage as a sailor on the lakes. Although only forty-seven years old, Eddie had made up his mind to retire at the end of this season—after twenty-five years on the boats, he would make one final swing to Superior and then call it quits.

He had begun as a coal passer aboard the *W. C. Richardson,* an Oglebay-Norton crane boat. He had quit his job with the Fairport Harbor Department of Streets because he was planning to be married and he wanted to make more money.

"I'd like to get a better job," he had told Helen one evening in 1950. "What do you think about my taking a job on the lakes?"

If he were looking to his fiancée for guidance and advice, he might have looked elsewhere.

"I don't pick work for anybody," Helen had told him succinctly. "If that's what you want, that's what you'll do."

He had, and he did. A few days later Eddie came into the Lake County Memorial Hospital kitchen, where Helen worked, and said, "I've got a job aboard the *Richardson.*"

Bindon quickly worked up to an oiler's job, and shortly after they were married, in 1951, Eddie told Helen, "I'm going to write for my third assistant's license. I want the money."

Over the next few years he studied for exams almost constantly, writing for the next highest rating as soon as he was ready. In 1973 he became first assistant engineer aboard the *Fitzgerald,* working directly under Chief Engineer George Holl.

A big man—he stood an even six feet tall and had weighed 240 pounds, with brown eyes and brown curly hair—Bindon suffered an attack of angina pectoris while the *Fitz* was in Two Harbors, and was hospitalized for several months, dropping 60 pounds during the period. His great passion in life—other than the *Fitzgerald*—was golf. "He ate and slept golf," Helen says, remembering their annual trips to Florida during winter lay-ups. "He lived on the golf course."

Retirement would permit him to spend all his time with

Helen and with his favorite pastime. *Just one more trip.*

"Why go?" she had asked him. "Why not stay home and help your Uncle Joe?"

He had shaken off her suggestion with a terse "I will not watch my uncle die."

*   *   *

At noon the *Fitzgerald* was between two and three miles northwest of Otter Head Light on the eastern Ontario shore of the lake. Winds were out of the southwest and had dropped to eleven knots; the barometer was down to 28.82 inches.

"We're right in the eye of the storm," Second Mate Jim Pratt advised Mike Armagost, the *Fitzgerald*'s third mate, who had entered the wheelhouse a few minutes earlier to take the watch.

Armagost scanned the weather forecast that had just come through. "The wind will be hauling around soon," he said. "I'd like to be beyond the Michipicoten Light before the seas build up."

Captain McSorley emerged from the stairwell into the chart room, where the mates were conferring. He stepped up to the chart table, took the weather sheet from Armagost, and then looked at the Lake Superior chart on which their course lines from Superior had been drawn. Second Mate Pratt tapped a finger on a spot near Otter Head Light, indicating where the ship was then located.

"I just ordered a change to 178 to set up off Michipicoten," he informed the captain, who nodded his approval.

"The winds will come around out of the northwest, and they'll increase," McSorley said. "The seas will be running funny down through here, Mike, between Michipicoten and Caribou. We'll want to be certain we make our turn just right to keep the wind on our stern."

Armagost placed a light pencil dot on the 178 course line. "This would put us about six miles off the Michipicoten Light."

"We'll make a decision on our turn when we see how the seas are running," McSorley said, turning to Pratt. "How's the radar?"

The *Fitzgerald* was equipped with two surface scan radar units, one of which had begun to malfunction periodically in the early hours of the morning.

"The sixteen-centimeter set is still unreliable," Pratt responded. "I've got it shut down."

"We should be all right with the shorter scale and the direction finder," McSorley said. "They'll tell us where we are."

*   *   *

In the chart room aboard the *Arthur M. Anderson,* Bernie Cooper was looking at his own charts. A better-than-average weather forecaster in his own right, Cooper looked with astonishment at the chart on which he had drawn the concentric arcs of barometric pressure known as isobars. He shook his head after rechecking his calculations. He must have made a mistake, he thought. According to his estimates, the back side of the storm now passing overhead would generate winds from the northwest with speeds of eighty knots. It couldn't be, he told himself. Bernie Cooper would later discover that his wind speed forecast would be more accurate than that of the National Weather Service.

*   *   *

One hundred and twenty-five miles southeast of where the *Fitzgerald* was steaming, the 490-foot-long Swedish saltwater motor vessel *Avafors* was being ushered through the Soo Locks at Sault Ste. Marie. The locks, first opened in 1855, permit ships to descend the twenty-one feet from Lake Superior to the level of Lake Huron.

Aboard the *Avafors* was Capt. Cedric Woodard of Duluth. As a licensed Great Lakes pilot, it was Captain Woodard's responsibility to guide and direct the ship through the tricky and frequently dangerous waters of the Great Lakes. He brought more than forty years of lake-sailing experience with him.

A few miles south of the locks, about noon on November 10, another experienced Great Lakes pilot, Capt. Albert Jacovetti, of Superior, was guiding the 709-foot saltwater motor vessel *Nanfri* through the winding St. Mary's River approach to the locks. He had climbed aboard the 13,500-ton Liberian freighter at Detour, Michigan, at the upper tip of Lake Huron, while the ship was under way, assigned to pilot the ship to Thunder Bay, Ontario.

A third Great Lakes pilot, Capt. Robert O'Brien, was a few miles south of the *Nanfri*, piloting the sister ship, the *Benfri*. O'Brien had come aboard at three o'clock that morning at Detour and immediately ordered the vessel to anchor until morning when visibility improved. Now the ship was under way, heading up the river to the locks and then across Superior bound for Duluth.

None of the three highly experienced lake pilots had any reason to anticipate that their respective voyages would be anything but routine. One would miss most of the excitement that was to permeate the area around the eastern end of Lake Superior later that day; he would be sound asleep.

CHAPTER 9

"He's In Too Close"

The weather satellite photographs transmitted to the National Weather Service during the afternoon of November 10 clearly portrayed the massive weather system which gripped the midwestern section of the United States. The swirling, counterclockwise circulation of clouds spread over all of Michigan, Wisconsin, Minnesota, Illinois, Indiana, Ohio, parts of Pennsylvania, New York, the Northeastern seaboard, and much of the Tennessee Valley. Trails of the system extended all the way down to the Florida Keys. The ice-laden air swooping down from Canada spawned tornadoes in parts of Indiana; winds were clocked at sixty-four miles per hour in Toledo; damage to buildings resulted throughout the Great Lakes area; trees were uprooted and temperatures plummeted. The sudden and drastic change came as a decided shock to those in the affected area lulled by the warm, pleasant weather of the previous week.

"It looks like winter is setting in" was a common reaction to the onslaught of biting wind and bitter cold.

The weather on Lake Superior was in an agitated state of flux. At one o'clock in the afternoon the motor vessel *Simcoe,* ten miles southwest of the *Fitzgerald,* reported winds from the west at forty-four knots, with waves seven feet. The Whitefish Point Weather Station had the winds from the south-southeast at nineteen knots, gusting to thirty-four, while the Stannard Rock Station, north of Marquette, reported winds from the west-northwest at fifty knots, gusting to fifty-nine knots. Aboard the *Fitzgerald,* ten miles northwest of Michipicoten Island, Third Mate Armagost checked the ship's anemometer and noted winds from the southwest at twenty knots; waves were twelve feet. In the Chicago office of the National Weather Service, the next regular forecast for eastern Lake Superior, to be broadcast at 1639 hours (4:39 P.M.), predicted: "Northwest winds 38 to 52 knots with gusts to 60 knots early tonight and northwesterly winds 25 to 35 knots diminishing Tuesday, waves 8 to 16 feet tonight decreasing Tuesday."

Michipicoten Island is located 106 miles northwest of Sault St. Marie, 25 miles due west of the Canadian shoreline. It is a rocky, largely barren land mass, measuring 17 miles east to west and 5 miles north to south. Twenty-two miles due south is Caribou Island, an even more desolate piece of real estate, measuring 3 miles north to south and approximately 1½ miles east to west.

In between, the depth of the water ranges from more than one hundred fathoms (six hundred feet) to a shoal area, north and east of Caribou Island, known as Six Fathom Shoal. Mariners sailing these waters rely on two basic sets of navigational charts to find their way across Lake Superior: U.S. Chart L.S. 9 and Canadian Chart 2310. Both series of maps are periodically updated to reflect changes in the geography of the region (new shoreline installations such as navigation lights or radio stations, newly created harbors, etc.) and also to identify possible hazards to ship navigation (wrecked ships, newly discovered shoal areas, etc.). Both American and Canadian charts in use on November 10, 1975, indicated the Six Fathom Shoal, also denoted as North Bank. Both based the location and depth of the shallow waters on the Canadian Hydrographic Service surveys of 1916 and 1919. The location of Six Fathom Shoal on U.S. Chart L.S. 9 was different from that noted on Canadian Chart 2310, with the U.S. chart placing the shoal approximately 350 feet farther south and a third of a mile to the east of the position indicated for the shallows on Canadian Chart 2310. Both charts were inaccurate.

*   *   *

At about 1340 hours (1:40 P.M.) Captain Cooper talked with McSorley.

"I'm going to haul to the west for a while," Cooper had told McSorley, indicating he wanted to alter his course to run farther beyond the west end of Michipicoten to put the anticipated wind change directly on his stern.

"Well, I am rolling some, but I think I'll hold this course until I'm ready to turn for Caribou."

The *Fitzgerald* at this time was nine miles ahead of the *Anderson*. The *Fitz* was extending its lead over the *Anderson* by virtue of its more direct approach to the passage between Michipicoten and Caribou islands. The lead would extend to seventeen miles, miles that also marked a separation in time; minutes between them would become precious, lost minutes that would not be recovered.

An overcast sky hung low over the lake as the *Fitzgerald* came around the point of Michipicoten Island, putting the West End Light directly on her port beam. The winds were swinging around, coming now from the west-northwest, and were down to a pleasant five knots.

McSorley asked to have sandwiches and coffee brought to the wheelhouse, deciding he would stay until the ship had gotten past Caribou. Gazing again at the chart, he laid a triangle down and drew a course line off the 178-degree heading Second Mate Pratt had drawn. Calling Third Mate Armagost over, he indicated the point where he wanted the

Fitz to swing to a southeasterly heading to clear Caribou
Island.

Pointing to a wavy line on the chart surrounding the
island, he told the young ship's officer "We want to get as
much of the lee from Caribou as possible, but we'll have to
watch this shoal area, and this one, up here." The shoal areas
were indicated on the chart by a light blue line tracing the
boundary of the shallow water. The line bore the numeral *6*,
signifying a maximum depth of six fathoms, or thirty-six feet.
The *Fitzgerald*, loaded with more than twenty-six thousand
tons of taconite pellets, had a draft of a little over twenty-
seven feet.

What neither Armagost nor McSorley knew was that the
L.S. 9 chart they were using had the shoal in the wrong place
and did not show at all the shoal area farther out from
Caribou Island, a shallow-water area to the north of the island
that has a maximum depth of 4.1 fathoms, or 24.6 feet.

*   *   *

In the cargo holds of the *Fitzgerald* a small quantity of
water was seeping under hatches 13, 16, and 21. Water coming
onto the spar deck was finding its way into numbers 2 and 3
holds through small weld cracks in the hatch end girders of 16
and 21 hatches and through a small notch in the deck plating
adjacent to number 13 hatch's coaming. The amount of water
entering the holds was very light.

Captain McSorley was aware of this minor hull damage; a
Coast Guard spar inspection conducted in Toledo on October
31 had discovered these discrepancies and noted them on Form
CG 835, completed by Lt. William R. Paul of the Coast
Guard Marine Safety Office in Toledo. A letter to the Columbia Transportation Division of Oglebay-Norton Company,
dated November 4, 1975, had been sent advising the ship's
operator that the discrepancies were to be corrected prior to
the 1976 operating season. The vessel was, however, considered seaworthy and free to operate during the balance of the
1975 season—during the stormy month of November.

At 2:45 in the afternoon, the *Fitzgerald* was about eleven miles due south of Michipicoten Island, holding a 141-degree heading. The winds had come around and were now out of the northwest at forty-three knots and increasing. The seas in this part of Superior were running sixteen feet and building rapidly. The ship continued working well in the growing sea, the wind now almost directly on her stern. A heavy snow had begun falling, reducing visibility to near zero.

McSorley had ordered a course change just before two o'clock, plotting the trackline to take the *Fitzgerald* to a point about five miles off the northern tip of Caribou Island. The plot for this trackline depended on accurately pinpointing the ship's position at the time the turn to 141 degrees was made. It wasn't; the malfunctioning large-scale radar had been shut down, and the increasing sea return showing up on the Sperry Mark 3 made reading radar bearings from Caribou and Michipicoten unreliable, although it wasn't realized by the men on the bridge of the *Fitzgerald.* Consequently, the vessel was farther to the west than they believed when the turn to 141 degrees was made. The *Fitzgerald* was heading directly for the Six Fathom Shoal area.

*   *   *

Second Cook Allen George Kalmon had three and a half hours to live. He didn't know it and was not making preparations for his death. Instead, at 2:45 in the afternoon he was in the ship's galley doing what he loved and what he did best: baking delicious breads and pastries. As second cook, Kalmon, in addition to other cooking chores, handled the baking aboard the *Fitzgerald.* Bob Rafferty, the temporary steward, was both envious and admiring of Kalmon's talents. Rafferty prided himself on his own abilities at the pastry oven, but he bowed in abject awe at the savory baked goods Kalmon produced with seeming ease.

The forty-three-year-old cook was a relative newcomer to a ship's galley, having gone on the lakes for the first time this season; the *Fitzgerald* was the only boat he had ever worked aboard—she was the only ship he would ever sail aboard. A shorebound restaurant cook for many years, Allen Kalmon had originally been trained and educated as a teacher.

He was born February 7, 1932, on a farm in Taylor County, Wisconsin, in a northeastern rural part of the state. After graduation from high school he attended a county normal college, studying to be an elementary school teacher.

While he was completing his student teaching requirements he met a pretty seventh grader, the daughter of a German American family of farmers. The girl's name was Irmengard. She was six years younger than Kalmon, and, as sometimes happens, she became thoroughly smitten with the handsome young student teacher. Several years after her graduation from high school, while attending a party, she again met Allen Kalmon. In 1957, when he was twenty-five and Irmengard nineteen, they were married.

Al found that teaching in the small rural schools of Wisconsin did not afford the salary or the promise a young man beginning a family needed. And so he left teaching for good. He tried a number of jobs, finally settling on cooking, for which he had a natural talent, working in various Washburn, Wisconsin, restaurants.

The Kalmon family grew—four girls and a boy—and their financial needs were continuing to stretch the resources like a tired rubber band. In 1973, Al began applying for jobs as cook aboard the lake boats, where he knew the pay was better than he could possibly make on shore, and in the spring of 1975 he was assigned to the Oglebay-Norton ore boat *Edmund Fitzgerald.*

He liked work aboard the big freighter; he liked the men, who, he said, tended to be easy to get along with.

"The guys who can't get along don't stay on the boats for very long."

Kalmon was of average height, stocky with blue eyes and dark blond hair. He was extraverted and liked hunting, fishing, and watching professional football. In every respect Allen George Kalmon was a typical pre-middle-aged man.

S.S. *EDMUND FITZGERALD*. This photo shows the vessel fully loaded and downbound from Lake Superior. (Photo courtesy of Oglebay-Norton Company)

Based on the extensive Coast Guard survey of the wreckage, a series of drawings has been prepared. In this artist's conception, the relative positions of the broken sections of the *Fitzgerald* are shown. (Drawing courtesy of United States Coast Guard)

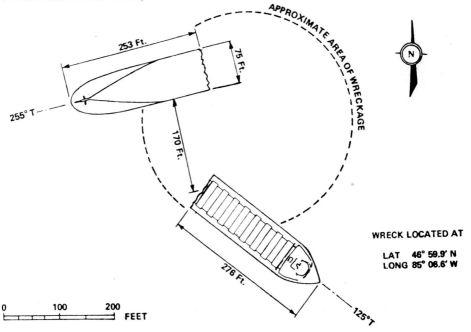

APPROXIMATE AREA OF WRECKAGE

253 Ft.

75 Ft.

255° T

170 Ft.

276 Ft.

125° T

N

WRECK LOCATED AT

LAT 46° 59.9′ N
LONG 85° 06.6′ W

0   100   200   FEET

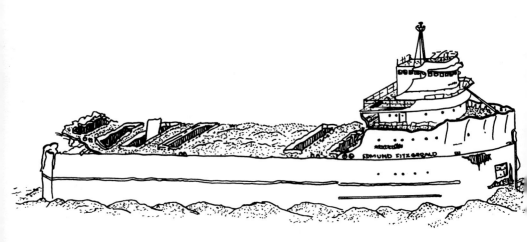

This drawing depicts the forward section of the *Fitzgerald*, showing the damage sustained by the bow and superstructure. (Drawing courtesy of United States Coast Guard)

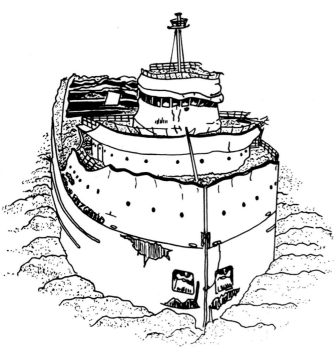

A bow on drawing of the forward section clearly depicts the distortion of the wheelhouse and forecastle deck. A large hole in the bow can be seen in this drawing produced from close-up photographs taken by the navy's remote-controlled underwater recovery vehicle (CURV III). (Drawing courtesy of United States Coast Guard)

The tremendous damage sustained at the point of separation is shown in this rear view of the forward section. Hatch covers and coamings are badly distorted, and a heavy layer of mud covers much of the spar deck. (Drawing courtesy of United States Coast Guard)

The stern section is upside down in the mud, resting on a portion of the approximately two-hundred-foot center section. Debris believed to be from the midsection of the vessel, hatch covers, coamings, and internal material can be seen extending outward from the point of separation. (Drawing courtesy of United States Coast Guard)

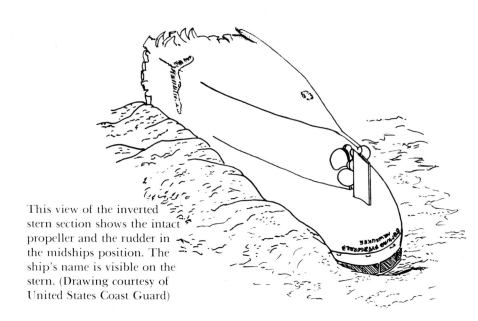

This view of the inverted stern section shows the intact propeller and the rudder in the midships position. The ship's name is visible on the stern. (Drawing courtesy of United States Coast Guard)

This photo was taken by the underwater survey vehicle (CURV III) and shows the severe distortion suffered at the wheelhouse. Windows have been smashed inward; the forward wall, in this external view, is bent inward. The straps of a life jacket can be seen dangling from the wheelhouse ceiling. The object at the right of the photo is an outside compass repeater. (Photo courtesy of United States Coast Guard)

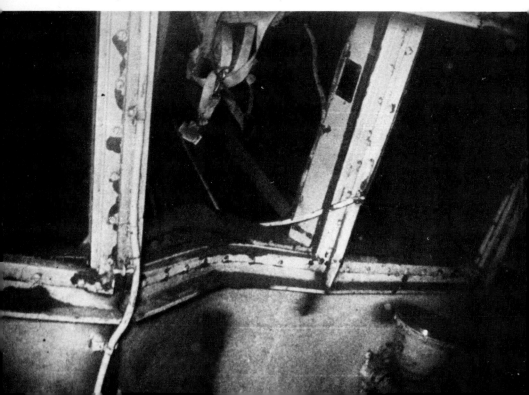

The rear of the pilothouse is shown. The windows have been blown outward, indicating that the glass was probably broken as the result of compressed air generated inside due to waves entering through the broken front windows. This portion of the pilothouse housed the chart room. (Photo courtesy of United States Coast Guard)

This underwater photo taken by the underwater survey vehicle (CURV III) shows the point where the stern separated from the midsection of the *Fitzgerald*. The tremendous forces exerted on the hull are clearly demonstrated by the torn and twisted plate which has pulled away from the one-inch-diameter rivets. (Photo courtesy of United States Coast Guard)

The hull plates were torn like paper, as this underwater survey vehicle (CURV III) photo demonstrates. (Photo courtesy of United States Coast Guard)

A portion of the twisted steel plates at the point of separation has been termed the "jungle" because of the incredible crumpling of the heavy steel plates. (Photo courtesy of United States Coast Guard)

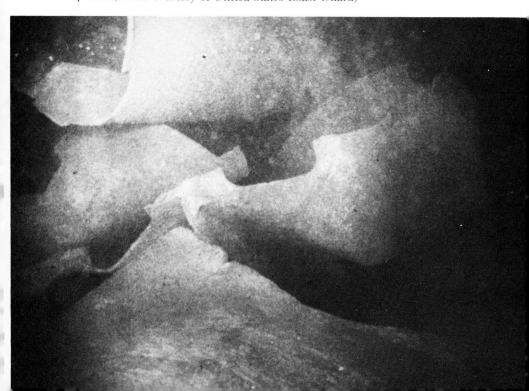

One of the life rings
recovered from Lake Superior
after the *Fitzgerald*'s loss.
The ring is heavily coated
with oil. The canister
attached to the line contains
a carbide light, which is
automatically activated when
the ring enters the water.
(Photo courtesy of United
States Coast Guard)

The Coast Guard cutter *Woodrush* participated in the search following the *Fitzgerald*'s disappearance and was the vessel which transported the cable-controlled underwater survey vehicle (CURV III) to the site of the sinking. (Photo courtesy of United States Coast Guard)

The final voyage of the S.S. *Edmund Fitzgerald* from Superior, Wisconsin, to the point in Lake Superior where the vessel foundered is depicted in this map. (Map by Robert Dunnegan)

"There was nothing about Al that would make him stick in your mind the first time you met him," Irmengard would later remember.

Nearing the end of his first season on the lakes, Kalmon had decided that he had found his "place in the sun." His plans were to continue sailing the iron boats indefinitely.

Working with Al Kalmon just before three o'clock in the afternoon was Porter Nolan Frank Church, fifty-five years old, from Silver Bay.

Church was also a recent addition to the *Fitzgerald*'s crew, coming from Oglebay-Norton's bulk carrier *Reserve*. He found the transfer much to his liking.

"He just loved the *Fitzgerald*," his wife, Thelma, says. "He said it was the nicest boat he had sailed on."

A World War II veteran of the Italian campaign, Church had spent about five years on the lakes.

The third son of four boys and two girls born to Thomas and Edith Church of Cass Lake, Minnesota, Nolan completed high school in Cass Lake. A small man—five feet, four inches and weighing 153 pounds—Church had blue eyes and blond hair that was beginning to thin somewhat. He loved children and seemed to be able to relate to the younger men in the crew, a generation and a half removed. He enjoyed hunting and fishing with his children and spent a great deal of time at his hobby, carpentry, which enabled him to pick up a little extra money during the winter lay-ups.

He had met his wife of twenty-eight years, Thelma, while she was employed at a hospital in Bemidji, Minnesota, in 1945.

"Nolan was still in the army at the time and was home on leave," Thelma recalls. "He came in with one of his brothers, whose wife had just had a baby."

Two years after their first meeting, Nolan and Thelma were married.

The couple first lived in Cass Lake, moving to Silver Bay before 1950. Five children were born to the Churches: Richard, Bonnie, Debbie, Marilyn, and Michael. During the years the family was developing, Nolan worked as a furnace operator with the Reserve Mining Company in Silver Bay.

"He decided that he wanted to try something different," Thelma says. "He had seen the boats coming and going and thought he might like working on them."

Beginning with the Cleveland Cliffs Transportation Company as a porter, Church switched to the Columbia Transportation Division of Oglebay-Norton because Silver Bay was their usual loading port.

Although the *Fitzgerald* had called at Silver Bay the week before, Nolan had not left the ship to spend a few hours at home. Doing so had not seemed terribly important at the time; after all, they would be wintering up in just a couple of weeks. He would have a lot of time to be with Thelma then.

*   *   *

In Sault Ste. Marie, Petty Officer Second Class Philip Michael Branch was completing his late lunch at the U.S. Coast Guard Station. Checking his watch, he noted that it was just after 1:00 P.M. He had almost three hours before he was due to report for duty. As a radio operator assigned to the operations office of the Coast Guard's "Group Soo" search-and-rescue facility, he stood an eight-hour watch from four in the afternoon until midnight every day. While it wasn't bad duty, it certainly cut into a young man's social life. Generally speaking, the job could get damned dull: monitoring the radio traffic crackling over five different channels from as many radios. His job was to monitor these frequencies for possible distress calls and to relay weather data from automated sites around the Michigan shoreline to the Weather Bureau at the Sault Ste. Marie airport.

He would be the only radioman working in the facility that night, although there would be the OD—officer of the day—and other personnel in the building. This late in the season there were few small boats putting out in the lake; therefore, there would be little reason to anticipate the need for search and rescue.

During the summer months there were frequent calls for assistance from boats that had run out of fuel or had broken down and were drifting. And there were the small sportfishing boats that were often poorly manned and would get caught in rough seas and overturn. And of course, in the summer, Branch could expect to handle the search for the pleasure boat that was overdue, lost somewhere along the southern shore of Superior. The reports were usually initiated by a distraught wife whose husband hadn't returned when he had promised. These "missing" usually turned up drinking beer at some marina bar or, at worst, bobbing in some sheltered cove, the passengers too intoxicated to know where they were or to much care. This added spice to Branch's job and made the hours pass much more quickly.

But that was during the pleasant-weather months. There wouldn't be, he thought, a great deal to keep him busy tonight.

*　　*　　*

The attitude of Radioman Branch was, in general, shared by other coast guardsmen at the stations around the upper Great Lakes. Many were aware that there was a storm approaching, but they felt no apprehension for those on the lakes that afternoon. The freighters plowing up and down Huron, Michigan, and Superior, hurrying to get in as many trips as possible before the season ended, would not be threatened by an early November blow—not the ships of 1975. The last ship to go down on the lakes was the *Morrell* in 1966—nine years earlier—and before that it was the *Bradley* in 1958. And the *Morrell* was sixty years old when it sank; not many that old were on the lakes anymore. The crews manning the Coast Guard stations had no reason to expect that much of anything would happen that night.

In the wheelhouse aboard the *Edmund Fitzgerald* the attitude was, if not as optimistic, certainly not dire. Other than the problems Captain McSorley and Third Mate Armagost were having with their one operable radar—which displayed so much sea return from the increasingly high wave tops that getting a good reading on Caribou Island was difficult—everything seemed to be going along normally.

"I'm getting two targets for Caribou and can't tell which is false and which is an actual target," Armagost said, frustrated.

McSorley turned from his position at the center window in the front of the wheelhouse and looked at the images registering on the lighted screen of the radarscope. The white bar extending from the center of the circular screen out to the edge swept around like the second hand on a large wall clock—taking about ten seconds to make a circuit—leaving behind it a series of white smudges.

"Take a range bearing on this one," McSorley said, indicating with a fingertip one of the two largest blobs. "The other one looks like clutter from the seas down there."

Armagost swung around the movable ring, mounted on the outer edge of the scope, on which had been inscribed the 360 degrees of the compass, and called out to the wheelsman, John Simmons "What's our present heading, Johnny?"

"One-four-one," came the reply.

Taking a relative bearing on the target suggested by McSorley and noting the distance as indicated by the concentric rings on the scope, Armagost was able to get the angle of the target off the ship's bow and the distance in miles from the object thought to be the small island.

Moving into the chart room, Mike ran a pencil line out from the island, using the bearing he had obtained from the radar, until it intersected the *Fitzgerald*'s trackline. He then measured the line from the island to the ship, using a pair of dividers. The distance to the island on the chart didn't correspond to the distance indicated on radar.

Assuming that McSorley had chosen the wrong radar target, Armagost returned to the scope and repeated the process. Again, the data from his radar bearings did not agree with the plot on the chart. The ship could not be on the trackline indicated on the map.

Using the bearing and distance from the first target, the third mate ran a line out from the island, marking off the distance shown on the radar rings. He shook his head at the results.

"I don't like this at all," he muttered aloud.

Aboard the *Arthur M. Anderson* the wheelhouse watch was about to change. First Mate Morgan E. Clark had come into the chart room for a cup of coffee, waiting for Roy T. Anderson, second mate, to sign off. Clark's watch was scheduled to officially begin at 1600 hours (4:00 P.M.) and it was now 1520. But the practice aboard the *Anderson* was to have the first mate report about a half hour early to allow the second mate to go to dinner; he would then return to the wheelhouse an hour later to permit Clark to have his evening meal before continuing his watch.

As he stood there, sipping his coffee, he overheard Captain Cooper and Second Mate Anderson in conversation at the radar consoles in the forward part of the wheelhouse. Sensing that something important was happening, Clark strolled over to where the two officers were conferring.

"Look at this, Morgan," Cooper said, indicating a small white dot on the radar screen. "That's the *Fitzgerald*; he's in close to that six-fathom spot."

Clark glanced at the image, then turned to the other radarscope that was also operating, clicking a selector knob to change the range of the set—in effect zooming in on the target. Looking first at the dot that Cooper had indicated was the *Fitzgerald* and then at the larger, solid image of Caribou Island, he said, "He sure looks like he's in the shoal area."

"He sure does. He's in too close," Cooper said. "He's closer than I'd want this ship to be."

* * *

Below the heaving surface of the lake, the sand, mud, and rock bottom directly under the *Fitzgerald* was rising from the two hundred feet shown on Chart L.S. 9, sloping steeply ahead of the ship, closing on a point thirty-one feet from the surface. It was Six Fathom Shoal, and the *Edmund Fitzgerald* was on a heading that would take her directly through the shallows.

CHAPTER 10

"I've Taken a List"

McSorley scrutinized the chart, rechecking Mike Armagost's bearings.

"We're not where we thought we were; that's for certain," McSorley commented, and then to Wheelsman Simmons, "Come left to 131 degrees."

At 3:00 P.M. First Mate Jack McCarthy walked into the wheelhouse and, seeing the concern apparent on McSorley's face, asked, "Something wrong, Mac?"

"Probably not, but I'm glad you're here. We've been heading too close to the shoals north of Caribou. It looks like we're going right through the shoal area."

As the ship's master and first mate watched, Armagost plotted an additional bearing, running the new course line out from their latest position.

"This new heading will take us slightly to the east of the shoal," Armagost said with some relief.

"Maybe," McSorley replied. "The Canadian chart shows Six

Fathom Shoal in a different spot. The actual shoal may extend further in both directions than anyone knows. I wouldn't normally get in so close to this area."

"But even if we run across them, we're only at the twenty-seven-foot marks," Armagost said. "The shoals are six fathoms—thirty-six feet—we'll still have a nine-foot clearance, unless . . ."

"Unless we get set down on them in the seas that are running down here," McCarthy interjected.

"Just being close to a shoal in heavy seas can cause hull damage," McSorley added.

Of course, Armagost thought. The pressure from the back-wash of current in shallow water is tremendous. Also, the pressure generated when a pitching vessel drops, or "sets," down close to the bottom can split a hull open. He was suddenly uneasy.

*   *   *

At 3:10 P.M. the storm's center was almost fifty miles inland over the Bremner River in Ontario. The spiraling winds on the backside of the system were now beginning to increase in the area between Michipicoten and Caribou islands, with readings approaching fifty knots; waves, now cresting at about fourteen feet, were building very fast—much faster and much higher than the National Weather Service was predicting.

> The revised forecast [broadcast at 4:39 P.M.] for Eastern Lake Superior [called for] "Northwest winds 38 to 52 knots with gusts to 60 knots early tonight and northwesterly winds 25 to 35 knots diminishing Tuesday, waves 8 to 16 feet tonight decreasing Tuesday."—National Transportation Safety Board, Marine Accident Report number NTSB-MAR-78-3, page 12.

*   *   *

At 3:15 P.M. the men in *Fitzgerald*'s pilothouse seemed to

relax; the ship was now three miles south of the Six Fathom Shoal area: they had apparently made it through safely. The seas were mounting by the minute, rolling out of the north-west, driven by the ever-increasing force of the howling wind, crashing over the stern and rolling along the spar deck.

Johnny Simmons, fighting to hold the ship on course, noticed that she wanted to swing to starboard, and he watched the bow carefully, trying to anticipate the pivot and to move the wheel to port just before it began. It was, he thought, almost as if the seas were running in two directions at once, a phenomenon sometimes found close to shore, where the undercurrent would try to suck the hull of a ship in toward the beach—or the rocks. He was about to comment on the starboard drift to Captain McSorley but was interrupted when a huge wave struck the ship, seemingly broadside to starboard.

"Where the hell did that come from?" a startled McCarthy said, echoing the question of four men in the pilothouse.

"The seas are building awfully fast," McSorley said. "You normally wouldn't expect the lake to start rolling like this for a couple hours after the wind came around."

"This is more like Erie," McCarthy agreed.

"We will want to stay in the lee of Caribou as long as we can. Better head 135 degrees for a while, as long as we have deep water," McSorley told Armagost.

Unknown to the three officers, the huge wave had masked a far more serious occurrence below the ship's waterline.

As the men on her bridge were beginning to feel more comfortable about the shoals, the *Fitzgerald* was actually in the center of a shallow area with shoals whose depth was only twenty-seven feet and not properly indicated on the chart that the ship's officers were using.

Just as the large and unanticipated wave struck the *Fitzger-ald,* her hull was sliding along a series of projecting rocks and hard-packed sand. The motion of the wave striking the ship's side first lifted her slightly—tilting her to the port, or left, side, a few degrees—and then dropped her back, tipping this time to starboard. This action caused the hull to slam against the shoal, punching in three plates at frames 68, 69, and 70 in

E strakes (strakes divide the hull on a horizontal line along the hull and are lettered from *A* at the keel to *M* at the deck edge). The site of the puncture was at the juncture of ballast tanks 3 and 4. The sudden pressure of the inward movement of plates compressing the trapped air in the tanks blew two of the air vents leading to the tanks, up through the top of the deck, breaking one off at the weld securing it to the spar deck and causing the other to be split and bend over. As the vent pipes were being blown upward, a large fragment of steel struck the side of the tank which shared a common wall with cargo holds 2 and 3, causing a tear in the steel plate about three feet below the top of the tank. The sudden blow to the hull of the ship when it came down on the shoal caused the ship to "hog," to bend downward slightly at the bow and stern. This bowing placed great stress on the fence rails, the three heavy wire strands stretched through metal poles along the spar deck to provide protection to the crew from falling overboard, and caused the cables to snap. The crash of the wave had totally masked the collision with the shoal below the waterline.

The slit in the hull and the loss of the vent covers permitted lake water to begin flooding into numbers 3 and 4 starboard ballast tanks, creeping upward, adding tons of weight to that side of the ship. As the water level moved up, the weight caused the *Fitzgerald* to begin listing slightly to starboard. It was a lethal flood.

Within ten minutes the list was noticeable in the pilot-house, and McSorley, McCarthy, and Armagost were seeking to discover its cause. An inspection with binoculars of the spar deck detected the damaged vent covers and fence railing, and a call to the engine room elicited the information that the King Gauges were showing a flooding in the two starboard ballast tanks.

"Start the auxiliary pumps," McSorley had ordered. Chief Engineer George Holl ordered that both two-thousand-gallon-per-minute pumps be switched on and that the necessary valves be opened to begin drawing water from the tanks and to pump it back into Lake Superior.

First Mate McCarthy and Third Mate Armagost made an inspection trip into the starboard tunnel. What they found was quantities of water coming into the tunnel from cracks in the vent pipe deck welds. They also determined that the broken vents would allow some water to gain access to the ballast tanks themselves.

"That big wave we took must have cracked off the vent covers," McCarthy reported to the captain. "The two auxiliary pumps will be able to handle the water coming in."

It seemed reasonable. The vent pipes were only eight inches in diameter; there was no reason to fear that two thousand gallons of water per minute would enter the ship through those openings on the deck. Still, as a mere precaution, he would be wise to notify the nearest vessel that he had a small problem.

"*Arthur M. Anderson,* this is the *Fitzgerald.* I have sustained some topside damage; I have some fence rail laid down, two vents lost or damaged, and have taken a list. I am checking down [slowing the ship]. Will you stay by me until I get down [into Whitefish Bay]?"

"This is the *Anderson,* ah, Charlie on that [I understand]. Do you have your pumps going?" Cooper asked.

"Yes," came McSorley's reply, "both of them."

The *Fitzgerald* had, in addition to the two two-thousand-gallon-per-minute pumps, four electrically driven seven-thousand-gallon-per-minute main ballast pumps.

Captain Cooper assured McSorley that he would make every effort to catch the *Fitzgerald* and stay close by.

"I knew he was too close," Cooper said. "He was right in those shoals."

Should he have warned the *Fitz* when he saw the ship heading into what he believed to be a dangerous area? An old retired ship's captain would later make this response to that question: "Hell, no. You don't get on the radio and try to tell a skipper how to run his boat. I wouldn't let someone try and tell me what to do."

Throughout the next forty minutes McSorley was in almost constant touch with the engine room. The water level in ballast tanks 3 and 4 continued to rise; the two pumps were not controlling the growing flood. Chief Engineer Holl recommended putting one of the seven-thousand-gallon-per-minute pumps on-line, and McSorley agreed. It didn't help.

"Mac," Holl said when the level continued to rise after an hour of futile pumping, "I think we've holed her. That much water isn't coming in through those damned vent pipes. The bottom's torn out on her."

McSorley said nothing, but his years on the lakes told him Holl was right. They could pump forever and never get the water out of those two tanks. If the hull had been significantly breached, the water would come in faster than they could pump it out. But as long as only two tanks were open to the sea, they could stay afloat. Just make sure the ship didn't fall into a trough, where the waves could strike her broadside. If that happened—with the added water in the tanks and a list—they would almost certainly capsize in the twenty-foot waves that were now rolling over that part of the lake.

"What about beaching her?" Armagost asked.

McSorley shook his head. "We're too far abeam of Caribou to do it now; we'd never be able to come about in these seas to reach the shore."

He quickly calculated their present position: about fifty miles northwest of Whitefish Bay; speed: about ten miles per hour (they had slowed from the sixteen miles per hour the ship was traveling earlier). Five hours, approximately, into the bay and shelter from the storm.

"We'll keep pumping," McSorley said finally. "As long as we stay on course and have no further damage, we should make Whitefish Bay."

It was a calculated gamble which depended on several factors: that the storm not grow too much worse (winds were now fifty-eight knots, it was snowing, and the waves were estimated at eighteen to twenty feet on their stern), that the list not increase, and that the damage to the hull not be such that the bending and twisting in the heavy seas would cause it to become more serious. Thoughts of the *Morrell* and the

Bradley breaking in two gripped McSorley, tightened his throat, and dried the inside of his mouth.

"Jack," McSorley turned to the first mate. "I want you to go into number 1 hold and check to see if there's any damage visible. Take one of the deckhands with you."

"Okay, although there's not much chance of seeing anything there. If the hull has broken up into the hold, the pellets would probably cover it up."

"I know, but I'll feel better having you check it, just the same."

McCarthy shrugged. It would be dirty as hell, stumbling through those damned iron balls, but if that was what McSorley wanted, that was what he'd do.

He left the pilothouse via the stairwell in the chart room, past the forecastle deck, down to spar deck level. Turning to his right at the bottom of the stairs and walking along a corridor, he turned right again into the forward crew's recreation room. Seated at a table, drinking coffee, were several crew members.

"We've taken on a list, Jack," Wheelsman Ransom Cundy remarked, as the first mate walked in.

"Yeah, we broke off a couple of tank vents. We're shipping some water."

Looking at the men seated there, McCarthy's gaze settled on Cadet David Weiss.

"Dave, want to come into number 1 hold with me? I'd like to check the cargo."

Weiss knew there was little reason to inspect the mounds of taconite in the holds; it never shifted, even in heavy seas like those they had begun to experience in the last two hours. But he didn't question the mate's reasons.

"Sure, Jack. I've never been down there in heavy weather," he said cheerfully, getting up to accompany McCarthy.

They walked across the room, exiting through a door on the opposite side from where McCarthy had entered. Moving along the narrow corridor on the port side of the ship, they dropped down a flight of stairs to the main deck. At the bottom of the stairs, McCarthy turned to the young cadet. "I'll undog the access door; why don't you go to your room and get a flashlight?"

The cadet nodded and dashed around the corner to the room he shared with Bruce Hudson.

McCarthy moved the six handles that clamped the water-tight door shut into the open position, swinging first the top dog, then one near the bottom. If there were water in the hold that had reached this level, he didn't want the door to be forced open and not be able to shut it against the flooding waters. The door opened easily and he swung it back, securing it to the bulkhead with a clamp fastened there to keep the heavy steel door from swinging as the ship rolled or pitched.

Weiss returned with a flashlight, and the two men started down the ladder just inside the access door, McCarthy in the lead. Just before starting down, McCarthy had thrown a switch that turned on a series of lights in the hold.

At first Weiss wondered why McCarthy had requested the flashlight, but he quickly reasoned that it would provide better illumination for any close inspection the mate might want to conduct. Also, if the ship should experience a power failure— a remote possibility—they would need light to find their way out.

It was a 14-foot climb down the ladder from the main deck to the point where the taconite pellets began sloping upward.

The 519-foot-long interior of the hold was divided into three cargo sections, separated by two "screen bulkheads," which were basically wire fences extending from the tank top deck 33 feet up to the underside of the spar deck. The taconite pellets had been loaded in three huge piles—resembling pyramids—one pile in each of the three sections, or holds. The tops of the piles extended up to approximately 12 feet below the spar deck level. Where McCarthy and Weiss stood— at the forward edge of the pellet slope in number 1 hold—was about 8 feet over the tank top, or floor, of the hold.

Moving to the starboard side, around the edge of the

mound, McCarthy and Weiss made their way aft toward the screen separating number 1 and number 2 holds. The screen served to prevent the cargo from spilling from one hold into another. It did nothing to inhibit the movement of any water inside.

Playing the flashlight along the plates, McCarthy, accompanied by Weiss, moved along the bottom of the sloping pile of rusty brown–colored pellets, each approximately one-half inch to three-eighths inch in diameter. At the screen bulkhead they stopped.

"Everything looks tight," Weiss said, his voice echoing metallically over the sounds of the waves hammering at the ship's sides and the tormented screeching of bending, twisting metal plates. He now knew the purpose of their visit to the hold.

"Yeah, but there could be tons of water seeping through the pellets where we can't even see," McCarthy responded before succumbing to a choking cough brought on by a thin cloud of iron dust floating in the air.

Aiming the beam of the light through the screen, the mate strained to see along the wall in number 2 hold.

On the other side of the hull, in the ballast tanks surrounding the sides of the hold, in ballast tanks 3 and 4, the water had now reached the gouge in the wall caused by the exploding vent pipe. The springing of the ship in the heavy seas was slowly, but steadily, tearing the opening wider. The water could now flow directly into the cargo hold itself.

"See anything?" Weiss asked McCarthy, not knowing exactly what the first mate expected to find.

McCarthy was about to answer in the negative when the beam of light reflected from something. Rubbing the dust from his glasses, he looked again at the spot where the light had glinted. This time he was able to see what had caused the reflection.

"I see something, all right, and it ain't good."

Back on the bridge, his clothes bearing splotches of the

rusty iron dust, his face and hands stained with a mixture of the dust and sweat, McCarthy spoke in hushed tones to the ship's master, as the third mate looked on.

"Mac, there's a stream of water coming from the ballast tanks into number 2 hold—lots of water."

Capt. Ernest Michael McSorley, forty-four years a sailor, master of one of the proudest ships to ever sail the Great Lakes, stood and listened to the most ominous news he had heard in all his years afloat: he was in danger of losing his ship.

CHAPTER 11

"She's Shaking Apart"

He could have gone out and bought himself a captain's hat. He was that good, and everyone knew that before too many years had gone by Michael Eugene Armagost, thirty-seven years old, would be master of his own ship, would be one of the youngest captains on the Great Lakes.

A big, bright, vital young man, Armagost had nineteen years experience on the lakes, working his way up from deckhand to third mate.

The first of the three sons and two daughters of Kendall and Loraine Berube Armagost, Michael was born October 14, 1938. Raised in Iron River, Wisconsin, he was very close to his grandparents, Frank and Florence Russell Berube, who owned a resort lodge in Iron River.

In 1943 the family moved to Naperville, Illinois. It was while living in the Chicago suburb that young Armagost discovered books, and reading became a passion that would stay with him all his remaining days. "My dear little friend Michael," a Naperville librarian called him.

When Mike's father was drafted into the military in 1943, the family moved back to Iron River. Filled with the healthy exuberance of a young boy, he became known as something of a hellion.

"When he was in the fifth grade he rode my new bike over the edge of a hill, breaking it in two pieces," his sister Suzanne remembers. "When he was older he once rode my horse in the front door of a bar in Iron River, rode through the bar, and out the back door."

In the years to come he would be remembered by Fred and Suzanne and the twins, John and Jeannie—his younger brothers and sisters—as someone who lived every day of his life to the fullest.

He would not have the full benefit of his father's wise counsel during the early, formative years. First, there were the years during World War II, when Kendall was away at war. Then in 1949, the elder Armagost took a job as office clerk with a timber company in Ely, Minnesota, in the northern part of the state, eighteen miles from the Canadian border. Kendall left the family in Iron River for several years before moving them to Ely. Then, in 1957, Mike lost any chance to enjoy a close association with his father. At the age of forty-seven, Kendall Armagost died.

Mike, who had talked about sailing the lakes when he had worked with his dad during the summer, fall, and winter of 1956–57, and who had received Kendall's blessing, took his first job aboard the boats a few weeks following his father's death.

In 1960, Mike signed on as a crew member aboard the *Eli V*, a Liberian oceangoing freighter leaving New Orleans for the Middle East.

"He didn't like it," his mother remembers. "The accommodations were not as nice as those on the lake boats. Nothing was as nice."

So he left saltwater sailing forever.

Following a two-year stint with the Red Diamond Division at Fort Carson, Colorado, Mike returned to the lakes, joining

Columbia Transportation a few years after his return. Serving aboard such ships as the *Ben E. Tate,* the *Ashland,* and the *Reserve,* sailing became ingrained in his life. His early ambition had been to work the boats just long enough to save money to put himself through hotel-motel management school, then to someday own his own tavern or possibly a resort lodge like the one his grandparents had owned.

But the lure of good money and his sense of obligation to his widowed mother and his brothers and sisters kept him on the lakes.

A big man at maturity, he stood six feet, one inch tall, weighed 230 pounds, and had dark wavy brown hair and blue eyes. He alternated between a full beard, a beard and mustache, just a mustache, and a clean-shaven face. His wide face was spread all over a bearlike head; his long Anglo-Saxon nose and his thick lips gave the initial impression that he was anything but a handsome man. This opinion was not affirmed by one Janice Marie Doyle.

One sultry August night, while seated in the lounge of Story Book Lodge, in Iron River, Janice looked up and saw among a party that had just entered a burly young man with wavy brown hair.

"What an interesting-looking guy," she thought. "Big and rugged, but handsome."

Although born and raised in Monona, Wisconsin, just outside Madison, Janice and her family had been coming to Iron River for one or two weeks' vacation every year since she was very young. But the University of Wisconsin coed had made few friends among the local residents. Later that evening, one of the few friends she had made in the area introduced her to the "interesting-looking guy." His name was Mike Armagost, and before the evening was over he had asked Janice to go out with him.

"I was reluctant to go; he was older—almost twenty-nine at the time—and 'wiser.'" Janice says. "But he was a real ladies' man; it was hard to say no."

The meeting between the lake sailor and the pretty young

"city girl" was quite coincidental; Mike was rarely home during the summer—the busiest time in Great Lakes shipping—but he had sustained a minor back injury on the boats and was recuperating when he decided to join a group of friends at Story Book Lodge.

Mike Armagost was a man in a hurry. After a flurry of letters, punctuated by high-speed dashes between Madison and Silver Bay, Armagost knew that Janice was the girl for him. There were moments when she questioned what she was letting herself in for—she had once met his boat in Silver Bay; he stayed too long, and the boat sailed without him. Janice and one of Mike's sisters had to drive him the 450 miles to Sault Ste. Marie to catch the ship as it went through the locks in the early hours of the morning—but it was difficult to say no to the intense, determined sailor. A few days after Christmas, 1967, they became engaged, and on October 5, 1968, with the Irish Doyles and the Scandinavian Armagosts looking on, Janice joined Mike at the altar of the Immaculate Heart of Mary Catholic Church in Monona, Wisconsin, to solemnly pledge ". . . until death us do part."

It had been an idyllic honeymoon; they had moved into an Iron River log cabin owned by Mike's mother and had spent a quiet, peaceful winter that seemed as if it might go on forever amid days of snowmobiling in the woods and untroubled, muted nights when it seemed they were the only two people in the world.

But as the protective winter abandoned its guardian post, allowing the awakening spring to intrude upon and stir the newlyweds from their blissful Eden, they found themselves rudely thrust back into the harsh reality of pragmatic life. Their very first spring together was to herald a ritual that Janice would come to anticipate with dread throughout the seven springtimes she would spend with Michael Eugene Armagost.

"At the end of March each year he would start getting antsy, knowing that vacation was nearly over," Janice remembers. "He had a short fuse, and it would get shorter as sailing time came closer."

Mike's explosive temper at times puzzled and frightened Janice, but she quickly learned that it was a relief valve for his frustrations. Still, it took her several years to come to terms with his mercurial nature.

"He would get over it . . . later he would laugh . . . and would be fine."

He loved to cook and would prepare many of their meals during his winters at home. He collected recipe books and enjoyed trying new dishes.

As he left her that first spring, Janice suddenly found herself confronted with the universal affliction of the young wife of a sailor—loneliness.

"I was totally unprepared for the life of a sailor's wife," she says. "There were adjustments to be made if you wanted to stay married to a sailor."

Mike's boat would come into Silver Bay, Minnesota—a two-hour drive from Iron River—every six or seven days and would be in port for as much as ten hours. The drive back to Iron River was too long, so the couple would often stay at a motel in Silver Bay. Mike never wanted Janice to go aboard his boat in the early days of their marriage; it wasn't until 1974 that he began taking her on board to have coffee or to sample the celebrated baked goods from the galley.

On December 21, 1969, Michele Lee was born to the Armagosts, and Mike began talking about building a home of their own—his mother's log cabin, their honeymoon cottage, had suddenly become too small. It was to be almost three years before the dream would be realized; it would require much patience and sacrifice from both, but finally, on November 10, 1972, with Janice "really pregnant" with their second child, the Armagosts moved into their new Iron River home. The date would not long mark a happy anniversary. Exactly three years later, Mike and his twenty-eight shipmates would perish on stormy Lake Superior.

Two and a half weeks after taking up residence in their new home, their second child was born. Mike was on the boat, and Janice called ship-to-shore to announce to him—and all listeners within radio range—"You have a son." Christopher

Michael had been born November 27, 1972, and Mike had to wait two weeks before he could get home to see his son.

A son: a boy child, someone who would bear his name, who would continue the lineage and thereby insure that some part of him would survive long after he was gone. It was a sobering thought, and it brought into sharp focus the colossal responsibility he must shoulder; he had a burgeoning family who depended on him for support, and he had his mother and his sisters and brothers, for whom he continued to feel a grave responsibility. He was thirty-four years old, and the transitory nature of life was suddenly a bitter reality that must be faced. Gone were the dreams of one day leaving the lakes, of someday owning a resort; sailing was the thing he knew, the thing he did best.

Very well, then. If he was to be locked into the occupation of sailor, then he would be the best sailor there was; he would strive to advance, to gain in professional stature. He would begin by becoming a ship's officer, and he would not stop until he had a command of his own.

In the fall of 1973, after months of almost constant study and preparation, Mike wrote the exam for his third mate's license.

"He was very apprehensive about writing the exam," Janice would later recall. "And he was so proud when he learned he'd passed. It did a lot for his self-confidence."

Armagost was more surprised at having won his new status than anyone in his family or among his circle of close friends. Those who knew his intelligence and intensity never doubted that his destiny was to be marked by achievement and acclaim. This confidence in Mike Armagost was shared by the former captain of one of the ships on which he had served. Capt. Ernest McSorley had seen in the bullish young sailor a discernible quality that perhaps reminded him of himself in earlier years.

A mutual admiration for one another had developed between the two men before Mike's elevation to ship's officer, and so it was not unexpected that Armagost should ask to be assigned to the *Edmund Fitzgerald,* where he might serve with his friend and mentor. Nor was it surprising that McSorley should seize the opportunity of having the bright, newly licensed officer join his command.

The next two seasons were ambivalent and frustrating times for Mike. On the one hand, he found his new responsibilities challenging and fraught with excitement, while on the other, the prestige and the money seemed often feckless when balanced against the long periods away from his wife and growing children.

"Here comes Daddy's boat," was a statement heard so often by little Christopher that in his ripening mind, *Daddy* and *boat* became synonymous; he began addressing his father as "Boat."

Mike took the first summer vacation he had ever taken, in 1975, in order to be at home when Michele Lee went off to kindergarten for the first time.

"For all his tough appearances, he was really devoted to his kids," Janice says.

In addition to his family, he was possessed with one uncontrollable passion: comic books.

"He positively loved the old comic books and kept a box of them under our bed," Janice recalls. "I would wake up at night to find him sitting in bed, eating a sandwich, and reading a comic book.

Aboard ship, he spent his off-duty hours engaged in the favorite pastime of his youth: books. He consistently read three or four books at one time, reading a chapter of one book, then switching to another, and another.

"He liked the old Western novels."

His life was slipping into an ever-deepening channel—not a rut, because that implies dull routine and boredom, and his life was anything but boring. He was wedded to the lakes, and there could be, at best, a temporary separation; divorce was unthinkable, impossible. There was little doubt that, barring catastrophe, Mike would spend his working years on the boats, eventually rising to his own command, finally to retire to live out his "golden years" with Janice, never certain that he had made the proper choice. But it was not to be.

Catastrophe lurked just around the corner—unseen, waiting.

On Sunday, November 9, Janice drove to Superior, Wisconsin, to meet the *Fitzgerald*. The ship seldom called so close to Iron River; it was an excellent opportunity for Mike to spend a few precious hours at home with the children. And yet he felt guilty about capitalizing on this good fortune.

"That's a tough dock. I should have stayed to help load," he repeated several times during the forty-minute drive.

Once at home, he and Janice opened the mail and wrote out checks to pay some bills, drank coffee, and watched the children play. After a while Mike suddenly decided to visit his mother. This somewhat surprised Janice; Mike rarely used the brief and precious time during loading to pay social calls. She was doubly bewildered when, as they were leaving his mother's house, he suggested they stop at the home of one of his closest friends, Jerry Darwin. Jerry was out hunting, so Mike and Janice visited for a hour with Jerry's wife, Judy.

Shortly before noon, Mike and Janice bundled the two kids into the car and started for Superior. The talk during the drive along U.S. Highway 2 was light and centered around the approaching end of the shipping season.

At the Burlington Northern gatehouse, Mike kissed the children and Janice and said he would possibly be home in about two weeks.

"As he walked away I thought how handsome he looked, how lucky I was," Janice remembers.

He stopped, turned, and waved, and then he was gone.

She took Michele and Christopher to a nearby fast-food restaurant for hamburgers and then drove down to the breakwater to watch the *Fitzgerald* depart.

It was becoming windy and turning cold as Janice seated the children on the wall at the edge of the breakwater, her arms around them to keep them from falling. The boat steamed by, so close that Janice could shout to a crew member on deck: "Where's Mike?" The sailor called back that he was somewhere below decks.

Slightly disappointed, the trio silently watched as the *Edmund Fitzgerald,* its huge propeller thrashing the water, sailed out into the lake. They watched it gliding away until the cold wind became too uncomfortable and then returned to the car for the lonely drive back to Iron River.

That night, with the wind screaming in the trees and a driving snow spattering against the windows, the power suddenly failed; the lights went out and the furnace shut down. Both children, frightened and cold, came to her room and crawled into Janice's bed to snuggle close for warmth and comfort.

Mike had never given Janice reason to worry about him when the storms blew upon the lakes. He never talked of the storms or the dangers. And so, as she lay awake through most of the storm-shattered night, the house dark and rapidly growing cold, her concern was for their problems at home. But the question she hurled into the darkness would have much greater implications than her fears about a temporary power failure, and the question would be much longer awaiting an answer.

"How am I ever going to take care of these two children by myself?"

*   *   *

In the engine room Chief Engineer Holl moved to the King Gauges; they indicated ballast tanks 3 and 4 were nearly filled. Each tank had a capacity of 1,095 tons of water—4,380,000 pounds—concentrated on the starboard side of the *Fitzgerald,* pulling her over to the right and dragging the ship deeper in the water, allowing still more water to enter and to be spilled into the hold.

Holl looked at the gauges and shook his head; he listened to the engine and detected a laboring that he had never heard before.

"She sounds like she's shaking apart," he said to Second Assistant Engineer Thomas Edwards.

*   *   *

While Chief Engineer Holl was having his problems in the engine room, the men on the bridge were being confronted with their own difficulties.

At about 4:00 P.M. a sudden, violent gust of wind tore the radar antennae from their masts atop the wheelhouse, hurling them over the bow into the grinding lake; the one functioning scope went blank. A few minutes later, between 4:10 and 4:15, McSorley called the *Anderson* to report that the *Fitzgerald* was now totally without radar navigational capabilities.

"Could you provide me with radar plots?" McSorley asked the *Anderson's* first mate (Captain Cooper was not in the wheelhouse).

"Certainly. I'll keep you advised of your position," Morgan Clark responded.

McSorley was not content with a total dependence on the *Anderson* to find his way into Whitefish Bay.

"We'd better take regular RDF fixes," he said to Jack McCarthy. "If the *Anderson* loses contact with us we won't know where we are."

McCarthy nodded, went to the radio direction finder, and began turning the wheel that controlled the loop antenna on the roof, attempting to pick up the three dashes and a single dot of Morse code that signified the Whitefish Point radio homing beacon. Having received the signal, McCarthy checked the bearing and noted it on a small pad. He would listen for the radio beacon again in about fifteen minutes—but when he did so, he would not be able to pick up the beacon's signal.

*   *   *

At approximately 4:30 P.M., as the *Edmund Fitzgerald* struggled in the rapidly growing wind and seas, forty-eight miles to the south the light and the radio beacon at the remote navigational station at Whitefish Point suddenly clicked off. The *Fitzgerald*, already crippled by the nonfunctioning radar, was now without homing capability from the automated system at Whitefish.

The strong winds had blown down the power lines which operated the station. A special backup gasoline-powered generator failed to take over as it was designed to do because an automatic relay stuck at that precise moment, leaving the station inoperative.

A small relay switch costing a few dollars had failed to function, and a severely damaged vessel costing several millions could not, at a critical time, use the radio beacon to take a bearing that would give the ship its exact location, nor could it use the light as a visual guide to find its way to possible safety.

At 3:30 Able-Bodied Seaman Gary Wigen was called into the Grand Marais (Michigan) Coast Guard station radio room to relieve Radioman S. N. McFarland, who had to go out to check on the station's thirty-six-foot launch and to move it to a safer mooring. Wigen wasn't due to begin his watch until 6:00 P.M. (1800 hours), but since he was in the operations building he agreed to stand in for McFarland while he and two others went out to tend to the launch.

At approximately 4:39 Wigen received a call from a vessel on Lake Superior.

"Grand Marais, this is the *Edmund Fitzgerald,* over."

The call came in on Channel 16—the distress frequency— and Wigen requested the *Fitzgerald* to switch to Channel 22— a general radio traffic frequency. The *Fitzgerald* complied with the request, and when it had reestablished contact, asked Wigen if the Whitefish radio beacon was operative.

"Stand by. We don't have the equipment here to tell if it is operating properly. I will call you back."

Wigen then got on the teletype machine, which connected him with Sault Ste. Marie, seventy-five miles east of Grand Marais. The Soo advised him that their monitoring equipment indicated that the Whitefish Point beacon and the light were both inoperative. They indicated that there had been a power failure and that when the power came back on, they would call back and provide information on the status of the navigational aid.

Wigen contacted the *Fitzgerald* and relayed the information he had received from the Soo.

"Okay, thanks," came the reply from the *Fitzgerald*. "We were just wondering, because we haven't been able to get it for a while."

"Everybody sounded like they were in real good spirits," Wigen later testified. There was nothing, in his opinion, to indicate that the call constituted anything but a normal radio communication.

As a matter of fact, the communication was anything but a normal one. The *Fitzgerald* desperately needed the Whitefish Point beacon, and was never able to receive it. Although the technicians at the Soo made attempts throughout the evening to reactivate the beacon and light, they were able to do so only on a sporadic basis on two or three occasions. The Soo station made no further attempts during the evening to contact the Grand Marais station to advise them that the Whitefish Point station was still inoperative. The *Fitzgerald* was left to fend for itself.

CHAPTER 12

"We Are Holding Our Own"

It was 4:45 P.M., and the winds on Lake Superior south of Caribou Island had reached eighty miles per hour; the center of the storm, having moved well onto the Canadian landmass, was giving the lake a vicious backhand, driving waves that were reaching thirty feet in height.

Amidst the fury of the storm, the *Edmund Fitzgerald* fought her way through the heavy seas, heeled over to starboard at a fifteen-degree angle. Below the ship's waterline, the water flooded into the split in her side faster than her pumps could empty it out. The tear in the wall separating the number 3 ballast tank and the cargo hold was slowly increasing, pulling the plates farther apart as the ship twisted in the crashing seas, allowing more water from the ballast tanks to flow into the hold, to mingle with the iron pellets. Like an inoperable malignancy—it could not have been gotten rid of.

There were no suction wells in the No. 1 or No. 2 cargo holds. The water in these holds drained aft along the length of the holds and through the sluices fitted in the lower portions of the screen bulkheads separating the holds, to the suction well at the after end of No. 3 hold. When the vessel was loaded with cargo, water entering the hold would have to filter through the cargo before it could be pumped. Experienced Great Lakes mariners testified that the cargo would restrict the flow and that the holds could not be pumped when loaded with cargo. . . . As an antipollution measure, the discharge from the engine room bilges was pumped onto the cargo.—Department of Transportation, Coast Guard Marine Casualty Report (USCG 16732/64216), page 7.

*   *   *

In the *Fitzgerald*'s chart room Captain McSorley held a somber-toned conference with his officers—McCarthy, Pratt, and Armagost—and Chief Engineer Holl.

"As far as we can tell, we've come down on a shoal and torn the hull," McSorley said, his voice carrying a barely detectable tremor. "We're taking water in number 2 hold through a fracture in the ballast tank wall. The pumps can't stay ahead of the intake. I don't know how long she will stay afloat."

McSorley discussed the options available to them: turn the ship around and beach it in the shallow waters near Caribou Island; abandon ship and hope to be picked up by the *Anderson*, which was then approximately fifteen miles astern of the *Fitz*; or sail on and try to make the shelter and shallow water of Whitefish Bay.

Turning the ship to attempt to make Caribou Island was out of the question in the monstrous seas; the wallowing, listing ship would certainly be capsized. Ordering the crew into the water was equivalent to a death sentence for them. The lifeboats could not be launched in the seas that were crashing fifteen feet above the boat deck; the life rafts (one forward and one behind the after deckhouse) would have to be inflated on deck and thrown into the water, with the men jumping after and hoping to reach them in the seas that would almost certainly keep them apart. Attempting to make a transfer to the *Anderson* under the conditions they were experiencing was unthinkable, and trusting in the *Anderson* to be able to maneuver in the storm to pick up men floating in the water was equally unrealistic. Besides, the *Anderson* was fifteen miles behind; given the relative speeds of the two ships, it would take over three hours for the *Andy* to catch up. Anyone in the water would drown or die of exposure long before that happened.

Their "options" in fact boiled down to making a run for Whitefish Bay. It was their only chance, their only hope.

Now there was the question of what to tell the men. Should they be alerted to the possible peril they faced?

"We are in no immediate danger," McSorley decided. "We are making headway, and there's a good chance we'll make Whitefish, where we can beach her if we have to. There is no need to panic the crew. There is nothing they can do; we can't get off. So we will continue a normal routine. If things get worse we can take some other action. If you are asked, you will state that we've lost some tank vents and are taking some water into the tanks, causing the list, but there is no cause for alarm."

It was decided that the Coast Guard would not be alerted. Again, there was very little that could be done in time; they would be into the bay before anyone would get to them. There was another reason.

"You don't get on the radio, where everyone on the lake can hear you, and talk about *possibly* sinking," an old lakes skipper would later state. "If you know for certain that you're going down, that's one thing; but to holler that you *might* be sinking is asking for trouble. If you make it in OK, you'll be the laughing stock of every boat on the Great Lakes—it ain't professional. What you do is hang on and make a run for it, and keep your mouth shut."

*　　*　　*

Sixty-three miles south of Whitefish Point, officials of the Mackinac Bridge, spanning the straits which connect Lake Huron with Lake Michigan, were growing increasingly concerned. The 3,800-foot-long center span of the nation's third largest suspension bridge was swaying precipitously in winds that were gusting to an incredible ninety-six miles per hour. At first, it had been decided that autos attempting to cross must travel in the company of semi trucks, which would act as wind breaks, avoiding the remote possibility that the cars might be blown off the bridge. However, when a semi was blown off its wheels and on top of one of the autos traveling alongside, it was decided that the bridge would be closed to all traffic until the winds abated.

At the world's busiest ships' locks, the supervisors at Sault Ste. Marie ordered the locks closed; the high winds and the waves washing over the lock gates made it too dangerous to continue operating.

Throughout the Midwest the storm was inflicting punishment; power lines down, trees uprooted, roofs carried away. On Lake Michigan, three youths were swept from a breakwater by the huge waves. One was quickly rescued by several bystanders; the other two were drowned.

Aboard the Swedish saltwater vessel *Avafors,* Capt. Cedric Woodard—the Great Lakes pilot—advised the ship's master that they should anchor until the storm abated.

"We go, pilot," the Norwegian insisted. "This is only a lake."

(The next day, after struggling through the storm, *Avafors*'s master would wryly comment, "This is a pretty big lake, isn't it?")

Woodard was concerned about taking the 490-foot vessel

into the lake; she was somewhat top-heavy with two large cranes on deck, and the pilot wondered what the fierce winds might do to the ship. A few minutes earlier he had answered a call for "any vessel in the vicinity of Whitefish Point." It was from the downbound ore carrier *Edmund Fitzgerald*. Captain Woodard knew Ernest McSorley very well, but the voice on the radio didn't sound at all like McSorley's. Answering the call, Woodard had asked, "Who am I speaking to?" The answer came back: "This is Captain McSorley."

Woodard was stunned; the voice didn't sound anything like the McSorley he had conversed with by radio for more than fifteen years.

"I didn't recognize your voice," Woodard responded, thinking that perhaps the man was very tired or possibly suffering from a cold.

The purpose of McSorley's call was to inquire if anyone could pick up the light or radio beacon at Whitefish Point. The *Avafors* was just pulling out of the bay and almost abeam of the light, and while Woodard could visually pick out the vague outline of the light tower, he could neither see the light burning at its top nor hear the Morse signal on the radio frequency assigned to the navigational installation.

It was snowing heavily, and the seas were monstrous.

"It was one of the biggest seas I have ever been in," Woodard would later testify. "The tops were blowing off . . . the sea was straight up and down, not like big rollers."

*   *   *

In the *Fitzgerald*'s forward crew's recreation room, a hushed conference was taking place between Cadet David Weiss, Karl Peckol, Bruce Hudson, and Paul Riippa. Weiss had been informed of the nature of the ship's injuries by First Mate McCarthy as the two were leaving the cargo hold following their inspection trip.

"Don't go spreading this around," McCarthy had cautioned

the cadet. But Weiss could not repress his desire to let his friends in on the excitement.

"Is the boat going to sink?" Riippa had asked.

"McCarthy thinks we have a good chance of making Whitefish; we're about four hours away, and he thinks she can stay afloat that long, if she doesn't break apart."

"And what if we do break in two?" Peckol asked.

"Then we'll only have a few minutes to get into the life raft if we want to keep from going down with her," Weiss advised. "As it is, we would have enough problems even then; the water is cold, and we probably couldn't last more than a half an hour unless we take some precautions. I'm going to change into the warmest clothes I've got, and I suggest you all do the same."

"You don't really think that it will come to that, do you?" Riippa asked.

"Maybe not, but I want to be prepared, just in case."

"Well, if this boat is going down, I doubt that any of us would have a chance in the water on a night like this. I'm going to stay put."

"Suit yourself, Paul. If you want to ride her down, I can't stop you," Weiss replied, turning to leave.

"Thanks a lot, Dave, but I think I'll just trust in the Lord. If he wants to take me, it'll be up to him, whether I'm here in the ship or out in the water."

Riippa had a deep and unfaltering faith in his Christian beliefs, having been "born again" while a teenager. He had been strongly influenced by a family who lived on his street in Ashtabula. The Cunninghams had conducted their own ministry, holding Bible classes for the youth in the neighborhood. Paul had been a part of this ministry and had carried his interest in the Bible into his adulthood.

At twenty-two, he was a big man, standing six feet, two-and-one-half inches tall and weighing about two hundred pounds. He had been active in sports throughout his teens, playing American Legion baseball and excelling at football while attending Harbor High School in Ashtabula.

Paul was one of six children—three girls and three boys—and would be remembered by his brothers and sisters as being soft-spoken and easygoing as a youth.

He had been very close to his father, Neil, who never failed to be in attendance at baseball or football games in which Paul participated.

After graduation from high school, Paul attended one full year at Wilmington College in Ohio before dropping out to save some money after his father's death.

He had gone on the lakes in 1973, serving aboard the *Ashland.* However, he wasn't happy on the ship. He felt that the men hadn't fully accepted him. He planned to enroll at Kent State in the Nursing School, and perhaps he became the brunt of cruel jokes because of his plans. Or it may have been his devotion to Christianity and his willingness to "testify for the Lord" that made him something of an outcast among the more earthy members of the *Ashland*'s crew. Whatever the reasons for his wanting to transfer to another ship, they were important enough to the sensitive young man to finally have convinced Columbia Transportation to approve the change. And in September of 1975 he was assigned to the *Fitzgerald.*

"He really liked being on the ship," Elaine Sespico, his sister, remembers. "He felt that all the men on the *Fitzgerald* had accepted him; he thought they were very nice."

Riippa sat in the recreation room for a few minutes after Weiss, Peckol, and Hudson had left, feeling the slant of the room pulling at him, trying to dislodge him from the chair. Finally he rose and walked slowly to his room. He would spend some time contemplating and reading from his Bible. Perhaps that would help show him what he should do if the boat did begin to sink.

In their own room, Dave Weiss and Bruce Hudson dug through the closet, searching for their heaviest clothing.

"I just don't understand how we could have hit a shoal," Hudson said. "Couldn't McSorley or the mate tell we were in shallow water? Didn't they keep their eyes on the Fathome-ter?"

"What Fathometer?" Weiss replied.

Hudson looked at his friend closely, not believing the implication in the cadet's words.

"You're not telling me that this ship doesn't have some kind of a depth-measuring instrument?"

"We have a lead line; you know, 'mark twain' and all that."

"But that's not possible; every ship has some kind of Fathometer," Hudson insisted.

Weiss shook his head. "The Coast Guard doesn't require them, and we don't have one."

*   *   *

In Whitefish Bay, other skippers were having doubts similar to those of Captain Woodard and had decided to anchor in the bay until the storm had blown itself out. The *William Clay Ford, William R. Roesch, Benjamin F. Fairless,* and the Canadian vessels *Frontenac, Murray Bay, Hilda Marjanne,* and *Algosoo* were all anchored in or near Whitefish Bay.

In addition to the *Avafors*—under Cedric Woodard's pilotage—the *Benfri,* about three miles astern of *Avafors* and piloted by Capt. Robert O'Brien, and also the *Nanfri,* about five miles in the rear and piloted by Capt. Albert Jacovetti, were pushing out into the stormy lake.

Winds on Superior were now being reported as 72 knots gusting to 84 knots (96.6 miles per hour), with wave heights as high as 30 feet.

At 5:30, Captain Woodard noticed the Whitefish Point Light suddenly flash on and begin rotating. Grabbing the radiophone, he called the *Fitzgerald,* relaying his observation.

"I'm very glad to hear it," McSorley replied, an obvious tone of relief in his voice.

"The wind is really howling down here," Woodard offered. "What are the conditions like up where you are?"

"We are taking heavy seas over our decks; it's the worst sea I've ever been in. We have a bad list and no radar."

Woodard thought and then responded, "If I'm correct, you have two radars."

"They're both gone," McSorley said.

Later, when he was asked if he hadn't been concerned with the reported "bad list" of the *Fitzgerald,* Woodard replied, "I didn't think too much about it. I thought that he knew what he was doing more than I did, and if he was in trouble, he would do the best he could."

*   *   *

The nature of Great Lakes shipping, with short voyages, much of the time in very protected waters, frequently with the same routine from trip to trip, leads to complacency and an overly optimistic attitude concerning the extreme weather hazards which can and do exist. The Marine Board feels that this attitude reflects itself at times . . . in the conviction that since refuges are near, safety is possible by "running for it."—Department of Transportation, Coast Guard Marine Casualty Report (USCG 16732/64216), page 103.

*   *   *

Throughout the *Fitzgerald,* crew members had either heard directly from someone in the engine room or from someone who had been on the bridge or they had guessed that the increasing list of the ship was due to a hole in the vessel's hull. While they gave the outward appearances of "business as usual," there was a creeping sense of apprehension among most of the men. Gathered in groups in the recreation room, in the crew's mess, or in their own cabins, the men discussed in hushed tones the threat posed by the storm and the damage to the ship. No imminent panic was present as the men seemed to take strength from the apparent calm of the others and from an unquestioning faith in Capt. Ernest McSorley. "Mac knows what he's doing."

Special Maintenance Man Joseph Mazes, of Ashland, Wisconsin, wasn't so sure. He had been in the engine room when the first call to check the King Gauges had come from the wheelhouse; he had seen the mercury rocketing up in starboard ballast tanks 4 and 5, and now he listened as the propeller shaft would suddenly increase its speed until the engine governor took over and slowed it down. He knew that meant the wheel was coming out of the water as the following seas raised the stern. The ship had been purposely loaded a bit more heavily in the after hold to keep the stern deeper in the water and to prevent the propeller from coming out of the water as often as it was now doing.

"She's down by the bow," Mazes thought. "The water is flooding the forward end, pulling her off balance."

George Holl had detected the same thing and had gone to the bridge to confer with McSorley. When he arrived, McSorley was on the radiophone, talking with Cedric Woodard. Turning to First Mate Jack McCarthy, the chief engineer shook his head.

"Jack, we have a bow rake; we're throwing the wheel."

"I know, George, but we aren't getting the water out of the tanks, and it's spilling into the hold."

"If we could level her off, we might be able to stop the water from getting in the hold."

McCarthy wagged his head. "How are we going to level her?"

"Let's pump some water into the port ballast tanks; let me go out and open a couple of portside vents and then put some water on that side. If we can level off, I think we might keep enough water out of the hold . . ."

Holl was interrupted by McSorley, who had overheard a part of the conversation.

"Don't allow anyone on deck. We'll leave the vents alone."

Holl and McCarthy exchanges glances, both understanding that the matter was settled.

When he had signed off the radio, McSorley joined the mate and engineer.

"George, I can't allow you or anyone else to go out on deck in this storm; you'll be washed over the side."

"OK, Mac. But we can't pump water into the port tanks with the vents closed. We'd blow them up."

"We've already taken on too much water, George. Loading any more in the tanks would make us more unstable than we are right now."

"Then it's make it into Whitefish the way we are?"

"It's that or nothing, George. Do you think she will hold together long enough?"

"I don't know, Mac. She's probably ripping the hole in the hull wider every time she's hit with a wave; maybe the hole in the cargo hold is spreading, too. It all depends on how much and how fast."

McSorley thought for a moment. Turning to McCarthy and Mike Armagost, he asked, "Do you want to alert the crew?"

Armagost said nothing; McCarthy rubbed the back of his neck with a hand as he debated with himself.

"Mac," Holl volunteered, "I'm afraid that we could have a problem on our hands with some of the crew if we start showing any real fear that we're not going to make it. A lot of the younger ones are going to want to take their chance in the water. They don't realize what will happen to them out there."

"I think George is right," Armagost chimed in. "This would be a bad time to try and explain that running for the bay is the only real chance they have."

McSorley glanced at his first mate. McCarthy nodded his head, agreeing with his fellow officers.

"Well, that is my opinion, too," McSorley said. "Mike, I'll want you up here with Jack and me when we get closer to Whitefish. Why don't you go down and try to rest for about an hour."

Armagost looked hurt, and McSorley moved quickly to reassure the young mate.

"Jack and I are going to be just about spent by the time we get down there. I'll want you to take the load off us when we have to negotiate into the bay, especially if we have to beach her then."

Armagost looked relieved and smiled slightly.

"Okay, Mac. I could use an hour in the sack," he said. "Just don't let me sleep through all the fun."

*   *   *

On the bridge of the *Arthur M. Anderson,* First Mate Clark kept a careful radar watch on the *Fitzgerald,* periodically calling the ship to inform her of the distance between the ore boats and the *Fitzgerald*'s position relative to Whitefish Bay. At 6:20 Clark had called to ask, "What course are you steering? You are widening out a little to the left of our heading marker."

"We are steering 141," the *Fitzgerald* had replied. It was the same course the *Anderson* was holding, and Clark was puzzled as to why the *Fitzgerald* should be straying to the left.

At seven o'clock Clark called again. "I am picking up the highland at Crisp Point. We're twenty-five miles from it, and you are ten miles ahead [of us]; you are fifteen miles from Crisp Point."

Crisp Point is a promontory twelve miles west of Whitefish Point.

"We haven't got far to go; we will soon have it made."

"Yes, we will," McSorley replied.

"It's a hell of a night for the Whitefish beacon to not be operating," Clark added.

The response was succinct: "It sure is."

It was snowing heavily, and the watch in the *Anderson*'s wheelhouse were unable to see the *Fitzgerald*'s lights. Their only contact with the stricken ship was the radar blip showing on the *Anderson*'s scopes.

As Morgan Clark was transmitting the 1900 weather observations, Captain Cooper decided to leave the bridge to get a
pipe from his cabin. At about 7:10, with Captain Cooper still
below, First Mate Clark noted a radar target coming out of
Whitefish Bay. He called the *Fitzgerald* to advise them: "You
have an upbound vessel nine miles ahead of you."

"Well, am I going to clear?" McSorley inquired.

"Yes, the way he is working, he is going to pass to the west
of you."

"Well, fine," McSorley said.

Clark was about to sign off when, as an afterthought, he
asked, "By the way, how are you making out with your
problems?"

McSorley responded, "We are holding our own."

"OK, fine. I'll be talking to you later," Clark replied.

He was wrong. Neither he nor anyone else would ever talk
with the *Fitzgerald* again.

The Whitefish Point Light had malfunctioned again. It
would remain inoperative throughout the balance of the
night. In Sault Ste. Marie, a large part of the city suffered a
power failure, and at Grand Marais, the Coast Guard's high-
level antenna—the antenna used to relay radio transmissions
from the Group Soo and Soo Control facilities at Sault Ste.
Marie—was blown down, limiting the range at which the
Coast Guard radios could transmit or receive.

On board the *Fitzgerald,* the lives of the twenty-nine crewmen were now being measured in seconds.

Red O'Brien struggled with the helm, fighting the ship's
tendency to swing to port as the following seas tried to push
the stern around into the wave troughs. The waves were
crashing onto the spar deck and rolling toward the bow,
pushing it down under tons of water, forcing the prow of the
vessel to fight its way back to the surface as each wave passed,
only to be driven down again as the next assault struck it.
Each time the forward part of the ship recovered there was an
imperceptible change in its attitude; it was falling deeper in
the water with each succeeding wave, and when the bow

surfaced again it was not coming back as far out of the seas as the previous time. The fracture in the hold's wall had increased to the point where water was pouring in uninterrupted, tons of it a minute. The *Fitzgerald* was foundering; the bow was settling into the lake an inch at a time in an action that was now irreversible.

Behind the *Fitzgerald* a series of waves larger than those which had pounded the ship for the last three hours was speeding toward the hapless vessel, as if the lake, now bored with the cat-and-mouse game it had been playing with the ship, had dispatched a huge paw to crush it.

Mike Armagost snapped on the light over his bed and looked at his watch: 7:15. He had slept for just over an hour.

In the officer's mess, Eddie Bindon lingered over a cup of coffee. He had come in at about six o'clock for a "snack." Although the regular evening meal was long past, Bindon had prevailed on Bob Rafferty to prepare a steak.

"I've never seen a man who could eat a steak like Eddie could," a former ship's steward would later recall. "He liked them no less than two inches thick and medium rare. He could eat two or three of them at a sitting."

In the engine room George Holl, Russell Haskell, and Blaine Wilhelm were watching the King Gauges.

"The water level is dropping," Haskell said. "The pumps must be catching up."

Holl shook his head and turned away. "Not necessarily. The side wall of the cargo hold may have opened up wider; the tank water may be draining in there a lot faster."

McCarthy was standing in the chart room, rechecking the ship's position: less than fifteen miles to go—ninety minutes. All they needed was another hour and a half. They wouldn't get it.

The first huge wave was thirty feet high. It struck the stern, rolling over the after deckhouse, producing a shudder of steel plates throughout the ship. When it hit the forecastle much of its force had been dissipated, but there was still enough power left to crash onto the bow and push it low in the water. Before the *Fitzgerald* could begin to recover, a second, larger wave was already sweeping over the spar deck with hundreds of tons of water. In cargo hold number 1, the flood reacted to the first wave's downward thrust, rushing as far forward as the bulkhead would permit while more water poured through the wide tear in the side plates to take its place, adding still more weight. The angle of inclination increased; the steering jib jutting from the prow dug into the water as the *Fitzgerald*'s nose buried itself in the lake. The second wave reached the prow and drove the forward section farther into the writhing water. The long expanse of spar deck bowed, the bow submerged, the lake covered first the forecastle deck, then the Texas deck; then the pilothouse dipped beneath the surface as the ship submarined toward the bottom of Superior, as the windows of the wheelhouse smashed inward, allowing the consuming flood to overwhelm the men inside, giving them time for but one final gasp.

Like a 700-foot-long whale, the ore boat slipped almost silently beneath the surface, its deck lights still blazing. It was approximately 7:15 P.M., November 10, 1975, and the 729-foot ore freighter *Edmund Fitzgerald* had just passed from the U.S. Maritime Registry.

CHAPTER 13

"The Damned Thing Sank"

When the wheelhouse windows smashed inward, McSorley was standing between the radar pedestals, his face almost pressing against the glass, trying to see beyond the huge waves. The force of the imploding water hurled him back against the heavy metal railing which surrounded the steering platform. He was instantly stunned and had no opportunity to cry out.

Red O'Brien, fighting with the big wheel, released his grip and stepped back, knocking over the stool directly behind him. "Oh, Jesus!" he cried, just before the onrushing wall of water overwhelmed him.

"Handsome Ransom" Cundy, standing on the starboard side of the wheelhouse, was inundated under a ton of water as the windows in front of and to the side of him disintegrated.

Jack McCarthy, bending over the map table in the chart room, heard the terrible crash of collapsing windows and the roaring flood. He had gripped the edge of the map table for support when the ship's bow began its downward plunge, and he was helpless to move. Paralyzed, he watched in horror as the wall separating the wheelhouse and chart room collapsed, the windows exploding in a blast of glass fragments, the metal divider folding toward the deck. The thrashing forms of McSorley, O'Brien, and Cundy were propelled from the wheelhouse as the cascading water rushed to fill every void. "Dear God!" McCarthy had managed to utter before he, too, was swallowed up.

It had happened in an instant; there had been no time to sound the alarm, no time to grab the radio handset, to shout a brief plea—"Save us!" The four drowning men were swept down the chart room stairwell as the flood sought every level.

The swirling Niagara thundered to the forecastle deck, smashing in the door to stateroom number 1, swamping the two neatly made beds, knocking over the bed stand and lamps. It was the same in stateroom number 2.

The pantry counter, next to the passenger lounge, was swept clean of dishes, coffee maker, cups, glasses—everything. The lounge submerged in seconds; the pleasantly stylish decor, designed and furnished with the best the J. L. Hudson Company of Detroit had to offer, was in an instant converted to a muckish, smashed, sodden mess.

McSorley's office was turned into a watery turmoil of papers, reports, charts, writing tools, lamps, books, the desk and shelves in the room wiped clear of anything not fastened down. His bedroom suffered the same fate as the staterooms, the clothes in his closet torn from their hangers, hats and caps flushed out into the room.

Even as the irresistible deluge sought to permeate all spaces in the forecastle deck, it was already flooding downward.

In his room on the spar deck Third Mate Mike Armagost had jumped from his bunk when the bow dipped low and had not righted itself. He had heard a loud explosion which seemed to come from up in the wheelhouse, and he heard the rumble from the deck above as furniture and loose fixtures tumbled under the water's onslaught. He threw open his door and struggled into the severely inclined corridor. Lake water was pouring down the stairwell in a torrent. Armagost knew there was no way to get up those stairs. Water was also rushing in through the undogged windlass room door. The ship was going down and Mike knew there was little, if any, time to get out alive. He threw open the door to Second Mate Jim Pratt's room, to warn the man, but it was empty. He struggled up the steep corridor toward the watertight door leading onto the outside spar deck. As he passed the open recreation room door he glanced in. The door on the opposite wall was also open, and Armagost saw Pratt and Wheelsman John Poviach in the corridor beyond, battling to open the door onto the spar deck on their side. He realized that the entire bow section must be underwater and that the pressure of the lake on the other side of the spar deck doors had sealed them shut. He and the others were doomed.

On the forward main deck, other members of the crew had been acutely aware that the *Fitzgerald* was in trouble.

In their room, Dave Weiss and Bruce Hudson had completed donning their warmest clothing to protect themselves as much as possible from the wind and the icy water.

"The biggest problem we would have is if she rolls over," Dave was lecturing Bruce. "If that happens, none of us is getting off alive."

"Wouldn't we have some chance if we were up on deck?" Hudson asked. "At least we might be able to jump free."

"If she flips slowly enough, we might. The problem is being able to keep from getting washed over the side. I think we should go up to the rec room and wait there. If she heels over much more, then we'll be close enough to the door to make a dash for it."

Karl Peckol, in his room on the starboard side of the deck, had completed his own preparations for going into the water and was about to rejoin his two friends Weiss and Hudson. As had been his habit, Karl had analyzed the problem thoroughly and had come to a conclusion: "No way. If this boat goes down in this storm, there's no way any of us will be picked up in time." But he would stay with his friends; he would go along with what they wanted.

Paul Riippa was alone in his room; his roommate, Deckhand Mark Thomas, was still aft. Paul had spent a half hour in prayer and reading the Scriptures. If the Lord would not still the rising waters, if He would not bring them safely to port, Paul was ready for the alternative. But in the meanwhile, he would trust in his Savior and would assume that everything would be all right.

The sudden forward dip sent both television and stereo crashing to the deck as Hudson and Weiss grabbed for a handhold to keep from falling themselves.

A shuddering in the deck plates, a thudding noise from somewhere above, and an unusual movement of air through their cabin signaled a serious problem.

"We must have hit something," Hudson said tensely, as the two held tight, waiting for the bow to right itself.

The door to their room flew open, and Karl Peckol stood at the threshold, his eyes wide. "We're sinking. Water's coming *down* the stairs."

Riippa was rolled to the floor when the ship started its dive. Instantly, he knew the *Fitzgerald* was on a one-way trip to the bottom. Pulling himself off his knees, he reached to the shelf above his bed, searching for his Bible. It wasn't there. Looking around, he saw that the contents of the shelf had been scattered around the room; he found his Bible on Thomas's bed amid items from Mark's own shelf. He felt no panic; he felt resigned and at peace.

The *Fitzgerald* was on a sloping dive, similar to the glide pattern of a large aircraft, but increasing its angle of inclination as the full weight of the cargo shifted forward and as the water flooded in through the pilothouse and other nonwatertight openings.

Bill Spengler had been lying on his bunk when the ship started its fateful dive. His concern with the list had been growing with the hours. His senses were fine tuned to the slightest change in the ship's attitude. He felt the shudder caused by the huge wave striking the stern, felt it rolling across the spar deck, felt the bow dip lower and lower, and realized that the ship was submarining. Spengler was off his bunk and out the cabin door seconds before the wheelhouse windows blew in. He knew there was no hope of getting up to the forecastle deck and then outside; his best chance was up the starboard tunnel. If the stern stayed on or near the surface, he might yet make it. His life jacket in one hand, Spengler dashed to the far end of the corridor and through the open tunnel, but the downward angle was increasing rapidly, forcing him to climb the deck, holding on to electrical conduits, recesses in the tunnel walls, anything that afforded handhold or foothold.

On the port side, Hudson, Weiss, and Peckol had also decided that the tunnel was their only avenue of escape; the bow was filling fast and there was no hope of reaching the forecastle deck. Get to the stern before it went under and take their chances in the open water.

"Maybe the bow will bottom and leave the stern out of the water," Bruce shouted as the three fled through the door of the portside tunnel. "How deep is it here?"

The question went unanswered. Forty feet up the tunnel the lead man slipped on the smooth deck floor, now pitched at a twenty-five-degree angle, sliding into and knocking the other two off their feet. The trio tumbled back to the doorway.

Spengler, in the opposite tunnel, was having more success, moving rapidly but carefully. Far up the tunnel a screeching, tearing noice stopped him: the pressure of the water coming into the torn ballast tanks was forcing the deck plates up. A sheet of water filled the air above the ever-widening tear, organizing itself into a tidal wave that began rushing down the passageway to where Bill Spengler, clutching at the wall, braced himself for what was coming, knowing he could not resist the impact of the advancing flood but unwilling to surrender even now.

The *Fitzgerald* was in an irreversible dive to the bottom of Lake Superior, the twenty-nine men in her beyond all worldly help.

As the bow bent down from the force and weight of the

large wave, the water in the hold rushed forward, deepening the downward angle of the ship. As the water rushed into the wheelhouse and down into the spaces below, the weight of additional water sealed the boat's doom, making it impossible for the bow to move back to the surface and increasing further the angle of the dive. Now the loose pellets in the cargo hold began to shift, to move forward, their momentum adding to the speed of the dive. The stern slipped under the waves, the propeller thrashing wildly, driving the hapless vessel even faster on its final voyage to the lake bed 530 feet below the squirming surface, most of the men inside her still alive, with agonizing, tortured minutes yet ahead of them.

Earlier, in the after section, Chief Engineer George Holl was monitoring the King Gauges in the lower engine room. Starboard ballast tanks 4 and 5 were still indicating a water level of twenty-eight feet. With all six pumps laboring, the water was not being controlled.

"We'd better find a beach damned soon," he muttered.

Holl's thoughts were interrupted by the sudden tilt of the deck as it dipped hard by the bow, accompanied by the loud screaming whine of the propeller shaft as the ship's wheel came out of the water. The engine's governor took over, slowing the shaft's spinning, but the pitch of the deck continued to increase. Second Assistant Engineer Haskell, standing at the Bailey System console, was keeping a close watch on the boilers' water level. Oiler Blaine Wilhelm was checking the pumps; they had been running hard and somewhat hot. All three men had to grab onto something to keep from falling when the bow took its dive; all stopped what they were doing, waiting for the ship to level itself. Suddenly a refrigerated drinking fountain, standing near the recording graph panel, tipped forward, tearing the water pipe from the back. The three watched the metal cabinet crash to the deck and slide to the forward side near the fireboxes. They knew then that the *Fitz* was in trouble.

Above them, men on the eight-to-twelve watch were having a cup of coffee before reporting to their stations.

Second Assistant Engineer Tommy Edwards sat in the

officers' dining room talking quietly with Eddie Bindon.

"Look at that," Edwards said, pointing to the coffee in his cup, which was almost to the rim on one side but far down in the cup on the other. "We're heeled over a good seven degrees."

Bindon nodded, but said nothing.

"Did George tell you what Mac wanted him forward for?" Edwards asked the first assistant engineer.

Bindon shook his head. "No, but Georgie was looking pretty pale when he came back."

"I think she tore her bottom back near Michipicoten; I think we're taking water in the cargo hold."

"If we are, then Mac is right in not talkin' about it. He knows we can't get off in this sea; he knows that the only thing to do is plow ahead and try to beach her at Whitefish Point; we're only a few miles from there. It won't do anybody any good to shout it to the whole crew. He's carrying the weight himself and trying not to panic everyone."

In the crew's mess, the topic of conversation also centered around the condition of the ship.

"You don't hold this much list for so long unless you've ripped the hull," Thomas Borgeson, able-bodied maintenance man stated flatly. "I went down and checked the King Gauges a while back—tanks 4 and 5 are filled to the top."

"I'll bet O'Brien won't be playing poker tonight," Oiler Ralph Walton chuckled.

"If he does he'll be playing alone," Wiper Gordie MacLellan laughed, just as the after deckhouse rose in the air and tilted precariously, sending coffee cups, catsup bottles, sugar bowls, and napkin holders flying from the table.

Walton slipped from his seat, bouncing off Borgeson, who grabbed the corner of the table in time to keep himself from falling to the floor.

"What the Christ!" someone shouted over the eruption of noises coming from the galley as pots, pans, trays, dishes, canned goods, and other loose items caromed around the large room.

Wheelsman John Simmons had left the mess room only

moments before the ship's bow plunged beneath the surface. He was not scheduled in the wheelhouse until midnight, but he knew Red O'Brien would be exhausted after four hours of fighting the wheel in the heavy sea and would welcome some relief. They would be moving into Whitefish Bay soon, and that was no time to have a tired man wheeling a wounded ship.

As the wheelsman who had "brought her out," Johnny Simmons was very protective of the *Fitz*. Years later his wife, Florence, would remark hauntingly, "He loved that boat, he really loved it. . . . I don't know why. The damned thing sank."

Turning the corner leading to the stairwell that would take him down to the tunnel, his glance fell on a porthole facing the spar deck. He casually peered out toward the forward deckhouse and was horrified at what he saw. A huge wave twenty feet over the level of the spar deck rolled toward the bow of the listing ship, crashing against the superstructure, driving the stem down into the water. The prow and the fore section of the spar deck bent down like a diving board under the weight of a diver, but as Simmons watched and waited expectantly, it did not spring back. Instead the ship humped over like a whale sounding, tilted sharply downward, and dove beneath the surface. Simmons saw the water wash over the wheelhouse, saw the ghostly glow of the chart room lamp briefly silhouetting figures inside being catapulted backward under the force of the rushing black water, then disappearing as the wheelhouse buried itself in the lake; the rest of the ship rushed to follow.

Transfixed at the awesome sight, Simmons did not move until the after deckhouse itself plunged beneath the waves. Then, grabbing a handrail along the wall, he began crawling up the steep sloping deck to escape the awful sight. Within seconds, the instant the icy lake water hit them, the boilers exploded.

Down below, in the engine room, George Holl, Rus Haskell, and Blaine Wilhelm died instantly in a flurry of flying metal and scalding water.

In his room just off the galley, Bob Rafferty was blown from his chair as the force of the explosion, coming up the draft fan casing, collapsed the wall. Dazed, he had but one fleeting thought before a merciful darkness closed about him: *This is my last trip.*

*   *   *

The Fitzgerald plummeted down through the ever-increasing blackness of the frigid lake, the taconite pellets now crashing through the screen bulkheads of numbers 2 and 3 holds to concentrate themselves far forward. The force of 26,116 tons of iron ore blew cargo hatches from their clamps; the pressure of the water buckled several inward, folding them as if they were cardboard.

The bow of the massive ship struck the mud and sand bottom first, folding the steering jib back against the pilot-house. The force of the impact tore the windlass engine off its mountings and hurled it through the starboard bow plates. The shell plating between the spar and forecastle decks wrinkled like aluminum foil. The Texas deck and pilothouse were nearly torn from their foundations and were distorted from the ship's impact with the lake bottom.

With the cargo gone from the after section of the vessel, the hull was extremely unstable. The jolt it sustained when the bow struck bottom caused the *Fitzgerald* to snap in two—the after section containing the heavy propulsion machinery, fuel bunkers, electrical generating equipment, and fire-fighting apparatus had greater mass than did the center section, which was devoid of pellets and was little more than a fragile shell. The stern continued its forward motion as the bow came to a sliding stop on the bottom, and it flipped over, ripping a 400-foot chunk away from the forward part of the ship. As the after section twirled in a gigantic somersault, 200 feet of the hull disintegrated, scattering large pieces of steel plating and girders over the lake bottom. The remaining 257 feet of the stern crashed down upon the debris, landing on the deck-house, crushing the two decks like eggs.

The men in the stern section died quickly, either from drowning, from injuries resulting from the exploding boilers, or in the final impact as the shattered piece of ship crashed down on itself.

A swift and merciful death was not a certainty for the men in the forecastle.

Of the fourteen men quartered forward, ten were probably there at the moment the *Fitzgerald* took her dive. In some portions of the spar deck and forecastle deck cabins, pockets of air would have collected, trapped—air that could, if located, sustain life for several minutes, perhaps an hour, until it was no longer breathable, or until the numbing cold of the lake bottom sapped all strength and took consciousness away while the ultimate process all must face was completed.

The immense cloud of silt churned from the floor of the lake, thrown upward by the vicious intrusion of the battered and broken ship. When it finally settled, the remains of the boat had come to rest at the spot it would occupy for eternity. Streams of bubbles poured from tiny chinks in her sides as water drove the remaining air out of her. Soon the bubbles would cease; the only movement aboard the vessel would be the endless waving of the strap of an unused life jacket, trapped on the ceiling of the wheelhouse, caressed by the currents moving through the broken windows.

The sinking of the *Edmund Fitzgerald* had taken less than five minutes from the instant she first dipped her prow below the surface of Lake Superior until she lay a shattered, twisted wreck on the lake's bottom. It required at least five minutes to dial a telephone and inform a horrified woman that her husband was dead. It took at least five minutes for a devastated mother to explain to a child that a beloved father would return to them no more.

In the years to come, on the anniversary of this frightful night, while the old ship's bell in the belfry tolls mournfully, a deacon standing in Detroit's Mariner's Cathedral will take a full five minutes to read the twenty-nine names of the men of the *Edmund Fitzgerald*.

CHAPTER 14

"I'm Going to Take a Hell of a Beating"

"He said he was holding his own," *Anderson*'s First Mate Morgan Clark informed Capt. Jesse "Bernie" Cooper when the ship's master returned to the wheelhouse shortly after 1910 hours (7:10 P.M.).

Cooper glanced at the radarscope but was unable to spot the *Fitzgerald*'s blip; the radar screen was cluttered with sea return. Clark had held the image of the ship, then nine miles out front, at about the time he had last talked with the vessel. But the combination of the increasing wave heights and the severe snow squall had virtually swallowed the ship, and Clark had watched as the *Fitzgerald* steamed into what Cooper would later describe as a "white blob" of sea return and clutter, and then disappear.

Now, at about 7:25, the snow squall abruptly ceased, and Clark could see the lights of an upbound vessel. It was the *Avafors*, and behind her was the *Benfri*; the *Nanfri* brought up the rear, and all three were now visible from the *Anderson*'s wheelhouse.

"We should be able to see the *Fitzgerald*," Clark said to Wheelsman Robert L. May.

But they couldn't see the *Fitz*. The saltwater vessels were no closer than seventeen miles and could be clearly seen, both visually and on radar. The *Fitzgerald* was supposed to be half the distance.

Checking the radar screens again, Clark thought he had the ship.

"We had something around six and a half, seven miles," Clark would tell the Coast Guard investigators later. "But it would hold, maybe two sweeps, and then it would disappear."

Clark attempted to readjust the radar, using the compressor, to eliminate the smaller targets and force the machine to concentrate on the solid target that should be the *Fitzgerald*.

Captain Cooper, now back in the wheelhouse, assumed that the ship might have suffered a power blackout and began searching the horizon for a silhouette. The others on watch began looking for the outline of the ship, also.

May thought that he saw a white light just to the right of a red one that proved to be a radio or television tower at Coppermine Point, Ontario. But no one else was able to see the white light, and soon May decided that he had observed the lakes phenomenon known as light flare, caused by straining the eyes to see far ahead at night.

The tension in the *Anderson*'s wheelhouse increased as the minutes wore on and no sign of the *Fitzgerald* could be found. Bernie Cooper and Morgan Clark alternated calling the ship on radio but received no reply. Finally Cooper, to check his equipment, called the freighter *William Clay Ford*, anchored in Whitefish Bay. The *Ford* replied that the *Anderson*'s signal was loud and clear. Cooper then asked if the *Fitzgerald* might have slipped into the bay and was told that it had not.

A feeling of horror gripped the men in the *Anderson*'s wheelhouse; the possibilities that the huge ore boat that had been with them throughout the voyage across the storm-tossed lake had met with disaster were growing rapidly.

Aboard the *Benfri*, Great Lakes pilot Capt. Robert O'Brien

was unaware of the apprehension that was being experienced aboard the *Arthur M. Anderson*. Shortly after 7:00 P.M., once he had cleared Whitefish Point, O'Brien went to bed.

At Group Soo, Radioman Philip Branch was occupied attempting to locate a sixteen-foot open boat that had been reported missing near Whitefish Point at about 6:00 P.M. The wife of one of the two men supposedly on board the small boat had contacted the Coast Guard and reported that her husband and another man had gone out before the storm had hit and had not returned.

About 7:39 P.M., Cooper called the Group Soo, using Channel 16, the distress calling frequency. The radio operator—probably Petty Officer Branch—told Cooper to switch to Channel 12. When the *Anderson*'s master complied, he was unable to raise the Coast Guard station. Bernie Cooper next radioed the upbound saltwater vessel *Nanfri*, just coming out of Whitefish Bay, speaking with Great Lakes pilot Capt. Albert Jacovetti. Cooper inquired whether Jacovetti could pick up the *Fitzgerald* on the *Nanfri*'s radar and was told that no contacts that could be the *Fitzgerald* were on his scope.

The frustrated and increasingly frightened Cooper, at 7:54, attempted again to raise Soo Control. This time he was told to watch for the missing sixteen-footer.

Cooper and Clark continued attempting to raise the *Fitzgerald* on radio and kept close watch on radar, but they were unsuccessful. Finally, at 8:32, Cooper again radioed Soo Control.

"This is the *Anderson*. I am very concerned with the welfare of the steamer *Edmund Fitzgerald*. He was right in front of us, experiencing a little difficulty. He was taking on a small amount of water, and none of the upbound ships have passed him. I can see no lights as before, and I don't have him on radar. I just hope he didn't take a nose dive."

"This is Soo Control. Roger. Thank you for the information. We will try and contact him. Over."

"This is the *Anderson*. Roger. Thank you, and also you might try WLC–Rogers City (the ship-to-shore radiotelephone station). Have him ring his buzzer on AM, and he might be able to contact him just to be sure that he is there. Over."

"This is Soo Control. Roger. We will try that. We will get back to you. Out."

Branch then made his own attempts at contacting the missing ship; first at 8:33, again just a few seconds later. At 8:40, Branch called WLC, requesting that they call the *Fitzgerald* on AM. Two minutes later the radio station called Group Soo to advise that there was "something wrong" with their AM antennae. "We'll take a look and get back to you." There is no evidence to indicate that the commercial radio station contacted the Coast Guard again that night.

If the personnel at WLC did not indicate any great fear for the welfare of the *Fitzgerald,* they were not alone. Paul Branch himself did not experience grave concern for the vessel and her crew.

> *Q.* And your testimony was you didn't consider that urgent, "I just hope he didn't take a nose dive," and you didn't consider that urgent?
>
> *A.* As I said, I considered it serious, but at the time it was not urgent.—Testimony before the Department of Transportation, United States Coast Guard, In the Matter of: Marine Board of Investigation, Sinking of the S.S. *Edmund Fitzgerald,* page 2976.

Branch advised the officer of the day and continued calling for the *Fitzgerald.* "I didn't completely disregard it (the *Anderson*'s report), but I didn't take it as urgent at the time." Calls at 9:07, 9:15, and 9:45 were all fruitless.

However, according to search-and-rescue procedure, the Coast Guard, following Cooper's 8:32 call, had informed the Coast Guard Rescue Coordination Center (RCC) in Cleveland that there was "an uncertainty concerning *Fitzgerald.*"

At 9:30, Bernie Cooper radioed with additional information concerning their position at the time they last had contact with the *Fitzgerald.* The Coast Guard, according to its final report on the investigation into the sinking, decided that this call constituted a formal "report that the *Fitzgerald* was missing" and relayed the information to RCC-Cleveland at 9:10. At 9:15, Cleveland directed the Coast Guard air station in Traverse City, Michigan, to dispatch an aircraft. At 9:16, the Canadian Rescue Center at Trenton, Ontario, was advised; at 9:25, Cleveland directed that the Coast Guard cutter *Naugatuck* get under way from Sault Ste. Marie and, at 9:30, ordered the cutter *Woodrush* to proceed to the search area—the *Woodrush* was in Duluth, over three hundred miles away.

Although under the provisions of the Coast Guard's search-and-rescue plan, the Traverse City station was required to have one fixed-wing search aircraft and one helicopter in "status Bravo-zero" (capable of being launched in thirty minutes) or "status Alpha" (in the air) at all times, the first aircraft launched—an HU-16 fixed wing—did not take off until almost an hour after the scramble order had been dispatched. The pilots had to wait while flares were loaded aboard. The aircraft was on the scene at 10:53. The helicopter departed Traverse City at 10:23 (over an hour after the call from Cleveland), arriving over the search area with a 3.8-million-candlepower searchlight at 1:00 A.M., November 11. A Canadian C-130 search aircraft was launched at 12:37 A.M.

The cutter *Naugatuck* left Sault Ste. Marie with orders not to proceed beyond the entrance of Whitefish Bay due to the fact that it was of a vessel class that was restricted from operating in open water when winds exceeded sixty knots. The *Fitzgerald* had disappeared out in the open lake, and the Coast Guard's closest rescue vessel was sent to operate no closer than fifteen miles from the last known position of the missing ship. It mattered little in the long run, however; the cutter broke an oil line and spent the balance of the night bobbing around while repairs were effected. She didn't get under way until 9:00 A.M. the next morning. The cutter *Woodrush* arrived on the scene in eastern Lake Superior shortly after midnight on November 12. The Coast Guard at Sault Ste. Marie had only a forty-foot patrol boat left to dispatch, which it did the next morning, once the storm had passed. The possibility of sending the thirty-six-foot launch from Grand Marais was discounted due to the severe conditions on Superior. The RCC forty-foot patrol boats stationed at Marquette, Bayfield (Wisconsin), and Duluth were too far from the scene to be effective.

The Coast Guard icebreaker *Mackinaw* was at its home port in Sheboygan, Michigan, but was under repairs preparatory to the winter ice-breaking season and was unable to get under way. The Coast Guard buoy tender *Sundew* was at its home port at Charlevoix, Michigan; it, too, was under repairs and unable to assist in the search. The forty-foot patrol boat and forty-four foot motor lifeboat at Saint Ignace were too far from the scene to be effective.

And so it went. In sum, there were no Coast Guard surface vessels anywhere near the scene that might have been useful in saving lives on the night of November 10, 1975. As far as the organization charged with the responsibility to search and rescue mariners on Lake Superior knew, twenty-nine men were in the icy waters, waiting, fighting to stay alive long enough to be saved by a flotilla that consisted of ships that were broken-down, under repair, too far away, or too small to be of any use. It was not to be a hallmark of pride that would go into the honorable and distinguished history of the United States Coast Guard.

Helpless and ineffective in their own right, the Coast Guard ultimately turned to the one who had battled to alert them of the possible peril to the *Fitzgerald,* who had insisted that they know that which they seemed not to be interested in hearing. At approximately 9:00 P.M., Group Soo radioed the *Anderson.*

"*Anderson,* this is Group Soo. What is your present position?"

"We're down here, about two miles off Parisienne Island right now . . . the wind is northwest forty to forty-five miles here in the bay."

"Is it calming down at all, do you think?"

"In the bay it is, but I heard a couple of the salties talking up there, and they wish they hadn't gone out."

"Do you think there is any possibility that you could . . . ah . . . come about and go back there and do any searching?"

There was a pause, and then Cooper replied: "Ah . . . , God, I don't know . . . ah . . . that . . . that sea out there is tremendously large. Ah . . . if you want me to, I can, but I'm not going to be making any time; I'll be lucky to make two or three miles an hour going back out that way."

"Well, you'll have to make a decision as to whether you will be hazarding your vessel or not, but you're probably one of the only vessels right now that can get to the scene. We're going to try to contact those saltwater vessels and see if they can't possibly come about and possibly come back also . . . things look pretty bad right now; it looks like she may have split apart at the seams like the *Morrell* did a few years back."

"Well, that's what I been thinking. But we talked to him about seven and he said that everything was going fine. He said that he was going along like an old shoe; no problems at all."

This was to be a consistent misquote that Cooper would broadcast throughout the night, the next day, and for weeks thereafter. The last words from the *Fitzgerald* had been: "We're holding our own." Whether or not Cooper, struck with a sense of subconscious guilt at not having voiced his concern for the *Fitzgerald*'s close approach to the shoal area near Caribou Island, felt some degree of personal blame for whatever had happened to the ship, or possibly felt that he should have been more quizzical about the persistent list the *Fitzgerald* continued to report for almost four hours, is not known. But in the face of corrections by the first mate, Morgan Clark, Cooper doggedly insisted that McSorley had stated that there was no reason to worry, even though Cooper had not actually heard the last conversation. Whatever his own feelings of responsibility for the missing vessel, Bernie Cooper was not anxious to turn around and put his own ship and men into the teeth of the storm that continued to rage out in the lake.

"Well, again, do you think you could come about and go back and have a look in the area?" the Coast Guard pleaded.

"Well, I'll go back and take a look, but, God, I'm afraid I'm going to take a hell of a beating out there. . . . I'll turn around and give 'er a whirl, but, God, I don't know. I'll give it a try."

"That would be good if you could turn around and head out that way, and we'd like to get as many other vessels that can possibly get under way and proceed to that area."

Cooper, worried and perhaps somewhat annoyed with the Coast Guard captain of the port—the man who was now asking that he put his ship in harm's way—suddenly asked an acid question: "Do you realize what the conditions are out there?"

There was no immediate response, so Cooper rephrased his question: "You do realize what the conditions are out there, don't you?"

"Affirmative. From what your reports are I can appreciate the conditions. Again, though, I have to leave that decision up to you as to whether it would be hazarding your vessel, or not. If you think you can safely go back up to the area, I would request that you do so. But I have to leave that decision up to you."

The buck had been passed.

"I'll give it a try, but that's all I can do."

Group Soo—now identifying itself as "Soo Control" because the vessels in the area insisted on referring to it as such—began attempting to recruit other ships in the search.

On board the *Benfri,* Captain O'Brien was awakened from a fitful sleep by the ship's master.

"The Coast Guard is asking to speak with you."

"I wonder what in hell they want now," O'Brien said, struggling out of bed.

On the *Nanfri,* Capt. Albert Jacovetti advised the Coast Guard that turning around would be impossible. "No way," he said. He did agree to slow the vessel some and to alter his course more to the north, to pass closer to the area where the *Fitzgerald* had last been reported.

Capt. Cedric Woodard, piloting the *Avafors,* had forgotten to switch its only bridge radiophone from Channel 11, after having talked to Captain O'Brien aboard the *Benfri* sometime around seven in the evening, back to the distress frequency—Channel 16. It was not until 10:30 that he suddenly began to wonder why he had heard no radio traffic for several hours. Getting a flashlight and standing on his tiptoes to see the face of the radio, he discovered the selector was still on the seldom-used frequency. Turning to Channel 16, the speaker erupted in a flurry of excited voices, all talking about the missing *Edmund Fitzgerald*. He soon learned that the Coast Guard had been attempting to reach him, unsuccessfully, to ask that he come about and search for wreakage and possible survivors.

It was too late; the *Avafors*'s master would not consider attempting the turn, and the *Avafors* sailed on, with the unrecognized voice of a stammering, weary Ernest McSorley echoing in Woodard's ears: "We have a bad list . . . a bad list . . . a bad . . ."

With none of the vessels closest to where the *Fitzgerald* was feared to have gone down willing to "hazard" their ships, Soo Control turned to the seven ships anchored in the lee of Whitefish Point.

"Is there any way possible that you could get under way and search for survivors?" was the question Soo Control asked.

"I'll have to notify the captain and call you back."

"I'm having problems with my gyrocompass; I would be in jeopardy with my crew."

"Well, I'd sure like to, but we've got a couple of big fractures in our port nozzle back there; I don't think it would ever stand it. I don't think I could, Soo Control. Golly, I'd like to."

The last statement, made by the master of the Canadian vessel *Algosoo*, was, of course, rubbish. None of the men, either experiencing the full force of the savage storm out in Superior or listening to the conversations of those who were in the storm, would "like to" gamble with their ships and crew in weather that had apparently taken one huge freighter and might yet take others.

Of the seven ships in the bay, only the Ford Motor Company's *William Clay Ford* and the Canadian *Hilda Marjanne* left the safety of Whitefish and proceeded out to look for debris or survivors of the *Fitzgerald*. The *Hilda Marjanne* determined after twenty or thirty minutes that conditions were too severe for the vessel and returned to Whitefish Bay. While other ships would join the search the following morning, when the storm had moderated and the seas had calmed, it was left to the *Anderson* and the *Ford*, assisted by aircraft, to brave the raging blast, in the rapidly waning hope that the *Fitzgerald*'s crew might yet be saved.

Shortly before getting under way, the *Ford*'s third mate suddenly saw something that brought a flash of optimism to all who fretted for the missing vessel.

"*Anderson*, this is the *William Clay Ford*. Over here, inside of Whitefish, I seen somebody shining a spotlight up in the air. Do you see that? I'm just wondering if that couldn't be him on the beach?"

"That was us here; we were flashing it for the aircraft," Cooper replied. At the request of Coast Guard search aircraft 7326, he had put his searchlight up in the sky to assist the pilot in identifying the *Anderson*.

"Oh, no, no, no. This was a long way from you; this was across the land. I'm anchored off Paradise (in Whitefish Bay), heading 310 degrees, and this is about 40 degrees on my bow. This is coming from the land. I can see a searchlight way across the land up there; it's inside Whitefish; it would be on your port side; I wonder if you can see it up in the clouds?"

Cooper looked outside. "I can't pick up any searchlight at all."

"They're not flashing now, but there definitely was somebody shining a spotlight in the air, between Crisp Point and Whitefish, someplace. It was too bright for any spotlight from a car. It definitely was a bright, bright spotlight being shined right up in the clouds, over the land there."

Might it have been from the search plane? Cooper wondered.

"When I saw the spotlight he wasn't in that area; he was over by Pancake Shoals, and we can see you from here, so it definitely was not you or it was not the aircraft. I just wonder if it was not him on the beach."

Other ships in the bay began radioing that they, too, could see the bright light flashing in the sky, as if it were a ship grounded on the beach, its radios out, trying to signal for help with its searchlight. Finally, the men in the *Anderson*'s wheelhouse also saw the light, and as hearts beat faster and hope flared throughout the eastern end of Lake Superior and on ships which were able to pick up the radio transmissions as far south as northern Lake Michigan and Lake Huron and the Straits of Mackinac, the search aircraft circled, looking for the source of the light.

*   *   *

Sometime after 10:00 P.M., word of a missing freighter began flashing across television screens and over radio speakers throughout the Great Lakes area.

In Superior, Doreen Cundy had just returned home from a bingo game.

"It was dreadful," she remembers. "I turned on the TV, and as the picture came on, there at the bottom of the screen it said, '*Fitzgerald* feared sunk.' It was such a shock; it was a terrible way to find out."

To the west, in Iron River, Janice Armagost was just returning from a meeting in Superior with several women from the Iron River area. Janice had not turned the car radio on, as was her normal habit, because she and her passengers had been chatting. After dropping off the last of the women, she drove home. As she pulled the car into the drive, the headlights reflected from the figure of her mother-in-law, hurrying toward the car.

"They've been flashing the news on TV," Lorraine Armagost said in a trembling voice. "Mike's boat is missing."

Thelma Church was watching the ten o'clock news on

Duluth's television Channel 10 when she first heard the report of *Fitzgerald*'s disappearance.

In Ashland, Florence Simmons and her grandchildren were watching Monday-night football on television when a knock came at the back door. It was her daughter, Patricia, tears streaming down her face. At the same instant the telephone rang; the news was being relayed by her daughter Mary's husband. Mary, in the hospital awaiting the birth of a child, had also watched football; she did not yet know of the tragedy.

Later that evening, with details still sketchy, Florence called the Coast Guard station at Bayfield, Wisconsin, asking to be put in touch with the Coast Guard at Sault Ste. Marie. In the background she heard someone shout to the coastguardsman on the telephone: "Tell her to call her [company] agent and stop bothering us."

*　　　*　　　*

The search aircraft had made several passes over the beach between Crisp Point and Whitefish Point in the area where the mysterious light had been reported and had now identified the source.

"That light you see flashing is hunters out there, chasing deer. They're right on the shore."

The light that had been a brief ray of hope to the hundreds who agonized over the fate of the *Fitzgerald* had been produced by a group of sportsmen, illegally "shining" for game.

Meanwhile, Soo Control was still trying to add vessels to the search.

"*William Clay Ford*, this is Soo Control. Do you have contact with the *Nanfri?*"

Capt. D. E. Erickson, master of the *Ford*, replied that he did.

"Do you think there's any possibility that Captain Jacovetti might talk the master of the *Nanfri* into searching the area that he's at?"

"He says he can't turn around, but he's doing the best that he can out there," Erickson responded.

Through the long, difficult hours, the *Anderson* and the *Ford* crisscrossed the area fifteen miles north of Crisp Point and fourteen miles west of Coppermine Point, while the Coast Guard HU-52 helicopter swept overhead, dropping flares and shining a brilliant searchlight on the lake's surface. Markers were dropped to indicate the areas already covered by the ships and aircraft, and with each passing hour the meager hope that survivors would be found slowly ebbed. The voices of the searchers mirrored their growing exhaustion and their bitter sense of defeat. They were operating now on sheer determination to complete the task of locating wreckage or the bodies of the crew, to confirm that which they all knew now to be true—the *Fitzgerald* was gone.

"If there were survivors, they would have drifted down this way" replaced the earlier, more confident "possible survivors" in the conversations crackling across the lake.

Looking for oil slicks and debris seemed to be the most pragmatic activity as the night wore sluggishly on.

A group of Canadian "beach watchers" were assembled to begin prowling the eastern coastline of the lake, looking for the corpses that frequently drift to shore after a marine disaster.

In Cleveland, the Rescue Coordination Center marshaled its forces for a full-scale search of the area: A C-130 from the Michigan National Guard was requested for the following morning; a Canadian C-130 was also asked to assist the "first light" activities; a Coast Guard HU-16 and two HH-52 helicopters would be sent from the Traverse City station; and the Coast Guard air station at Elizabeth City, North Carolina, was to send an additional C-130 to the area.

As dawn approached, bits and pieces of flotsam began to be sighted by the prowling *Arthur M. Anderson*: a piece of life jacket, an oar, a life ring, a propane cylinder. In addition to these items, search vessels and shore-bound parties later recovered the severely damaged number 2 lifeboat and a sixteen-foot section of the forward part of number 1 lifeboat; both inflatable life rafts were found, and one twenty-five-man raft was found inflated and floating near the shore in the vicinity of Coppermine Point. It was recovered by the ore freighter *Roger Blough* at 9:42 A.M. Tuesday. A second inflatable raft was found south of Coppermine Point at 11:00 that same morning. It was partially deflated when recovered by an Ontario provincial police shore party.

Throughout the day, other items from the *Fitzgerald* were spotted and/or recovered by search teams. They included twenty-one life jackets or life jacket pieces; eight oars or oar pieces; eight flotation tanks, identified as having come from the lifeboats; one piece of a ballast tank sounding board; one built-up wooden fender block with line attached; two propane cylinders, identified as having come from the galley storage area on the poop deck; thirteen life rings, with pieces of line attached; one piece of line approximately eight feet long; two two-inch-by-twelve-inch planks, one approximately twelve feet long, the other approximately fifteen feet long; one wooden stool similar to the type used on the *Fitzgerald*; one heaving line; one stepladder; one-half of a boat cover like those used on the *Fitzgerald*'s lifeboats; one floodlight, identified as the type installed on the pilothouse and afterdeck of the *Fitzgerald*; one plastic spray bottle, white, marked "pilothouse window"; one broken extension ladder; and pieces of assorted broken scrap wood.

No survivors were found; no bodies were recovered.

Jesse Cooper stood in the wheelhouse of the *Anderson*, leaning against the forward windows, his body slumping over, his eyes burning and his mouth and throat dry.

"We're now in the area of the debris," he said wearily. "This is the spot."

Outside, the inky blackness of predawn closed more tightly around the ship, the sound of the wind now changing from an enraged shriek to a melancholy moan, as if a ghostly choir—composed of all the mariners ever claimed by Superior—was chanting a dirge of grief for the twenty-nine men newly recruited to their ranks.

CHAPTER 15

"Presumed Dead"

"Is my dad dead?"

It was a question that was asked many times during the day of November 11, 1975.

Pamela Johnson, daughter of Bob Rafferty, asked the question.

Pam's husband, William, a career soldier, was on leave, awaiting the birth of their fourth child. They had spent the time in their rented quarters near the post at Fort Benning, "just sitting around and playing cards, just waiting the time out." In the early afternoon on November 11, Pam had strolled next door to a neighbor's; Bill had been watching television. A short while later, Bill came to the neighbor's house.

"What are you doing here?" he had asked. "Why don't you come on home?"

Pam said that he had a strange look on his face, and she assumed that perhaps he was angry. Back at their home, Pam said, "You want to go somewhere, right?" and grabbed the newspaper, looking for the movie section.

Bill closed the newspaper in her hands.

"Listen," he said, "I've got to tell you something. Your dad was on a boat . . ."

"I knew when he said that, that something was wrong," Pam recalls.

She went to the telephone and called her mother in Toledo.

"Is my dad dead?"

Brooksie Rafferty had first heard the news in a radio broadcast at five that morning, but she had not believed the early report. It was not until about 9:00 A.M. when she had turned on the television and heard the network news broadcast, that the truth had finally hit home.

"I ran through the house shouting at my son, who was still asleep, 'Randy, your dad's dead, your dad's dead, he's dead . . .'" And then I thought, 'What a terrible way to wake somebody up.'"

The parents of David Weiss heard the news on the same network broadcast in their home in Canogha Park. They spent the rest of the day on the telephone, calling the Coast Guard and the Great Lakes Maritime Academy, attempting to learn exactly what had happened, hoping that later reports would divulge that their son had not died on the ship.

Helen Bindon was in her home in Fairport Harbor when her sister-in-law, Margaret Majoros, called at eight in the morning.

"Helen, where is the *Edmund Fitzgerald* at?"

"I think she's standing in for weather," Helen had replied.

Margaret was silent for several seconds, saying not a word. Helen was puzzled and finally asked, "Margaret, what's the matter?"

"Helen, if you're standing up, you'd better sit down. The *Edmund Fitzgerald* sunk last night."

At about the same time, in St. Joseph, Florence Bentsen was preparing to leave for work at a nearby gift shop when her employer, Carol Greening, telephoned to ask, "Tom wasn't on the *Fitzgerald*, was he?"

Florence answered that he was.

"Did you hear the news? They're saying on the radio that it has gone down."

Lois Beardsley had called her brother, Roger Holl, to say that the *Fitzgerald* was missing.

"What do you mean, 'missing'? You don't lose a seven-hundred-foot boat!"

At six in the morning, Bill McCarthy, brother of the first mate, Jack, had gone to his parents' home to relay the news.

"I told Dad that Jack was gone, that the ship had sunk and there were no survivors. He looked at me for a minute and then, with no tears, no screaming, he said, 'Do you want some coffee?' "

Later that day, John Lychester McCarthy would take his rosary and go upstairs to his room, where he would sit and pray for the soul of his lost son, alone with his memories and his grief. It's the way of the Irish.

Those who had heard the news the night before and had spent agonizing hours waiting for official word, who had faced a bleak, unfriendly dawn, red-eyed and worn, were now joined by those who were just getting the frightful news for the first time. Stunned and horrified, they were forced to run a painful and puzzling gauntlet of friends and relatives who were phoning and banging on their doors and hordes of newspaper, radio, and television personnel who had been dispatched by their editors to perform a seemingly heartless and brutal ritual—an endless series of tormenting questions, personal and probing, all of which stung and burned and left their victims reeling, still unable to fully comprehend the magnitude of what had happened. Wives and mothers, fathers, brothers and sisters, suddenly thrust into the glare of television lights, blinded by flashguns, prodded by questions—the cold, bitter questions: When did you see him last? What were the last words you remember him saying? Did he ever talk about the storms on the lakes? Was he afraid of the ship? The questioning would go on for days after the sinking. And when it seemed that there would finally be a merciful end to their torment, a new report would surface; some additional bit of gossip about the ship or her captain or the crew would start the painful process all over again.

And there were the anonymous telephone calls late at night, the poison words uttered by faceless, nameless people with poisoned minds: "Your husband was sleeping with a woman in Duluth. . . . Your son is rotting at the bottom of the lake. How does that make you feel? . . . Your brother borrowed money from me and never paid it back. You don't want that to ruin his memory, do you?"

A year after the *Fitzgerald*'s loss, it was the song; that *song* that was played endlessly, day after day, retelling the story of the terror and death in a November storm on Lake Superior.

"If I was driving my car and the song came over the radio, I would have to pull to the side of the road until it was over—but I couldn't turn it off," was a common comment made by those the *Fitzgerald*'s crew had left behind.

The most difficult thought they had to face—a fact that has continued to haunt them down the lonely years—was that there would be no body to pray over and to lay to rest in some quiet, beautiful place where those who loved him would be able to visit, to gently lay flowers or to spend a few silent moments close to him.

"It just doesn't seem that it's over with; it's somehow incomplete," Pamela Johnson would say five years after. "If there had been a real funeral, with a body to bury, I could find it easier to accept the fact that he's really gone."

"He said he wanted to be buried with his ship," Lois Beardsley, niece of Chief Engineer George Holl, said. "But it felt so strange attending a memorial service. I kept asking myself, 'Why are we here?' It still doesn't seem final."

*   *   *

The wounds would not be permitted to heal. In the days

immediately following the tragic loss, there were the daily accounts in the papers and on television as the legal process of investigating the disaster went on.

First it would be the United States Coast Guard Board of Inquiry.

At ten minutes past ten in the morning on Tuesday, November 18, 1975—just a week and a day after the ship disappeared—the Marine Board of Investigation convened in the thirty-first floor auditorium of the Federal Building in Cleveland.

With Rear Adm. Winfred W. Barrow as chairman, Capt. Adam S. Zabinski and Capt. James A. Wilson as members, and Cmdr. C. S. Loosmore as recorder, the board heard testimony from forty-five witnesses over a period of twelve days; 361 exhibits were entered into evidence; 3,001 pages of testimony were transcribed into the record of the proceedings.

On July 26, 1977—twenty months after the sinking—a formal report was issued. It was hailed as the most comprehensive investigation into a Great Lakes maritime disaster ever conducted and was professed to be the "definitive" examination of the loss of the *Fitzgerald.* However, the report ultimately posed more questions than it sought to answer. It's "probable cause" for the sinking ignored or attempted to ignore vital bits of evidence that, if addressed carefully, would have totally discredited its conclusions.

Almost immediately after the ship's disappearance an extensive search was initiated to locate the spot where the hulk lay on the bottom of the lake.

During the period of November 14 to 16, a search was conducted from the cutter *Woodrush* using an Egerton, Germershansen and Greer (EG&G) model 250 side-scan sonar provided by the U.S. Coast Guard Research and Development Center. Wreckage, which later proved to be the *Fitzgerald,* was located at a position 49°59.8'N, 85°06.7'W.

Because this first side-scan search had been conducted in adverse weather conditions, it was determined that a second, similar search should be undertaken. On November 22 to 25, 1975, the second search was conducted, using a commercial contractor, Seward, Inc., of Falls Church, Virginia. The survey was performed from the *Woodrush*, using equipment similar to that employed in the first search operation.

Based on the analysis of this side-scan search, the marine board determined that the wreckage was very probably that of *Fitzgerald*, but that positive identification was necessary, and the configuration and arrangement of the wreckage and the bottom conditions were such that a detailed visual survey was both feasible and necessary.

From May 12 to 16, 1976, a third side-scan survey was made to reestablish the accurate position of the wreckage for a photographic survey and to define the planned mooring radius for anchor placement clear of the wreck.

Immediately following the latest survey, a visual inspection of the wreckage was begun, using the U.S. Navy CURV III system under contract with the Coast Guard.

The CURV (Controlled Underwater Recovery Vehicle) consisted of a frame—approximately six feet by six feet by fifteen feet—supporting two horizontal propulsion motors, one vertical propulsion motor, one 35mm still camera, two black-and-white television cameras, lights, a manipulator arm, and other machinery. The vehicle operated on electric power supplied through an umbilical control cable from special generators placed on the *Woodrush*, and it was operated from a control van also placed on the vessel. In addition to the remote control mechanism and sonar presentation, the control van contained videotape recording equipment.

The underwater operations began on May 20, and over the next nine days the CURV made a total of twelve dives, logging fifty-six hours, five minutes of "bottom time" and recording 43,255 feet of videotape and 895 color photographs.

Because of the extreme darkness of the water at 530 feet below the surface and the murkiness caused by the silt that was stirred up by the passage of the CURV near the bottom, the tapes and photographs had to be taken at very close range. But they provided a stark view of all that remains of the once-proud Columbia flagship.

The wreckage of the *Edmund Fitzgerald* lies in 530 feet of water in eastern Lake Superior, approximately seventeen miles northwest of Whitefish Point, just north of the international boundary, in Canadian waters. The wreckage consists of the upright bow section, approximately 276 feet long, lying on a heading of 125 degrees true; an inverted section approximately 253 feet long, lying on a heading of 75 degrees true; and debris scattered in between. At its closest point, the stern section is approximately 170 feet from the bow section. An area of distorted metal lies between the two pieces and to both sides over a distance of 200 feet. Both the bow and stern sections and all the wreckage in between appear to have settled into the bottom mud, and a great deal of mud covers the portion of the spar deck attached to the bow section. The bottom mud in the area of the wreckage shows extensive disruption, and in some locations, the bottom mud has been formed in large mounds, apparently caused by the skidding of the sections along the lake floor. The mud appears to have been plowed up at the bow and at the stern sections. The name of the vessel is clearly visible, both on the stern section and on the bow section.

The bow section is sitting nearly upright on the bottom, inclined approximately fifteen degrees. The spar deck of the bow section extends to a location between hatch number 8 and number 9. At the separation, the starboard side of the hull is bent inward toward the center line and is folded under the deck, while the deck is bent upward from a point approximately two hatches forward of the separation. Mud is spread and piled all over the spar deck area, and the deck edge on the port side is completely covered with mud. At some locations it is possible to distinguish taconite pellets or the mud-covered outline of them. The forward coaming of number 1 hatch is severely damaged. The after coaming of number 1 and the forward and after coamings of number 2 hatch show less damage. Number 3 and number 4 hatches are covered with mud. The hatch covers for hatches 5, 6, 7, and 8 are missing. The forward coaming of number 5 hatch is laid down and damaged. The degree of damage to the deck and hatch coamings increases from number 1 to the separation. The access hatch, located between cargo hatch numbers 7 and 8, is present, with the cover on and dogged. No fence rail stanchions are present. The sockets into which the portable stanchions were fitted are undamaged. The twenty-eight-foot draft mark is visible just above the mud line, and the hull beneath is buried in the bottom of the lake. The bow above the mud is damaged on both sides immediately adjacent to the stem. On the starboard side, slightly aft of the stem, the hull immediately below the spar deck level is holed and badly distorted. The shell plating between the spar deck and the forecastle is badly damaged and distorted, and aft on the starboard side this plating is badly bent and laid in toward the centerline. Throughout this area the plating is heavily wrinkled; the white paint which had been on the hull in this area has broken away, and the plating beneath it has rusted. The steering jib is bent completely back, and the end of it lies up against the forward section of the Texas deck bulwark. The plating of the bulkhead of the forward house between the forecastle deck and the Texas deck is badly damaged. The forward section of the pilothouse is damaged on both the port and starboard sides, and the forward section of the sunshade above the pilothouse windows is damaged on the port side. Most of the pilothouse windows are missing. The radar and the radio direction finder antennae and the ship's bell, which had been installed on the top of the pilothouse, are also missing. Foundations for the radar antenna are visible, but no antenna can be seen.

The stern section is upside down, inclined approximately ten degrees. All of the bottom plating and the side shell plating that is visible above the mud line is intact. The separation is estimated to be at frame 155, which would correspond to the after end of hatch number 18. At the separation, approximately twelve to fifteen feet of the hull extends above the mud. At the after end, the overhead of the spar deck—the underside of the poop deck—is lying approximately even with the mud level. The aft superstructure is buried in the mud. The rudder and propeller are clearly visible and undamaged. The rudder appears to be at the midships position. There is no hole or rupture in the exposed stern section of the hull other than at the separation. One dent was found slightly to port of the centerline, approximately fifty feet forward of the rudder post. A large inward dent, which appears to be a buckle, was found on the starboard side of the stern section at a position approximately twenty feet from the separation, extending vertically from the mud line to the turn of the bilge and across the hull for ten or fifteen feet. There was no breach of the hull at either dent. At the separation on the starboard side, the plating is twisted outward from the hull, while on the port side, the plating is, in general, twisted inward.

Extending outward from the separation at the bow section and at the stern section is an extensive area of debris. For the most part, this debris cannot be identified as coming from a particular part of the vessel, although much of it appears to be pieces of interior structure. This debris is covered with mud, and in some cases, taconite pellets are visible within or on top of the mud. A set of three damaged, but regularly spaced, hatch coamings and a hatch cover are located adjacent to the inverted port side of the stern section. One of these coamings has the numeral *11* on it. Although a systematic survey of this debris was attempted, no regular order to it could be determined by visual examination.

All of the areas of the separations, which were examined in detail, show curving, twisted edges like those associated with ductile failure. No separations were seen that appear to be the sort of straight or flat separations common to brittle fracture. All of the hatch coamings found have hatch clamps attached; the great majority of the hatch clamps observed appear to be undamaged. One coaming, which could not be identified by number, has a line of clamps, with one distorted and several completely undamaged clamps on either side. One distorted piece of structure, which was identified as a badly damaged corner of a hatch coaming, was observed to have undamaged hatch clamps attached to it. This general pattern was seen at every location where a hatch coaming was found.

A few deck vents were observed, primarily on the starboard side of the bow section. It was not possible to determine whether the vent covers were in the open or closed position. One vent was observed to have been torn away from the deck, and an opening in the deck at the base of the vent pipe could be seen.

The survey had been comprehensive, but it was not sufficient to enable the Coast Guard to support a finding consistent with the conclusions they mysteriously settled upon.

> In the absence of more definite information concerning the nature and extent of the difficulties and of problems other than those which were reported, and in the absence of any survivors or witnesses, the proximate cause of the loss of the S.S. *Edmund Fitzgerald* cannot be determined.

> The most probably cause of the sinking of the S.S. *Edmund Fitgerald* was the loss of buoyancy and stability which resulted from massive flooding of the cargo hold. The flooding of the cargo hold took place through ineffective hatch closures as boarding seas rolled along the spar deck. The flooding, which began early on the 10th of November, progressed during the worsening weather and sea conditions and finally resulting in such a loss of buoyancy and stability that the vessel plunged in heavy seas.—Department of Transportation, Coast Guard Marine Casualty Report (USCG 16732/64216), page 92.

The marine board concluded that damage reported by Captain McSorley at about 3:30 in the afternoon of November 10 "could have been caused by the vessel striking a floating object which was then brought aboard in the heavy seas. This could have resulted in undetected damage opening the hull plating above or below the waterline and additional unreported damage to topside fittings, including hatch covers and clamps. Intake of water into the tunnel or one or more ballast tanks through the damaged vents and opened hull would have produced the reported list and increased the rate of cargo flooding."

As to the identity of the mysterious floating object—massive enough to have snapped three steel deck railing cables, sheared off two eight-inch steel vent pipes, punched a hole in the steel hull plates, and possibly have caused additional damage to hatch covers and clamps—the board concluded the object may have been "a log."

The board also concluded—in July 1977—that the twenty-nine crewmen on board the *Fitzgerald* "are missing and presumed dead."

The National Transportation Safety Board (NTSB) conducted their own investigation into the sinking of the *Fitzgerald* and came up with their own theories as to the cause of the vessel's loss.

On May 4, 1978, the NTSB, in a fifty-one-page report, concluded that the "probable cause of this accident was the sudden massive flooding of the cargo hold due to the collapse of one or more hatch covers."

In a classic example of suppositional overkill, the board tossed in the Coast Guard's "improperly secured hatch cover and floating object" theory, plus the possibility that the hatch crane or spare propeller blade had broken away, causing topside damage.

Both the Coast Guard and the NTSB rejected the possibility that the *Fitzgerald* had struck a shoal, breaching her hull and causing damage to the cargo hold, which resulted in the massive flooding they decided had ultimately taken the ship to the bottom of the lake. Their reasons for discounting the shoaling possibility were basically twofold:

1. The underwater survey of the wreckage did not develop positive evidence of a hole in the vessel's bottom.

2. The inability of the *Anderson*'s officers to reconstruct the *Fitzgerald*'s exact trackline during its passage between Michi-

picoten Island and Caribou Island did not allow the board to
conclude that the *Fitzgerald* had, indeed, grounded on Six
Fathom Shoal.

While this method of evidentiary logic helped to avoid
outside claims that the Coast Guard had reached conclusions
that were not supported by physical proofs, it hardly lent itself
to a satisfactory explanation of what caused a demonstrably
safe, relatively new cargo vessel to succumb to a storm that
claimed no other ships on the lake that night and which did
only minimal damage to vessels other than the *Fitzgerald*.

And yet the Coast Guard had abundant evidence to find that
the *Fitzgerald* had a serious break in her hull—a hole that
almost certainly resulted from striking or passing too near a
shoal or reef. Capt. Jesse Cooper and First Mate Morgan Clark
of the *Anderson* testified that the *Fitzgerald* passed close to the
Six Fathom Shoal area. Captain Cooper, in a recorded telephone conversation with U.S. Steel officials as soon as he
docked at Sault Ste. Marie on the afternoon of November 11,
said: "He [the *Fitzgerald*] went in close to the island [Cari-
bou], and I am positive in my own mind—we had him on
radar—we never had him visually, but we had him on radar
all the time, and I am positive he went over the six-fathom
bank." Later, in the same recorded conversation, Cooper said:
"And I know damn well he was in on that 36-foot spot. . . ."
He also stated: "I wondered when he was making water if he
had some cracks down below and making water and not
coming in through the vents, because he had both pumps on
to hold his own."

The conversation was a four-way telephone hookup, with
Cooper and three company officials able to hear and converse
with each other. When Cooper indicated that he had "wondered" about the possibility of water coming in from below,
one of the company representatives stated: ". . . Bernie, I think
we want you to say only what occurred as a matter of fact to
your knowledge, what was said to you, what conversations
you had, what you did."

"I know," Cooper replied. "You don't want to infer anything."

"I don't want you guessing as to what happened on their ship beyond the information that was directly related to you," the company official insisted.

Thus the plan was apparently to deny the investigative board the benefit of Cooper's knowledge and experience and his thoughts and fears based on the events that were occurring as he stood in the *Anderson*'s wheelhouse and watched.

Someone at U.S. Steel had second thoughts, however, and almost three weeks following his initial appearance before the board, Cooper returned to the stand to testify about the telephone conversation.

Yet the thrust of the questions posed by the panel of Coast Guard officers seemed to be designed not to explore the *possibility* that the *Fitzgerald* struck the shoal, but to discredit Cooper's claim that it had sailed into an area where it might have hit the shoals.

The questioners hammered away at Cooper, apparently seeking to create confusion or uncertainty in his mind as to whether the *Fitzgerald* had actually passed over the Six Fathom Shoal area.

After hearing the taped telephone conversation, the marine board's chairman interrogated Cooper extensively concerning the position of the *Fitzgerald* relative to Caribou Island and the shoals.

> *Q. (by Admiral Barrow).* . . you have stated, "He went in close to the island, I am positive in my own mind . . . he went over that six fathom bank." . . . That is a rather positive statement. Did you believe that to be true?
>
> *A.* I still believe that as far as the small-scale chart was concerned. That is what I was using.
>
> *Q.* You believed that to be true at the time you stated it?
>
> *A.* If that chart says 36 feet and the Corps of Engineers are right or whomever it was that got that, then he went over a 36-foot area.
>
> *Q.* You believed at the time you made this that he went over a 36-fathom bank?
>
> *A.* Yes, I do.

Q. And further on in the transcript [tape] it says, "But it just seems to me that it was just before he called me and told me that he had broken some vents off. And I know damn well he was in on that 36-fathom spot, and if he was in there, he must have taken some hell of a seas." That is an accurate description of what you stated at that time?

A. I believe so. If he was not on that six fathom bank, when you have a shoal area as shallow as that north end off of the north end of Caribou, the seas could be extremely nasty in there.

Q. And you believed that to be true at the time you stated it?

A. Yes, I do.

Q. And the third part of the transcript says, "We were concerned that he was in too close, that he was going to hit that shoal off of Caribou."

A. The shoal water that extends out from Caribou, yes.

Q. In earlier testimony before this investigation, you had concluded that the *Fitzgerald* was perhaps some four to five miles off Caribou. Would you care to comment on what appears to be a contradiction between these two positions here?

The two positions were not contradictory. Cooper's earlier testimony was that the *Fitzgerald* came down from the north over the six-fathom area into an area close off the eastern side of Caribou, where there are also shoal waters. Cooper was flustered at this point and had to fall back on an imprecise response to the admiral's question.

A. All we can do is give you what we hauled down as an impression. It was my impression definitely . . . that he was closer than I wanted to be.

Later in his testimony, Cooper stated flatly: "I believe that she was cracked somewhere . . . from an opening in the hull . . . water coming in from below."

In his introductory remarks on the first morning of the marine board's hearings, Rear Adm. Winfred W. Barrow outlined the purposes of the inquiry as follows:

> This investigation is intended to determine the cause of the casualty, to the extent possible, and the responsibility therefor. . . . The investigation and determinations to be made are for the purpose of taking appropriate measures for the promotion of safety of life and property at sea and are not intended to fix criminal and civil liabilities.
>
> The investigation will determine as closely as possible:
> 1. The cause of the casualty;
> 2. Whether any failure of material, either physical or design, was involved or contributed to the casualty so that recommendation or the prevention of a recurrence of a similar nature may be made;
> 3. Whether any act of misconduct, inattention to duty, negligence or willful violation of law on the part of any licensed or documented seaman contributed to the casualty so that appropriate action may be taken under Revised Statutes 4450, as amended, against the license or document;
> 4. Whether any Coast Guard personnel or other representative employee of the Government or any other person, caused or contributed to the cause of the casualty.

In a seeming attempt to conform to this high purpose, former masters, officers, and crewmen of the *Fitzgerald*; masters and officers of other vessels; and naval architects and engineers were called to testify and were all asked the same basic question: "What in your opinion happened to the *Fitzgerald* to cause the vessel to sink so suddenly that no member of the crew was to get off?"

While the response to this question varied to some degree among the witnesses testifying, one glaring fact stood out: not one of the witnesses voiced the opinion that the *Fitzgerald* was lost as the result of "massive flooding of the cargo hold . . .

through ineffective hatch closures." Yet the marine board managed to conclude that that is exactly what did occur.

The overwhelming consensus among the expert witnesses testifying was that the list reported by McSorley could not have been caused by the loss of two ballast tank vents, since the pumps available were more than adequate to control flooding through this source. Yet the marine board determined that this is what happened.

Reliable and experienced witnesses, when asked, voiced their certainty that the *Fitzgerald* had most probably struck a shoal, causing a breach in her hull that was enlarged over a three-and-a-half-hour period. And yet the marine board determined that the vessel had not sailed through a shoal area prior to her foundering.

Ironically, given the board's insistence that the "most probable cause" of the *Fitzgerald*'s loss was "massive flooding of the cargo hold," the recommendations issued at the conclusions of the Coast Guard report into the sinking offered no suggestion that watertight bulkheads be installed to separate the three cargo holds, an alternation which would enable a vessel's crew to contain any intake of water and make it possible to remain afloat in the event that the hull were flooded by any means.

It is also significant that the marine board's recommendation number 14 stated: "That navigation charts showing the area immediately north of Caribou Island be modified to show the extent of the shoals north of the island and that this modification be given the widest possible dissemination, including Notices to Mariners."

The National Transportation Safety Board, issuing its report on the tragedy, held, basically, to the Coast Guard's conclusions that hatch covers were not properly secured to prevent water from gaining access to cargo holds in heavy seas, although there was conclusive testimony from ship's officers and crew members that the *Fitzgerald* had never arrived at an unloading port with water in the holds, even after passage in severe weather. No evidence was introduced to indicate that "wet cargoes" had ever been a problem on modern bulk freighters employing the one-piece hatch covers secured with Kestner clamps.

Unlike the Coast Guard's report, the NTSB report included a dissenting opinion to the conclusions reached by the agency. Member Philip A. Hogue, arguing against the majority opinion, stated:

> The most probable cause of the sinking of the S.S. *Edmund Fitzgerald* in Lake Superior on 10 November, 1975, was a shoaling which first generated a list, the loss of two air vents, and a fence wire. Secondarily, within a period of three to four hours, an undetected, progressive, massive flooding of the cargo hold resulted in a total loss of buoyancy from which, diving into a wall of water, the *Fitzgerald* never recovered. . . .
>
> The record indicates that the *Fitzgerald* was in all respects seaworthy prior to the commencement of her final voyage. Testimony as to the prudence and competence of her Master, Captain McSorley, is abundant. Paraphrasing the words of various witnesses, he was the best captain of the best ship in the fleet operated by Oglebay-Norton Company. In recognition of this reputation, crew members specifically sought employment on the S.S. *Edmund Fitzgerald*. Further, available evidence indicates that Captain McSorley would not commence a voyage into predicted bad weather without first insuring that all the hatch covers were specifically secure.
>
> Like the Marine Board of the Coast Guard or the majority of the members of the National Transportation Safety Board, I could speculate or surmise in the first instance that flooding into the cargo hold took place through ineffective hatch covers or in the second instance that flooding took place due to the failure of hatch cover number 1 due to massive seas. I reject these arguments because neither of them is fully cognizant of the ramifications of the first reported list, the loss of two vents and fence railing at

approximately the precise time the *Fitzgerald* was reportedly in or over shoal waters.

Between the first reported damage and the time of the sinking, approximately three to four hours later, seas of 25 to 30 feet and winds gusting to 80 knots were variously observed. Without exception, expert testimony has affirmed the fact that seas in the shoal waters are inherently more violent and wild than in open water. It follows, therefore, that subsequent to her initial sustained damage, the *Fitzgerald* suffered progressive damage from laboring, rolling and pitching for the next three to four hours as it proceeded toward Whitefish Point Light.

At or about 1730, Captain Woodard aboard the Swedish vessel *Avafors* received a report from Captain McSorley stating that the *Fitzgerald* had a "bad list," had lost both radars and was taking heavy seas over the deck in one of the worst seas he had ever been in. In approximately two hours from the initial report of a list, the *Fitzgerald* had acquired a "bad list" and sustained the loss of both radars.

Approximately 1 hour 40 minutes later at or about 1910, the *Fitzgerald* reported it was holding its own. This was the last transmission ever heard from the *Fitzgerald*. Aside from the expert testimony elicited at the Coast Guard Marine Board hearing, it is self-evident that Captain McSorley had a damaged ship, and that he did not know how damaged she was.

It is true that initial damage to the *Fitzgerald* could have been sustained by other means, but it would be a most unlikely coincidence that damage sustained at the same approximate time that she was reported by Captain Cooper of the S.S. *Anderson* to be in close or over shoal waters.

Despite the difficulty experienced, in retrospect, by Captain Cooper days later before the Coast Guard Marine Board, in pinpointing the position of the *Fitzgerald* over various and sundry shoals, the fact remains that in his most fresh, spontaneous and free report of the accident to his company less than 24 hours after the accident, Captain

Cooper variously stated: "I am positive he went over that six fathom bank," and "I know damn well he was in on that thirty-six-foot spot, and if he was in there he must have taken some hell of a seas." "I swear he went in there. In fact, we were talking about it. We were concerned that he was in too close, that he was going to hit that shoal off Caribou, I mean, God, he was about three miles off the land beacon."

In other testimony before the Coast Guard Marine Board, Captain Cooper testified that he told the mate on watch on the *Anderson* that the *Fitzgerald* was closer to the six fathom shoal north of Caribou Island than he wanted the *Anderson* to be.

No one knows of a certainty how long the *Fitzgerald* had a list or had other topside damage prior to the conversation between Captain Cooper and Captain McSorley at about 1530. Neither does anyone know for sure exactly which vents were initially lost.

It is reasonable to assume, from all that is known of Captain McSorley, that his first report of damage was based on damage sustained immediately prior to 1530 and that it was no small consideration that caused Captain McSorley to ask the *Anderson* to stay with him, saying, "I will check down so that you can close the distance between us."

Considering the fact that no testimony has ever been produced to show that the *Fitzgerald* had ever arrived in port without dry cargo and the overall success of the hatch covers generally in use on the Great Lakes for many years, I have great difficulty accepting the argument that one or more of the hatches on the *Fitzgerald* on the day of the accident were either nonwatertight or that they failed prior to the first report of damage. If, in fact, hatch failure or loss of weathertight integrity occurred prior to the *Fitzgerald*'s sinking, I can only surmise that such failure or failures occurred subsequent to the first list reported on or about 1530 and prior to the sinking on or about 1910.

I place great credence in Captain Cooper's testimony that

the *Fitzgerald* was in proximity or over shoal waters; first because his judgment is the most expert to be found at the scene and as much as anything else, the *Fitzgerald* reported her first casualties at that almost exact time. I could have doubts of one fact or another, but putting two and two together plus the subsequent events, I am strongly convinced that the *Fitzgerald* received her first damage as I have indicated and that from that time until the sinking, the *Fitzgerald*'s condition deteriorated beyond the Captain's knowledge and beyond recovery.

After studying all available information, it is my firm conclusion that the *Fitzgerald* shoaled and sustained her initial damage shortly before 1530 and that thereafter the various workings of the vessel and loss of watertight integrity led to her sudden and totally unexpected sinking.

*　　*　　*

While Great Lakes shipmasters tend to agree with Philip Hogue's contention that the *Fitzgerald* shoaled and thus ripped out her bottom, very few agree that McSorley was totally unaware of the serious nature of the ship's injuries.

"You don't pump water for over three hours without correcting a list and not know that something serious is wrong," one ship's captain explained.

"If you take a sudden list and your pumps don't straighten the ship out in a hurry, you start looking around to find out what the hell has happened," another stated.

"McSorley had to know that the ship was badly damaged, but what could he do? His only hope was to run for Whitefish and beach her," was the conclusion of still another experienced Great Lakes skipper.

The chairman of the National Transportation Safety Board investigation into the sinking summed it up succinctly: "The usual practice on the lakes seems to be that nobody ever turns back."

In an admittedly self-serving protest, the Lake Carriers' Association, an organization composed largely of shipping companies, refuted the Coast Guard's findings, arguing that Capt. Jesse Cooper of the *Anderson* was correct in stating that the *Fitzgerald* had passed over a shoal and that the ship had struck the shoal, tearing a hole in her bottom. The organization insisted:

. . . The navigation position data near Caribou Island furnished by the Master of the *Anderson* is materially strengthened by direct radar observations, in contrast to the confusing reconstructed track line produced by the Marine Board. On page 2149 of the Board Report, Captain Cooper stated he simultaneously had both the *Fitzgerald* and Caribou on his radar, and he was positive that the *Fitzgerald* went over the shoals. Captain Cooper meticulously avoided the shallower waters because of the heavy seas normal there in such storm conditions.

The significant point is the simultaneous radar observations of Caribou and the vessel. When one object is fixed (Caribou), the distance can be rather accurately determined without any concern for relative motion, bearings, track lines, position, speed or heading. The radar is equipped with concentric ring scales enabling the experienced to estimate distance between objects on its screen.

The result of the hydrographic survey of the Caribou Island shoal waters conducted by Canadian Hydrographic Service, at the request of the Coast Guard Marine Board looking into the *Fitzgerald* sinking, is described on Pages 86 and 87 of the Report. It should be particularly noted that the survey identifies a shoal less than six fathoms deep more than one mile farther east than any in the Six Fathom Shoal cluster depicted on the latest navigational charts. This verified shoal was in the track of the *Fitzgerald*, as observed by the *Anderson*, thus making shoaling even more certain as the start of the fateful events leading to the sinking.

While the reasons for the Lake Carriers' Association's distaste for the Coast Guard's findings were unabashedly pecuniary—the possibility that the government might require installation of more secure hatch covers or the redesign of the entire cargo hold system, which would involve the expenditure of millions—the motives of the Coast Guard to insist that the *Fitzgerald* was lost as the result of improperly secured hatch covers was far more difficult to analyze. Why would the board issue findings that were improper and incorrect? The most charitable explanation is, of course, that they were simply and honestly mistaken in their conclusions. The most damning indictment of the board would be to suggest that by arriving at conclusions which were arguable but nonetheless benign in placing blame on either the company or the captain, the board had protected the reputation of the ship's master and had saved Oglebay-Norton from very expensive law suits by the families of the lost crew.

Under maritime law, monetary judgments against the ship-owner have traditionally been limited to the salvage value of the ship and cargo. In the case of the *Fitzgerald,* the salvage value would be nil. If, however, a negligence on the part of the company or the captain (as agent for the company) could be proven, then the liability of the company would be greatly increased. If it could be demonstrated that McSorley was careless or reckless in allowing his ship to stray into shallow waters, and if it could be further demonstrated that the company was aware of this carelessness, a damage claim brought by surviving relatives of the crew could be catastrophic to Oglebay-Norton.

While no suggestion is made that such considerations played any role in the board's deliberations, the conclusions which were arrived at are puzzling in light of the evidence that was readily available.

Curious, too, was the board's apparent attempt to preserve McSorley's reputation from assault. In questioning former *Fitzgerald* crew members, the matter of fire and lifeboat drills came up. Capt. Delmore Webster, who had served under McSorley on a number of occasions, testified that drills were held at least every seven days. "We had boat drills once a week. It was noted in the log."

When Gerald Lange, a retired first mate who had served under McSorley, was asked about boat drills, his answer was almost identical to that of Captain Webster: "We had weekly drills, and these drills were so noted in the pilothouse log."

However, when Charles H. Lindberg, Thomas E. Garcia, John H. Larson, and Donald Hilsen—all former *Fitzgerald* crewmen—were asked about boat drills, three testified that there had been no boat drills at all during their service under McSorley, and one testified, "I wouldn't say he never had a drill, but I can't say how often he had one. . . . I would not say it was once a month. He did not have them that often. . . . He did not have them regularly."

The board's frustration with the obvious contradiction between what two former *Fitzgerald* officers claimed regarding boat drills and the testimony of four former crew members became evident when Donald Hilsen testified.

Under questioning by Capt. Adam S. Zabinski:

Q. Mr. Hilsen, you indicated that the lifeboat station was the No. 1 boat. Was that on the port or starboard side?

A. There again, I can't be specific. I always get that mixed up.

Q. Mr. Hilsen, who are you kidding? Any boat you ever went on—how many ships did you say you were on?

A. About 25.

Q. Every ship you were ever on, Boat 1 was on one side, and Boat 2 was on the other side, and don't try to kid me.

A. I am not.

Q. Don't tell me you were on 25 ships and you don't know where No. 1 boat is. This is a serious matter here, and you have been evasive on every answer you have given, and I am fed up. Now, you answer. What side is No. 1 boat on?

A. Port side.

Q. Are you sure of that?

A. No sir, I am not.

Q. You're damn right you are not. You are not sure about

anything. I don't know where you got your lifeboat
certificate, but I will be darned if I don't check up on it.

Who are you kidding? What boats were you on? You
say you have been sailing since '64. What boats have you
been on since '64?

A. Well, we will go back to the *Fitzgerald*, and before that
was the *Mathiott*, and I have been on the *Armco*. I have
been on a number of them.

Q. Mr. Hilsen, I am not going to dignify you by asking
you another question.

Hilsen fared little better under questioning by the board
chairman, Rear Admiral Barrow:

Q. As closely as I can tell, when you first started testifying,
you said that you can't recall any boat drills being held
on the *Fitzgerald*; is that correct?

A. That is correct.

Q. I have testimony here taken just yesterday from two
people. In that testimony it was stated by one person,
"We had boat drills once a week. It was noted in the
log," in describing the boat drill. Another witness: "We
had weekly drills, and these drills were so noted in the
pilothouse log." Both stated that in testimony under
oath. You testified here that you had no boat drills on
the *Fitzgerald*?

A. None that I can recall.

Q. You persist in that?

A. Yes, sir.

Hilsen, the last of four devastating witnesses, would endure
one final scuffle, this time with Thomas A. Murphy, attorney
for Oglebay-Norton and oddly enough, the lawyer who should
have been representing Hilsen, an Oglebay-Norton employee.

Murphy, addressing the board:

I am just as concerned about this as you are. I want to say
for the record that the entire testimony as it has come in
today is just as much a surprise to us as it is to the Board.

We are just as much concerned at getting to the bottom of it as the Board is. . . .

Q. Mr. Hilsen, do you say on oath that you never had a boat drill during the period that you were aboard the *Fitzgerald* with Captain McSorley? Are you telling these people that?

A. As I said before, I can't recall, I can't say that there never was one held, but as far as I can recall there was none.

Q. But you are saying, then, that they were not held on a regular basis; is that what you are saying?

A. Yes, that is true.

Q. And you are saying that under oath?

A. I am saying that. I can't recall one being held.

Rear Admiral Barrow to Hilsen: Do you have anything further to add to your testimony?

A. Well, I apologize for any shortcoming I may have shown here. I have tried to be helpful.

Barrow: I think the point, Mr. Hilsen, is that you have qualified everything you have said before this Board by you can't remember or you can't recall, just about everything that you have said.

Of course, that was an exaggeration; Hilsen was no more unresponsive than most other witnesses when pressed by the board. But then, Hilsen's answers to questions about boat drills aboard the *Fitzgerald,* coming as they did immediately after three other witnesses, all contradicting the pair of ship's officers, posed serious problems for the board if they wanted to avoid any possible claims that safety measures on the boat were ignored or treated frivolously.

The board managed the apparent serious conflict simply. Their final report would address the question with a single, misleading sentence:

Lifeboat drills were held on the *Fitzgerald* during the 1975 season, but were not held on a weekly basis as required by regulations.—Department of Transportation, Coast Guard Marine Casualty Report (USCG 16732/64216), page 99.

CHAPTER 16

"With Loss of Life"

"The S.S. *Edmund Fitzgerald* sinking in Lake Superior on 10 November 1975 with loss of life."

That was how the government had put it: *with loss of life.* It seems somehow cold, and unfeeling, to phrase it just that way. It had been more than "loss of life" to the families who were left behind. It was a loss of hopes and dreams and plans stretching out for years in the future. To the widow, it was a loss of a partner with whom she might raise the children—to watch them grow and to glory in their successes and to weep at their misadventures and to do it together. To the orphaned, it was the loss of a father—someone who, even if he were away much of the time, was still a real, living dad, who, when he was home, would share their happiness, would counsel and direct them, would sit with them in the gathering dusk of a pleasant evening, and would offer an attentive ear to catch a shy, half-whispered "I love you, Daddy," and would respond, "I love you, too."

To mothers and fathers, it was the loss of a son, some of whom were still in the beginnings of their lives, with the beautiful years still before them. To these survivors, the *loss of life* meant the loss of an important member of the family; in some cases the *loss of life* was a loss of a family. John O'Brien and Gene Beetcher had little more than their fathers; there was no family with them gone. To the women, such as Helen Bindon, who had no children to draw close and to take some comfort from, this *loss of life* meant years of loneliness, of emptiness, of sustaining themselves on memories that were incomplete but would not die.

For all, it meant picking up the broken pieces of their lives, going on, struggling to adjust to a new existence. Some of the wives, such as Karen Pratt—wife of the *Fitzgerald*'s second mate—sought to begin a new life, remarrying and moving to another part of the country, turning their backs—as much as possible—on the devastating memory of a drowned husband whose body would never be recovered. For some it was a matter of continuing their lives with a minimum of disruption, of providing a stable home for children who might yet be too young to face the loss on their own. For Janice Armagost, it was returning to the University of Wisconsin to pick up her education where she had dropped it when she had married Mike, and to await and be prepared for the questions she knew would eventually come from her two children: "What was my dad like?"

For Mary McCarthy, it was living quietly with her grief for a time and then going beyond the grief, to do all her crying alone and then to confront the years ahead just as she had faced the years in the past, with resolve and determination. "She's not become hard, but she's had to be tough," her priest would say of her.

Nellie McSorley, living with a pain-wracked body, now faced a life of much greater pain, an agony that was impervious to medical nostrums.

For all, it was a loss that could never be replaced. Bruce Hudson had been the only son of Odis and Ruth. They would be condemned to live their lives with a ghost that never left their home. His dog, Kelly, will not permit the door to Bruce's room to be closed, but from the morning the news of the tragedy came, the dog has not entered the room.

The news reports of the sinking all stated that there were no survivors; the Coast Guard and the National Transportation Board indicated in their reports that none of the crew survived the wreck of the *Edmund Fitzgerald*. They were wrong.

Richard Bishop, the *Fitzgerald*'s first cook, lives a haunted life, unwilling to talk about the ship or the men who died in her, refusing to share his pain with even his closest friends or his family. He still sails the Great Lakes, passing a hundred times each year near the spot where his shipmates lie in death. And in his dreams he still hears the same bitter question other shipwreck survivors have heard before him: "Why you?"

The public will let none of the grievers forget the tragic days of November 1975. Each year the story is resurrected, the song fills the airwaves, the ship's photograph appears in the newspapers and on television, and memorial services are held. There is a curiosity, an interest in the ship, that continues, that has thrived years after it plunged to the bottom of Lake Superior. This fascination is such that a world-renowned underwater explorer was drawn to the story of the boat's death.

On September 24, 1980, the research vessel *Calypso* anchored over the spot in eastern Lake Superior where the *Fitzgerald* rests. Jean-Michel Cousteau, son of the famous explorer Jacques Cousteau, supervised preparations to send a two-man submarine to the bottom, where the remains of the *Fitzgerald* would be filmed for a proposed television special on the Great Lakes.

Colin Mounier and Albert Falco climbed inside the squat, yellow diving saucer and were lowered over the side. Five hundred and thirty feet below the surface—just where the Coast Guard said it was—the two men found, in the melancholy gloom, the hulk of the huge ore freighter.

Moving slowly along the bow section, the two men were

suddenly petrified. Just ahead of them, out of the murkiness, they saw a pale light glowing from one of the ship's port-holes.

It was several long seconds before they realized that the light was the reflected image of their own brilliant diving lights, rebounding from the glass and coming back to them as if the glow were inside the ship.

For thirty minutes they slowly drifted around the two sections of the broken ship, seeing no bodies, retrieving no artifacts. Finally, the first humans to visit the ship since the stormy night she was lost silently floated away, leaving the corpse alone once more.

It would provide some small comfort to those loved ones of the *Fitzgerald*'s crew if they could point to a constructive result coming from their loss, mitigating against the pain they feel. It would be somewhat reassuring if they could feel that their men had sacrificed their lives so that the tragedy would not be repeated, so that other families would not suffer the deep anguish and the bitterness that they have endured. Unfortunately, little has come from the *Fitzgerald* catastrophy to prevent a similar incident from occurring again, at any time.

Fathometers were encouraged equipment aboard Great Lakes commercial vessels for a time, but they are once again optional, unnecessary. Survival suits, which are designed to protect men in freezing water, are now required for each member of the crew on all ships operating on the lakes. A new navigational system—known as the Lorain C System, employing a computerized radio receiver which instantly provides a visual readout of the vessel's location within a few hundred yards—is now standard equipment on all but a few lake boats. And there have been some experiments with hull stress detectors, which would alert the bridge of any imminent failure of the vessel's shell plating. But they have not been made mandatory. The weather service now issues "large craft warnings," designed to alert ship's masters of the danger of severe storms on the lakes. But the warnings are purely advisory; they do not require that ships stand in until the weather moderates. After all, the Great Lakes shipping industry depends on getting cargoes through, and ship's masters know all too well the importance of making on-time deliveries.

No permanent memorial exists to perpetuate the memories of the twenty-nine men who were lost in Lake Superior in 1975. It will be up to the sons and daughters and the grandchildren of the men to keep their heritage somehow alive.

On November 12, 1975—two days after the loss of the *Fitz*—Patricia Florence Simmons Louko was born. Only 3 pounds at birth, the girl was, in every other respect, normal and healthy. Five weeks later, on December 16, Jeremiah Johnson—8 pounds, 9½ ounces—made his appearance. These were the much-awaited grandchildren of Johnny Simmons and Bob Rafferty, grandchildren they did not live to see.

In their steel tomb at the bottom of the "Big Lake," in never-ending darkness, the crew of the steamer *Edmund Fitzgerald* repose in endless sleep, safe at last from the gales of November.

BIBLIOGRAPHY

Bowen, Dana Thomas. *Lore of the Lakes.* Daytona Beach, Florida: Dana Thomas Bowen, 1940.

Boyer, Dwight. *Ships and Men of the Great Lakes.* New York: Dodd, Mead & Co., 1977.

Boyer, Dwight. *Strange Adventures of the Great Lakes.* New York: Dodd, Mead & Co., 1974.

Dills, Michael, and Greenwood, John. *Greenwood's and Dills' Lake Boats '73.* Cleveland: Freshwater Press, 1973.

O'Brien, T. Michael. *Guardians of the Eighth Sea: A History of the U.S. Coast Guard on the Great Lakes.* Washington, D.C.; Government Printing Office, 1976.

Ratigan, William. *Great Lakes Shipwrecks and Survivals.* Grand Rapids, Mich.: William B. Eerdmans Publishing Co., 1977.

Trimble, Paul E. "Year-round Navigation on the Great Lakes." *Inland Seas,* Summer 1976.

Wolff, Julius F. "One Hundred Years of the Coast Guard on Lake Superior." *Inland Seas,* Summer 1976.

United States Congress, House Committee on Merchant Marine and Fisheries. Coast Guard Activities in the Upper Great Lakes. *Summary of Results of Survey of Wreckage of Edmund Fitzgerald.* Serial No. 94-39. *Hearings before the Subcommittee on Coast Guard and Navigation.* 94th Cong., July 16, 1976.

United States, Department of Transportation, Marine Board of Investigation. *SS Daniel J. Morrell Sinking with Loss of Life, Lake Huron, 29 November 1966.*

United States, Department of Transportation, Coast Guard, Marine Casualty Report. *SS Edmund Fitzgerald; Sinking in Lake Superior on 10 November 1975 with Loss of Life.* July 26, 1977.

The Blade (Toledo, Ohio), November 10–13, 15, 1975.

Detroit Free Press, November 11–13, 1975; September 26, 1980.

Detroit News, November 11, 12, 1975.

Marquette Mining Journal, November 12–14, 19, 21, 22, 1975; December 13, 1975; November 11, 26, 1976; December 31, 1976; September 29, 1977.

Milwaukee Journal, November 12, 13, 1975.

New York Times, November 11, 1975.

Plain Dealer (Cleveland), November 11, 12, 1975; January 21, 1979.

Sault Evening News (Sault Ste. Marie, Mich.), November 11, 1975; May 20, 21, 1976.

Steere, Mike, "The Riddle of the *Edmund Fitzgerald.*" *Toledo Magazine*, November 2, 1980, pp. 4–15.

Index